How to Participate in the World

A Manual of Creativity and Connection

with lots of theory and digression

Mary Lounsbury

Published by Leaf and Lizard Publishing Company

© 2025 Mary L Lounsbury. All Rights Reserved.

contact: mary@mythos-sphere.com

Paperback ISBN: 978-0-9845488-2-8

Dedication:

To all the helpful spirits, great and small, who have travelled this path with me.

Most especially, to my children and their families, and to my dear husband and partner, Sal.

And of course, to the furry boys who have been by my side every day of this writing.

Thanks to all for your unwavering support.

Table of Contents

Preface xi

Book as Container xi

Book as Journey xi
Whys + Hows
Inners + Outers
Navigating

Book as Friend xiv
A Wish

Part I : Opening Space

Opening Space 3

What is Human Nature? 3

Opening Space for Creativity 5

My Goals for This Book 6

Integration 7

Essential Ideas 8
Everyday creativity is nourishing
An ecological understanding puts humanity in perspective
Thirdness establishes continuity

- Mythological awareness is helpful
- Healing the wound in the social tissue

Everyday Tools and Practices For Creative Expression   30
- Everyday tools
- Everyday practices

Why   32
- Why develop an everyday creative practice
- The value of creative engagement is social cohesion
- Why you should start a creative group
- Moving beyond the myth of individualism
- Therapeutic not therapy

My Point and Mission   38
- My point
- My mission
- Who am I to say?

Experience Comes First   42

Part II : Being Creative

Being Creative   47

First Show Up   47
- Noticing psyche in everything
- Participation

Join the Conversation   49
- Who's here?
- Archetypes, intuition, and imagination

Expression   63
- Creative Expression ≠ Art
- Projects, Skill Building, and Messing Around
- Honoring the creative process
- What I "make" doesn't have to be good or beautiful
- But what if I want it to be? (good or beautiful)
- Watch out, ego! Don't be a troublemaker!

Fear and Anxiety   73
- FEARS
- Relieving anxiety
- The many faces of resistance
- Trauma and avoidance
- The use of everyday creative expression for working out traumatic memory
- Habitual resistance
- Actually, it IS scary and dangerous

Play & Risk   86
- Play = Risk
- Play as goofing around
- Play as movement
- Play is pretend and it is real
- Magic circle as container

Ways Into Play   90
- Embrace metaphor
- Act silly
- Be ambiguous—sometimes...
- And here we are in the third

The Personal Third   94
- Inner+Outer continuity
- Unfolding
- Being fluid
- The insider-outsider dilemma
- Fluid narrative
- Reframing our narratives
- Word magic

Alchemy and Transformation — 110
Mind-body
Alchemy in depth psychology
The alchemy of making things
The alchemy of dreams
The alchemy of aging

Your Everyday Practice — 120
Set the stage

Practices: The How-To Guide — 130

Part III : Being In Between

Being In Between — 185

Navigating the Third — 186
Where's the boundary? Know where you are.
Containing the third
Crossing boundaries: entering the third
Recognizing a metaphor when you see it
Letting the geni out of the bottle
It's not all good times
Just start
Engaging with multitudes of imaginal others

Guidelines: Best Practices for Being In-Between — 200

On Imaginal Guidance — 203
Intro
Evolution of numinous energy: A Theory
From *The Gift* by Lewis Hyde (67-68):

Consulting with Guides — 212
On working with imaginal beings
A Guide to Guides
The imaginal interview: vetting your guides

Cosmologies and World-Making: Mapping the Territory — 232
Explore the territory
Keep a journal
Make your own map
Compare notes
My Cosmology

Journey's End: Exiting the In-Between — 240
How do I get out of here?
What should I do with all this weird stuff I've made?
Compost the unfinished expressions.

Mary's Adventures in the Third — 243

Part IV : Being Together

Being Together — 283

Everyday Connection — 283

Human = Social — 284
Humans need connection
Coherence
Cultural sense of individual consciousness
All our relations
Splitting

Continuity   293
inner+outer experience and the psychoid
particles, waves, you, me, everyone. everything

Cultural Participation   300
Toward a healthy society
Society needs connectivity

Healing Social Wounds   304
Scapegoating
Sociopathy
Healing trauma TOGETHER
Metabolizing trauma through the body
Ritual is physical
Shared metaphor
Cultural pluralism

The Social Third   323
Group alchemy
How to share the imaginal
Enter the Mythos-Sphere
Sharing is the best/Sharing is scary

Starting a Group   335
Why *YOU* should start a group
Can you do it?
What kind of group?
But I don't know anyone!
Start somewhere

Group Process: Some Specifics   337
Planning and maintaining the group
Surrender is not submission
Shared ideas belong to everyone
Being inner + outer + introverted + extraverted

Shared Creative Practices   345
Sharing the imaginal through creative engagement
Basics of Creative Sharing: A Summary

Group Practices: The How-To Guide   *350*

Part V : Full Circle

Full Circle   385

   From Flatland to the Mythos-Sphere   385
   Sharing Reality   385

Bibliography   389

Image Credits   397

Index   401

Preface

Hi there, Reader! Welcome to my book! Let me orient you as you make your way in.

How to Participate started out as a revision of my doctoral dissertation,* and it is still that, but it has morphed a lot. As I worked with these ideas which are so important to me, I knew I wanted to make them accessible, useful, and friendly. The new structure and tone reflect my work as a group facilitator and my conversational style.

Originally titled "Crafting the Mythos-Sphere: Toward the Integration of Intellect and Intuition"(2018), you can find it on Proquest if you're interested in the academic version.

Book as Container

A book is a container holding worlds of words and images and ideas. I'm for the physical book. E-books definitely have some advantages, like the search function, and always having something to read in the airport. But the physical book — its heft, its geography, its mystical quality as a container of worlds — the physical book will always be tops for me. It's easier to recognize it as an experience that you are having, that's engaging you, taking you somewhere, changing you…. You open and close it. You enter into it and step out again.

As I write this in 2024, I'm thinking about the way we read today. Not the same for everyone, of course, but generally speaking, our reading habits have changed quite a bit since the last century. Reading sessions may be shorter or less focused as our attentions are called in more directions by the busy, busy world.

This book doesn't ask you to swallow it whole, or to eat it all at once, but to engage with it as you like. This book is holding deep, thought-provoking ideas alongside wisps and whimsies. Images and metaphors unfold over time. Seriousness mixes with silliness to enrich and leaven the text in a palatable, digestible way. This book hopes to provide sustenance for you as you need it.

Book as Journey

Books are vessels carrying ideas across space and time. When you enter a book, it will carry you, too. You don't always know where it's going to take you, or how it may change you; so, if you're like me, before you commit, you start by flipping around, reading a bit here and there, getting a sense of whether it's going somewhere you want to go. And then, if you are sufficiently charmed, you dive in! Here's an overview of the journey ahead:

Whys + Hows

This book delves into both the "Why" and the "How" (two of my favorite things): in other words, both the theory and the practice of creative engagement and social connection.

Part I introduces the ideas of myth and psyche that run throughout the book; Part II is oriented to the personal creative experience; Part III explores the "in-between-land" of the Third, which is so relevant to both creative expression and social connection; Part IV is devoted to the social sharing of creative expression; and of course Part V wraps it up with some conclusions and suggestions for going further. There are lots of useful resources at the back of the book.

There are "Hows" all the way through, but in particular, the *Practice Guides* located after Parts II and IV are the How-To manuals for your everyday creative explorations and your group experiences. *The Travelogue* section after Part III has excerpts from my own imaginal journey journals, to illustrate my method and inspire your own explorations.

Inners + Outers

Everything has an inner, an outer, and an in-between — including you and me — but sometimes we feel flattened out or disconnected. This book is designed to help you expand and connect by engaging all of these parts: inner, outer, and in-between. The inner <–> outer movement shifts your perspective, your mind set, and of course your actual physical position.

As far as the doing? The actual practices? Do them! Listen, Reader, I don't like people telling me what to do, I really don't. Maybe you don't either. You don't have to do every single thing or do them in a certain order or at a certain time. Make it your own! But the ground of this book is the doing: the physicality, the engaged experience, the practice — that's the whole point. *And I'm only saying this because I know how easy it is to buy a book and READ about doing things without actually DOING them. Reading them isn't doing them.*

As the book travels back and forth between ways of knowing and ways of experiencing, between thinking and doing, between self and other, I hope this movement will open up space for your own ideas and inspirations to flow in.

> *Warning: It's not always a rational route! Be willing to wander!*

I'm a wanderer. I do digress! I feel like digressions make life worthwhile. And there is a method to my madness (so I claim), but if you ever feel lost on this journey, the Table of Contents is essentially a map of the journey. so it will show you where you are and where you're going. Go ahead and take a shortcut if you like. Some people feel like it's cheating to skip around in a book but — *It's not cheating! It's your book! It's your journey!*

Navigating

Of course you can read from beginning to end, but if you want to go off-road a bit, here are some formatting hints to help you navigate the book with ease.

Meditations
highlighted in lavender
are good places to pause, breathe, consider.

Definitions
are placed alongside
the text like this

Or pulled out in the text body like this

Sidebars are scattered around to provide more info on relevant topics I may have glossed over in the body of the text.

PRACTICE GUIDES

are after Parts II and IV. You'll find them easily as the pages have blue or green borders.

Practice Tips are also scattered through the text in blue or green type.

The Travelogue

follows Parts III with examples from my own Inner+Outer journeys.

Most illustrations are my own. Other artists are credited alongside and in the Image Credits in the back, where you'll also find the usual Bibliography and Index. Additional resources, like websites, worksheets, and suggested reading, can be found on my website.

Book as Friend

I'm a book lover, and I mean, I love my books as friends, advisors, teachers, entertainers.... They are beings in the world. They have presence. They have conversations with each other on my shelves, or when they happen to bump into each other on my desktop. They may rest quietly for years, and then suddenly jump out at me with just the message I need to hear. They enrich my life immeasurably. Above all, they whet my curiosity and inspire me to live my best life.

A Wish
My wish? That you may have a satisfying, friendly relationship with *this* book! Dip in or dig in as you like. Go from first page to last, or take another route. Some sections may inspire you to linger and daydream; some may offer a deeper understanding, provoke a deeper think, or catalyze a deeper project; sometimes you may just flip in for a quick how-to recipe or reminder. As a manual, it's intended to accompany your practice: a reference you can return to over time, rather than a "once and done."

Just as with your other friends, you may at times find parts of the book annoying or flawed. In that case, I hope you will give grace to the foibles and focus on the parts that feed you.

magic wishes flowing into the world

Part I : Opening Space

Opening Space

An introduction to the essential ideas presented in this book.

What is Human Nature?

What is human nature?

If we were born to do something, to be something, what would it be?

The egg hatches, the seed grows.

Birds build nests. Bees make honey.

What do humans do?

We make things. And in making things, we make meaning.

Creative Participation: it's how we engage with the world
• •

As a species, humans sure seem like bad actors: doomed to make ever more catastrophic mistakes that we urgently try to fix. Is that our "nature"? Or have we strayed from our nature? Is that even possible, to be something other than one's nature? These questions haunt me. I'm sure I'm not alone.

The closest I've come to an answer is this: If we could slow down and tune in more immediately and directly to our drives and impulses, rather than compulsively, chaotically acting them out without consideration, maybe we would be more balanced and grounded, less pathological.

I'm one who loves to make things. All kinds of things. Everyday. I guess it's my nature.

This would have been great for me, maybe two or three hundred years ago, because I enjoy doing so many things that once gave form to daily life: baking, building, sewing, spinning... practically anachronisms, now. So what to do with all that? How to make a life — a living, let's say — of hand-making things in this industrialized capitalist world? Which I grudgingly admit is now the way of things, despite my resistance.

I'm not too interested in selling things; and I don't care all that much about teaching you how to make the things I make (though I'm happy to share, sure — just ask). Mainly, I make things up as I go along, and by the time I figure out what it is I've made, I'm ready for something new. But it's *THAT*—the making things up as I go along—*THAT* is the thing I want to share, the thing that has so much value for me, you and the rest of humanity. I know it. It's much more important than my brownie recipe or my collage techniques or how to spin a yarn – because it encompasses all that.

Making things up = creative engagement

Here's what I care about: I want more people to really get the radical value of everyday creative engagement. **NOT obsessively making things*—that is **not** what I mean—but being creatively engaged with the world in which you live, every day, in such a way that you become a better listener and a better collaborator in the process.

This is a book about participating with the world.

Opening Space for Creativity

Frustratingly, the more convinced I become that making stuff up everyday is vitally important, the rarer and more endangered it seems. (One notable exception being the making up of "facts.") It's true, these most important practices of creative engagement don't jive with attempts to maximize production, efficiency, and profit. And when people are struggling, whether to just get by, or to do "better" somewhere along the economic continuum, they are stuck on the task of money making. It's hard to get off that track; in fact, it seems ever more challenging to keep up. Industrialized capitalism has so deeply effectively pervasively (either) colonized or cannibalized our lives and minds that it simply doesn't make sense to spend time on such quaint pastimes.

Take another look at the metaphors invoked in that last phrase: "...*make* sense ... *spend* time..." Yes, it's all about money, my friends. How difficult — or even impossible — is it to step outside of the capitalist model? How rare and fortunate have I been to follow my creative whims despite the lack of income generated from them? It's a privilege, for sure! *AND*... along with my privilege, I've been underestimated unrecognized underpaid or unpaid or even actually paying to be able to do my work because I don't want to play that f—ing industrialized capitalist game. Yes, I've been privileged to be able to say "I don't want to play" and to find ways to make that work. I'm not independently wealthy and it hasn't been without sacrifice, but I have a few high cards in my hand that have allowed me the freedom to decide how *I* want to play the game.

It's not just about me, though. Please. Don't patronize me — cause I do have a chip on my shoulder about it. Seriously! You get that when people underestimate you. I've spent my whole life on these ideas, not because I'm a nitwit, but because they're so important! Now, more than ever, in our world of change, we need to know how to interact with *what is*. And *that* is the very definition of creative engagement.

We may think of "play" as "for children." Yet teachers have a never-ending battle to convince parents and administrators that children need time for creative play; a need so obvious that it seems to me ludicrous to have to justify it. That led me to the "aha" that, if we want **adults** to understand, then we need to give **adults** time and permission to play. Many people struggle day in and day out with lives that allow no time — no space — for authentic personal expression or true interpersonal connection whatsoever. The two are related, and the consequences are dire. Without personal expression or interpersonal connection, we are cut off from the sense of a meaningful life, or even from understanding the nature of our presence in the world; and then we act out...

Well, it ain't gonna fix itself.

> *And thus, the need to proactively open and hold space in our lives to engage with the imaginal world through creative practice.*

The spaciousness we need is available to us, if we know where and how to find it. The space is in you – the space is in your relationships – the space is in your world.

My Goals for This Book

My goals for this book are simple:
- Get people into a regular, healthy flow of creative expression in their daily lives.

- Get people comfortable in sharing creatively with others.

- Get people into the settings that <u>allow</u> the sharing of creative expression.

And by "people," I mean you. Because an everyday creative practice will help you explore and discover your inner nature and your place in the nature of the world. Giving form to the imaginal impulse is human nature. Let it happen.

Integration

Everyday creative engagement, practiced over time, is a process of integration. It helps you to fit the pieces of your life together: to integrate your inner world with your outer world, your thoughts with your feelings and dreams, and you with the others in your life. Through this process, life becomes meaningful.

Listen to the promptings of imagination. Bring the pieces of your life – the inner and outer, the conscious and less conscious – into relationship with one another. Unblock the inner+outer flow.

When you give form to imaginal content through creative expression, you encourage the different parts of yourself to work together. Your intuition functions in concert with your intellect. Your inner world and your outer world become more cohesive. And it gets even better — more rewarding — when we practice and share creatively *together*. Then, we can bridge divides in understanding in a way that rational discussion alone will never do. It's a beautiful thing.

Integrating the various aspects of life is a matter of balance; and balance is a moving target: dynamic, not static. Balance is an ongoing practice, and we find it as we move back and forth between poles, in the space between.

We *make* meaning as we *move* back and forth *between* intellect and intuition.

We *make* connection as we *move* back and forth *between* inner and outer.

The *moving* is important, the *making* is important, and the space *between* is important.

What I'm Getting At: There's a *between* between everything; including *between thinking and doing*; including *between you and the world*.

> The "between" space is important because...

This is the space where the creative process happens, and this is the space where relationships develop. It's essential to a balanced **human experience**!

balance - balance - balance

Essential Ideas

Here's an introduction to these important concepts in this book:

- *Everyday creativity is nourishing*
- *An ecological understanding puts humanity in perspective*
- *Thirdness establishes continuity*
- *Mythological awareness is helpful*
- *The wound in the social tissue cannot be healed by individuals*

Everyday creativity is nourishing

Everyday creativity is nourishing. It's human nature. It's how we contribute to the world. When you do your thing, you feel charged, alive, satisfied.

But ——
Is it wise to follow our human natures, or...
better just to try to stop doing anything?

Because —

Look at the state we're in. Look at the trouble we've caused by being human — despite clear and abiding wisdom on how we might live sustainably, responsibly, as stewards of our common ground.

Other species seem able to play their parts without too much pathology. Other species are not implicated in climate change or mass extinctions or ethnic cleansing or nuclear waste. What is WRONG with us? Our species seems uniquely inclined to live in such destructive ways!

Have we somehow defied nature? Is that even possible? Or is it actually human nature to be a—holes? I can't claim to know all, but I know this: if we are to recover from the fine mess we've gotten ourselves into, we must begin with seeing the problem. Right now, right here. Look within and look around. Recovery begins with awareness.

An ecological understanding puts humanity in perspective

Indigenous Traditions

I don't want to generalize about indigenous traditions, which exist in so many forms, the wide world over. Each is unique. Still, it can be said with confidence that ***indigenous traditions DO NOT create the imbalances that now threaten our world.*** Although indigenous peoples have been scarred horrifically by the atrocities of colonizers, yet where indigenous traditions survive, they show connection to the land, reverence for the web of life, respect for all beings, awareness of life processes, a deep sense of community, and an understanding of interspecies support systems gained through generations of observation and living integrally within local ecosystems.

indigenous
adjective
originating or occurring naturally in a particular place; native

RECOGNIZE:
We are part of the web, not free agents

Indigenous practices and indigenous peoples, by definition, grow out of the land, and indigenous traditions demonstrate this ecological relationship. To those of us who are not (not *anymore* or not *yet*) indigenous: we must get our roots into the soil. We must learn reverence and appreciation for the web of life that supports and sustains us, of which we are but one strand. We can learn this through direct experience, and by honoring and studying the wisdom of those who were here before us.

According to some Native American lore, the human, as the youngest species to arrive on the scene, is not the boss of the world but rather has much to learn from other creatures, who are not so confused as we humans are!

soil layers

Human Humus Humility

Listen, Humans! You're not **all that.** We will end up in the ground, as humus. Get it? So practice humility.

"Everyday creative expression": at first glance it might sound...boring? mundane? nothing much?

Ok. It has a humble quality: not glamorous nor earth shattering. That turns out to be its great value. Can we stop shattering the earth? How about if we let ego take a break? How about some everyday humility?

TAKE NOTE: I'm not encouraging you to mediocrity. I'm encouraging you to ease of expression, and a big part of that is: ***just stop trying to impress people.***

Keep in mind:

> - it isn't all about you,

> - it isn't just *your* expression ... *and* ...

> - it probably isn't original.

Releasing creative ownership goes along with releasing self-consciousness and releasing ego. Revise your notion of self.

> *What? What is that supposed to mean?*

> **Stay with me...**

For parents, your children exemplify this idea. Yes, they are part of you, they are born of you, yes, and you are crucial to giving them life and sustaining them; but they are more than you. They separate from you as they grow, becoming more and more their own unique expression of life. The wise parent lets this happen, though of course it is sometimes challenging. In just the same way, when you bring a creative idea into form, it is yours and also it isn't yours. You can love it and also let it become whatever it is. Let it happen. Please, get over yourself!

"On Children" from **The Prophet**

Your children are not your children.
They are the sons and daughters of Life's longing for itself.
They come through you but not from you,
And though they are with you
yet they belong not to you.

You may give them your love but not your thoughts,
For they have their own thoughts.
You may house their bodies but not their souls,
For their souls dwell in the house of tomorrow,
which you cannot visit, not even in your dreams.

You may strive to be like them, but seek not to make them like you.
For life goes not backward nor tarries with yesterday.

— *Kahlil Gibran*

You/Not You
If what's coming through you is NOT YOU specifically, but rather you giving form to psyche that wants expression, you do not have to take credit or blame for how fabulous or stupid it looks.

---

psyche is breath, life, soul; the animating principle of the universe

A creative idea is yours and also isn't yours. Sure, when you apply yourself to any project, you have a right to take credit! You're giving it shape. You're giving it voice. You're giving it a place in the world. Be proud! I'm not calling for *false* humility, I'm just pointing out – it ain't all you. It never was and never will be. So, like – your every day creative engagement — it doesn't have to be earth shattering. It can be humble — and you don't have to feel either egotistical or ashamed about that.

Matter of fact, we need less earth shattering events and more humble every day comfortable grounded creative expression. The airwaves are stuffed with people clamoring for attention: trying to be the loudest, the coolest, the newest, the trendiest, the zingiest, the wisest, the deepest, the dopest—pfffft...Who cares! So much noise! What a cacophony. But why is it happening?

When social media platforms and self-promotion are the main ways we communicate with each other, it's like we're all in this big arena, everyone trying to build a platform high enough and loud enough that people will see and hear us for a second. That's a crappy way to communicate; and a **terrible** way to build community. It's like you're always selling something, when what you really want is to be in relationship with others.

Sharing everyday creative expression builds social mycelium.
Individuals will starve for lack of social connection. Consider the role of "social mycelium" in keeping us nourished and networked.

In a healthy ecosystem, mycelial networks play a crucial part, carrying nutrients from constituent members and redistributing where needed. Mycelial networks are disrupted by industrial farming practices such as monoculture and pesticide use. Imagine "social mycelium" as a naturally occurring support system that has been disrupted by the imposition of our industrialized economic system. When we humans are organized for maximum productivity and divvied into our demographic silos to maximize efficient consumption, we are simply one more crop being cultivated for economic gain. Like any other monoculture, imbalances are created that lead to poor nourishment and result in disease. You can think of that metaphorically or literally; either way, it's true.

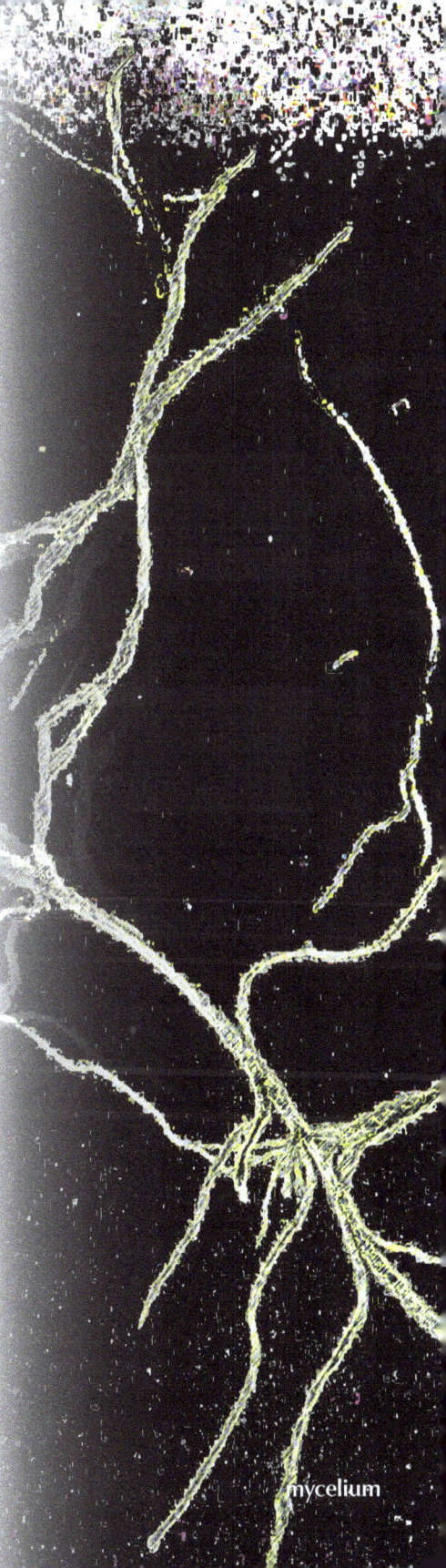
mycelium

Mycelium

Kick up a little dirt on the forest floor. See that white stuff? That unassuming mat of fibers?

Mycelium, affectionately known as the "wood wide web," is the mass of white filaments that form the plant body of the mushroom. When a spore germinates it develops into a thread-like hypha. Hyphae grow and branch out by digesting and absorbing nutrients from the soil, interlacing to form a vast underground network. This mycelial network is the main body of the plant, of which the mushroom is a short-lived fruit.

Mycorrhizal mycelium digests and distributes nutrients among other plant species as needed, literally growing into the roots of other plants to exchange nutrients. Mycelium provides nourishment for a host of other species in its ecosystem, and can also transport water and spikes of electrical potential.

"Scientists believe 92% of all plants form a mycorrhizal relationship in the soil....The mycorrhizal fungi do not simply grow in accordance with one individual but instead connect many individuals throughout the soil. Often one species of mycorrhizal will actually connect species of different plants as well. This type of mycelial network is essential to the health of ecosystems because the mycorrhizae aids in plant communication and even transfers nutrients amongst species. It has been found that plants will actually give nutrients to weaker trees in the community which effectively helps the entire forest."(Baldi)

"Social mycelium" is what we humans need, to nurture and support the health of our human common ground, which will starve, atrophy, calcify, (die!) without the creative participation of individuals. The "social mycelium" uses the nutrients provided by our personal creative engagement to nourish our societies. When our individual ideas and creative contributions circulate amongst us, it creates a healthy social ecosystem. The health of our common social connection is essential to the survival of humanity.

Personal creative experience must have a pathway for social expression, and it's a two way need for nourishment. The best functioning self is fed by social connection. The best functioning society is fed by individual contributions.

Eco-participation and psyche in everything

To participate in the world, be present. Simply by being present, curious, and engaged, you naturally become aware of location and the presence of "the other." What's "the other"? Sounds so mystical. Ok. "The other" is simply "that which I don't consciously identify as me." The other is not limited to other people!

If we imagine that psyche is continuous in everything — and certainly we don't know that it is not — then we naturally open to a different experience of the world. That is a world of possibility, in which we are all participants — humans and "others" alike.

You may notice, wonder about, and feel things without being sure what they are. That's OK. In fact, it's helpful to recognize that many things you think you know are not so sure. Our lives are full of guesses, assumptions, and mysteries that we often pretend are known entities, just to make life easier or less scary. But mysteries don't always resolve themselves just because we want them to. It's ok, you can just let them be. Even celebrate them.

Celebrating Mysteries
In the rational world, a mystery is often considered a problem to be solved. In the world of the sacred, a mystery is a source of awe and revelation, something to be revered and celebrated. A sacred mystery is bigger than us, beyond our understanding, something to which we can surrender.

From the Eleusinian mysteries of ancient Greece to the Christian sacraments, sacred mysteries are celebrated in spiritual traditions. If you're outside of such traditions, how can you partake? Simply this: Where do you feel awe? Where can you lose yourself? Perhaps in the mist of a sunrise, or staring out to sea. In the arms of a lover, or in the eyes of a child. In the hum of cicadas or the silence of winter. Via ecstatic drumming or mycelial magic. This world, this life, is bigger than you, more than you...

Once you start noticing, you discover the abundance of awesome mysteries around you! Find your own way in... Create your own celebrations of awe, and share them with those around you!

...now...where I am...what's happening...now...

Notice the moment. Wonder...and perhaps, wander.

Follow my curiosity, while staying in my commitment to the moment.

What am I noticing, following, feeling right now?

*Be with my feelings. Acknowledge them. Express them.
Feel them.*

*Become more aware of the wisps of ideas and images
that float through me and around me—the ones that I
usually shoo away.*

*Expand awareness of my continual participation with
"Other."*

Contemplate the idea of psyche continuous in all things.

*Include:
   the soil beneath me,
   the person next to me,
   bird, grass, sun,
   the breeze on my skin,
   the unconscious,
   a thought or impulse that comes to me out of
nowhere...*

*In my direct experience of being present,
I feel, see and hear things that I am not sure about.*

*Are they inside, or outside?
Am I imagining, or sensing?
I must admit to not knowing.*

I notice sounds and scents, breath and air, moisture inside and moisture outside... As I become more aware of my body, I also become more aware that I am continuous with the world around me.

In this way of noticing and allowing, we become more porous and the world flows through us.

There are parts of you that have become walled off because they aren't recognized or accorded value, or because you don't know how to deal with them; so that even you yourself may forget about or devalue these parts of yourself. This happens to others as well—other people, other things, other beings, and also to other places and parts of the world. When they are not noticed or not recognized, they may stop communicating.

Notice them. Give a little extra attention.

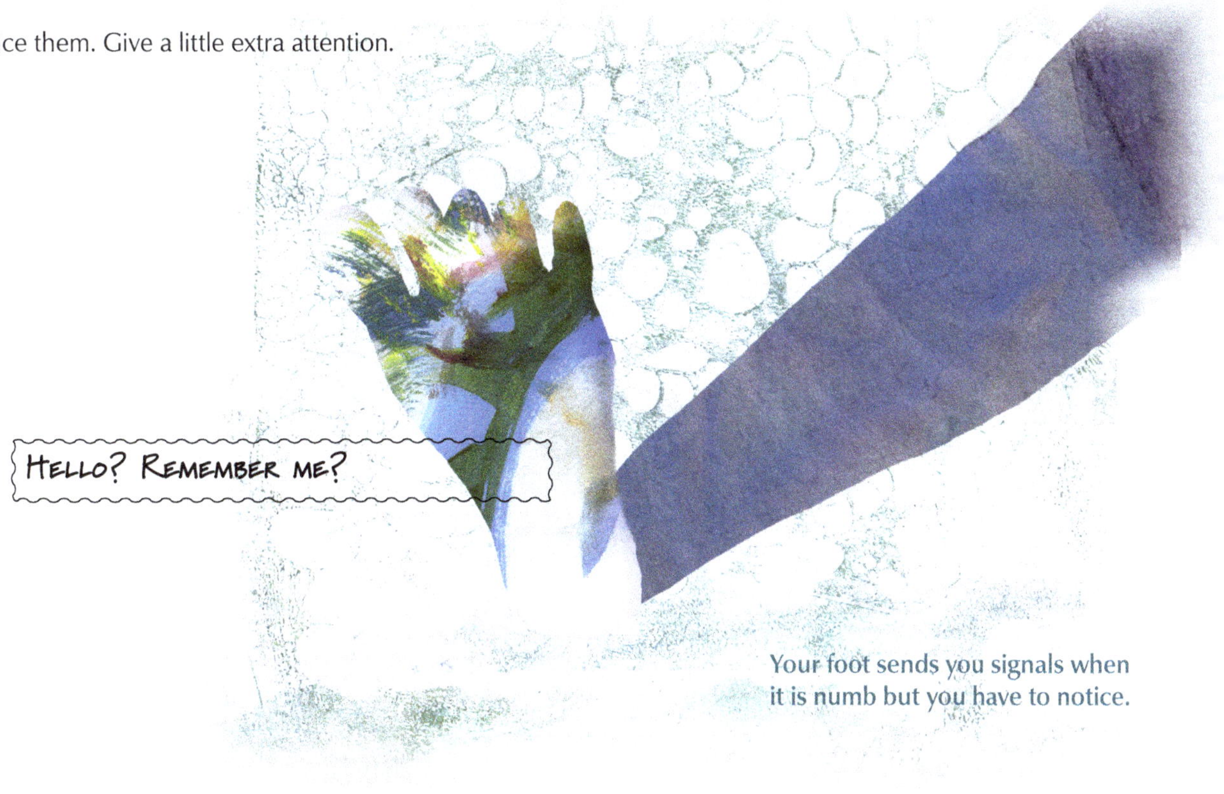

Hello? Remember me?

Your foot sends you signals when it is numb but you have to notice.

18   HOW TO PARTICIPATE IN THE WORLD

Thirdness establishes continuity

As we open to the unknown and allow ourselves to acknowledge that we don't know everything, there is a sense of expansion: new space actually opening up. A space of possibility. We can call this "the third."

In between known and unknown, this space is characterized by ambiguity and neutrality. Here, events are not clearly one thing or another; they are possibly both/and.

The third is any liminal "in-between" space, and it is essential: for the healthy function of the individual, for healthy relationships, and for a healthy society.

What is quite mystical and magical about it is that it can easily be expanded — or collapsed!

The Third:

In logic, the third is the space between true and false; in relationship, the space between you and me; in creative process, the space between real and pretend. The third is the possibility of another option between Yes and No.

Characteristics of the Third:

neutrality, openness, incompleteness, ambiguity, synthesis, mediation, detachment, transcendence, transformation, participation

Concertina Expand!

Expanding the third
The third is collapsed when we refuse to imagine, or to entertain possibility.

In an environment where a thing must either be **True** or **False**, the third is collapsed.

In a relationship where all interpersonal dynamics are ascribed solely to one person or another, the third is collapsed.

Where pretending is not allowed, where unknowns are not admitted, where ambiguity is not tolerated, the third is collapsed.

In these tight places, individuals will find it hard to express themselves or to find true connection with others. Paradoxically, it is having space between us that allows a healthy and functional relationship between individual and group. Room to breathe...room to move...room to express and connect.

That, my friend, is why I feel it's so important that we create social opportunities for creative play and sharing. Expand the third! We need it. And it's not hard or expensive to do. Everyday creative expression is just the thing to open up the space. This book will show you how.

Continuity is real
Traditional stories and rituals connect the individual with the larger worlds of culture and nature, past and future, through imagery of inner-outer continuity: a mythic worldview that includes us, inside and out, and connects us to land and creatures, and other beings around us.

Our continuity and relatedness seem obvious—a matter of common sense. Yet in contemporary western culture we often must remember to imagine ourselves into the world (even though we are already here). So much are we in our heads and in our computers that we forget or neglect being in body, being in place.

Even when we are "in-bodied" and "in-placed," the common western attitude leads us to think of our experiences as isolated and individual (just as we think of our body parts as distinct from one another: the heart...the elbow...the salivary gland...); but the boundaries between self and other (and self and world) are conceptual. Of course you can define the edges of your body. You know where your skin is. You can distinguish your body from the chair you sit on or the dog at your feet. So, the sense of being an individual is not just conceptual. We do function as individuals and it's pretty easy to see why and how we recognize each other as such. BUT...there are so many, many things that regularly cross the boundaries between "you" and "not you," many of them invisible. The aroma of flowers, when you notice it. You or not you? The song you sang along with on the radio that's now stuck in your head. You or not you? The surly look from that guy in the gas station, that's now smirking up your own face. Your files and photos stored on your hard drive...The air you breathe...the food you eat...the water you drink...the sun warming your skin...the microbes in your gut...the memory of your mother hugging you... You or not you?

Western culture concretizes the distinction between inner and outer experiences, but it's never so solid. Think of bodies of water to understand that inner-outer boundaries are approximations only; they are useful ideas, not objectively "real."

There are no definitive lines separating the Gulf of Mexico from the Caribbean Sea or the Atlantic Ocean, except the lines that we make up. We can describe where they are and we can discern differences between these "bodies," but the waters mix freely. Lines of separation are invisible and ambiguous. Border "territories" would be a more accurate way to think of it, and you can think of that ambiguous territory as an example of the third, which is "both" and "neither."

Building a wall in the ocean (or desert) in order to enforce distinctions would cause problems for the ecosystem, and the same is true regarding the building of walls between your inner and outer, yourself and others, or consciousness and the unconscious. We have done it; and it has caused problems. Like dam building, it is done for a reason, but not without ramifications. You can see why we need to allow the transitional third space to exist.

Fortifications have ramifications.

Mythological awareness is helpful

I think of mythology as the quintessential expression of thirdness; so if we need more thirdness, "in myth" is a great place to look. It is "me" and "not me"; true and not true; inner, outer, and in between.

Mythology is a continuity in human experience, connecting humans to one another and to the world around us, connecting our inner experience to our outer experience. It has ever been so. Mythology infuses our beings, our thoughts and our actions. Different mythologies flow into and through each other, and, like bodies of water, though we can name and describe different sources, we can recognize continuities and influences, but lines of separation are ambiguous.

We're never fully aware of the mythological beliefs that guide us. We cannot be. Yet, just as we can become more aware of our own personal feelings, intentions, and drives that are not fully conscious, but kind of pushing against the boundary, pushing up into consciousness: so we can also become more aware of the cultural psyche—that is, the mythological sea in which we swim.

Myth is metaphorical
Composed of fact and fiction, mythology uses metaphor to connect what we know with what we believe, what we sense, and what we imagine. It pulls from all our different ways of knowing, understanding, and perceiving, in order to create models or narratives that inform the way we live. It simply is always a part of the human experience: the very definition of how humans make meaning.

Engaging with myth
Myth is always growing and changing, and a growing mythological understanding keeps us healthy. Mainstream western culture does not recognize our immersion in myth, so, as individuals, we must! Not only recognize it but champion it!

Instead of pretending we've left it behind (so it can sneak up on us), we're better off to try to understand it. Instead of trying to get away from it, what if we intentionally enter into it? How? Let thinking and imagining swirl together. Encourage fluid movement between intellect and intuition. Explore the wilds that extend beyond rationality. Notice where you're pretending to *know* things that would more accurately be described as *beliefs*. Most important of all, do things with other people.

Myth grows and changes. We are more aware of the beliefs we outgrow and cast aside, because they no longer fit. Weirdly this image of fossils (right) is generated by AI–something I am willfully, quixotically avoiding; but when I searched for an image of fossils to use for reference to create an illustration here, this image came up, perfectly fitting what I hoped to show: an image of something from the distant past, created by the technology which is propelling us into the future; which only goes to show ya that myth grows and changes, and the current moment, as AI moves into culture, is no different.

MYTH IS:
A web composed of facts, beliefs, memories, traditions, ideas, dreams, stories...

This web of mythology grows out of our shared experience, holding us and shaping us, becoming culture.

Mythology performs the crucial function of bridging what we know with what we don't. This occurs at the interface between consciousness and the unconscious. This mysterious area between "real" and "pretend" is where dreams and theories, habits and traditions, and all manner of creative things come into being.

Myth is certainly revealed in story form, but is also expressed in very many other ways: through all of the arts... through government and religion, architecture, craft, and design...dreams, memories, habits...speech patterns, foodways, family traditions...even scientific procedures, economic strategies, and political ideologies... In short, every human construction is mythically infused.

Kaleidoscopic and paradoxical, myth cannot be reduced to a defined meaning, but speaks on many levels. It is not falsehood. It is metaphorically true though not literally true.

Everlasting Dreams - stock.adobe.com

One way to do all of this is by giving form to imaginal content through creative expression. It's a way of both engaging with and creating space between you and the imaginal impulse, gaining perspective by moving this content out where you can take a look at it and interact with it. By this practice, you make invisible things visible and help others to see more of what you see; and you are creating a cultural milieu in which intuitive understanding can be shared.

Mythology is cultural
We view ancient cultures as mythological, but our own? Harder for us to understand our current ways as mythological. Is Science a mythology, or Capitalism, or the American Dream? They truly are; but when you're living it, when you're immersed in it, you simply can't be fully conscious of the ways your beliefs guide you and shape you.

We live *within* belief systems, so it is very difficult, if not impossible, to see the myths playing out in our lives. When you always see and act through those beliefs, you are not fully conscious of them, yet you can become *more* aware. It's a matter of degree.

People sometimes refer to "personal mythology," but this is almost a misnomer, because mythology is a *cultural* expression of psyche. We do each have our own relationship, or our own standing in relationship to the mythologies in which we live, it's true, but mythology is bigger than you — it's always bigger than you. That goes a good way toward explaining why you can't simply choose to reject a mythological tradition that you are steeped in, even if your relation to it is contentious; but you can work to become more aware of it, and its presence in your life. You can call it out and help others to see what you see. Becoming aware of the myths we inhabit is a sign that we are outgrowing them, but it is an ongoing process. New myths will replace the old.

Mythology weaves us together
Imagine mythology as an invisible weaving, and we are the weavers. The work proceeds, with or without our awareness; but awareness helps us align with the rhythms and patterns that shape our lives. Awareness elucidates our continuity with location, elements, and the influences of anima mundi. Awareness helps us better understand each other and ourselves. Awareness helps us recognize our own contributions to the web we are weaving.

Coming together around the liminal loom, we become more aware of our invisible threads. What are others thinking, feeling, and noticing? Where do our threads cross, align, or diverge? We weave a sense of group mythology, to which each relates in their own way.

Myth is social mycelium
Myth holds us together. It grows out of our shared experience. It feeds us.

Just like the way mushrooms and mycelium are everywhere so important and powerful, yet often humble or hidden so that at first you don't notice them. And then you do. And once you see one, then you see that they are all around!

As we learn more and more about the omnipresence and superpowers of the fungal kingdom through the groundbreaking work of such researchers as Paul Stamets and Merlin Sheldrake, it strikes me that the "everyday-ness" of mycelium is quite significant—not that they don't exhibit a mind-blowing and fabulous array of features! Yet they are ubiquitous and constant, working, growing, morphing, and interacting. As western culture has obsessed over *Amazing Individuals Performing Incredible Feats Against Overwhelming Odds*, meanwhile the extensive *Kingdom Fungi* is knitting the world together; as always, ceaselessly becoming.

"There have never been individuals...
We are all lichens." Gilbert

Lichens are a complex life form that is a symbiotic partnership of two separate organisms. USDA Forest Service

Healing the wound in the social tissue

Each of us has suffered trauma to some degree. In the western world, until recently, it was common to try to keep your painful experiences to yourself as best you could; but the repression of significant trauma can generate a cascade of health problems, not least of which is allowing injurious actions to continue unchecked. Today it has become more accepted to recognize that wounds, whether visible or not, need care. How to care for our invisible wounds? Notice them, listen to them, and sometimes, share them. As more and more personal stories come to light, we have learned that by compassionately bearing witness to each others' traumas we can help heal what we are unable to cope with alone (see Kalsched, Herman).

There are wounds, also, that are not "yours" or "mine" – wounds in the social tissue that cannot be healed by individuals in isolation. When the wound is between, we must attend to it together.

The mind/body split is such a wound disclosed in western culture, a wound that shapes the way we think, speak, and act, a wound that has impacted the health of the world. It is historical and it is mythological. This way of viewing the world takes us out of experience by its focus on fragmented forms and the translation/reduction of experience to logos. The attention to discrete, defined, constituent parts unfortunately does not easily allow simultaneous understanding of relationships and processes. Dualistic thinking has propelled us to new capabilities while also setting us on a dangerous course.

"Ruh roh! This isn't where we wanted to go!"

Wounds are injuries. They may leave scars and disabilities, and also leave us with gifts of new insight and understanding that can make us wiser. This can be said of the mind-body split. Let us acknowledge what we have learned along this path while also recognizing the critical need to redress the injury and put a stop to the injurious behavior.

Philosophers and physicists have shown us the limitations of mind-body dualism, while many mytho-cultural views (native american, taoist, and yogic traditions, for example) offer alternate ways of understanding. We can see the error in our thinking, yet we still labor under the misapprehension. We cannot heal that wound as individuals because it is a wound in the social tissue: the wound is located "between."

Sharing the imaginal experience is essential to a cultural healing of the subject/object, mind/body split. Restoring a natural permeability and sense of continuity between inner and outer, self and other, encouraging the imaginal flow between us, we can regenerate that social connective tissue that keeps us healthy and whole.

To Recap:

- Mythic understanding is valuable.

- Mythic understanding is third-like, helping us to imagine, make meaningful connections, and see from new perspectives.

- Mythic understanding grows from engaged creative participation.

- Making and sharing creatively with others builds myth and metaphor, nourishing a healthy social network [mycelium].

I hope this book will convince you and catalyze you to cherish the mundane creative act practiced with awareness

- for you

- for your communities

- for the eco-psyche— and the more-than-human world

Remember, mythology is not falsehood. It is a web composed of facts, beliefs, memories, traditions, ideas, dreams, stories...

Everyday Tools and Practices For Creative Expression

What do you need to practice everyday creativity?

Everyday tools
Tools for creative expression are **EVERYWHERE**, and, really, **everything**. At the top of the list: hands, voice, mind+body...

Beyond the self, my personal favorites include paper, paint, pencil, glue and scissors, needles, yarn, and fiber, flowers, a camera, and kitchen tools! I particularly like the process of physical making, because of the material evidence it brings forth, if you will. Creating form outside of yourself where you can look at it and interact with it and turn it over and show it to someone else gives a particular boost to the practice; but all kinds of creative engagement are worthy. You'll find the tools that you most love to use. Name your pleasure! It may be an ever-evolving list.

The point is, *"Everyday Creative Expression"* is really an approach to life: a mindset. You can be creative in any moment, in any way you choose. Movement, song, voice, drama, poetry, comedy, cooking, gardening, wildcrafting...are just a few options. All are fantastic vehicles for engaging and expressing.

So if you're wondering what stuff you need to go along with this book—well, count on me to give you permission to treat yourself to art supplies, musical instruments, gorgeous yarn, fresh produce, beautiful flowers...but what you *need*? You probably already have.

Everyday practices
The everyday creative practices I'll be sharing all extend from these basic ideas:

- reverie
- creative exploration
- archetypal awareness
- eco-participation
- journaling
- imaginal dialog

Everyday social connection grows through sharing

- inner and outer experiences
- imaginal exploration
- ideas, feelings, differences and correspondences

We'll delve into all these great things in the pages ahead. But—WHY??? Why should you care? Why does it matter?

Why

Why does this matter in a world run amok? Isn't it kind of...trivial?

Why develop an everyday creative practice

I live in a society that overvalues rational analysis and pretends that you can get to the bottom of things by following the whys all the way down, *AND* I'm personally prone to overthinking things. So let me point out from my own experience that you can get trapped in an endless cycle of "whys" that ultimately spirals into frustration and anxiety. It's not just 5-year-olds who do it.

Still, a judicious amount of "why-ing" provides orientation and motivation. So why develop an everyday creative practice?

1. First of all, because it's fun...enjoyable...feels good

2. because you will learn things about yourself that are worth knowing

3. because you will work through some problems that have been bothering you

4. because you will become clearer about your direction

5. because you will become more confident in your voice and vision

6. because you will experience healthier connections with the world and the others in it.

The value of creative engagement is social cohesion

The most valuable "why" of creative engagement is not the thing you make, but the process of participation—being in conversation with the images, the ideas, the materials, the elements...and the sharing of that with others. Not only are we – individuals – hungry for social connection; but the social mycelium, if you will, demands the nutrition that comes from our personal creative experience. It's the network you nourish through your creative involvement that sustains us all.

Why why why? It's turtles all the way down]

Why you should start a creative group
I basically think EVERYONE should start a creative group; so YOU, being a member of EVERYONE, should start a creative group. But what do I mean by "a creative group"? It's wide open, indeed! There are countless forms this might take, so there is surely a creative group for you. You don't really have to even think of it as a group. More on all that in Part IV...

The main thing is, we need opportunities to be around other people in real life without the intermediary of a computer; and we need to do things together where each of us can feel we are "being ourselves" (whatever that means—yeah, more about that later, too). We need opportunities to share ideas within smaller, local communities, where differences of opinion can be not only tolerated, but explored and entertained.

For now, let me emphasize this: the matter is urgent. Our social contracts are failing. People are lonely and isolated, frustrated, angry, sad...and they're acting out in desperate ways. The internet, the computer, the phone, social media all have their uses, no doubt, but they cannot provide the connection and support that is most needed now. It's like eating junk food when you're starving: it doesn't satisfy your nutritional needs, so you're still hungry, so you just keep eating it, even though it's making you sick.

The antidote to loneliness and isolation is participation.

Ultimately, your creative practice is not for you alone. Your creative engagement is you working in concert with the world. You are the instrument of bringing the imaginal into form. Be a well-crafted instrument.

Moving beyond the myth of individualism
It's About You!
Sharing your unique, creative self is something *YOU NEED*—and I don't even know you! (probably). As long as you're human, you need the connection to community. To be healthy and happy, you need the opportunity to share ideas, skills, and resources.

To feel fulfilled, you need to be able to contribute to the social group in a way that's meaningful to you. Not necessarily in the way that someone else thinks you should; because it's you, with your unique traits, in your unique ways, that has something special to share, just by being you. Individual differences strengthen society.

Revise your notion of self.
Release self-consciousness and release ego.
Be aware that when you give form to a creative idea
— it is about you
and also
— it isn't about you.
Let it happen.
You are in concert with
the imaginal impulse
the materials
the elements
and who knows what all else
a story your mother told you
a book you forgot you read
a sculpture that inspired you
a breeze in the trees

That's not even scratching the surface of all the invisible
and unknown influences that play a part in your expression,

So – Get over yourself!

Be a well crafted instrument.

therapeutic
adjective
1 having a good effect on the body or mind
2 contributing to a sense of well-being

therapy
noun
1 treatment intended to relieve or heal a disorder
2 the treatment of mental conditions by verbal communication and interaction

Therapeutic not therapy
If you are thinking, "This sounds intense" or "I'm not qualified to organize a group," it's not really, and yes, you are. I'm simply talking about bringing people together to share everyday experience, in a way that's meaningful to you. Whether it's fun or deep or quiet or raucous, there are countless forms this can take. It's something you've done before and will do again, probably: *a normal thing* — except for many people it has become much less normal — but I want to be sure you know how IMPORTANT it is.

The experience of creative sharing can be quite therapeutic — that's why I'm writing this book; but I am not suggesting that you must be a therapist or a teacher or an event facilitator — unless of course you choose to!

Really, I'm just saying, reach out and gather some folks to do something together.

In Part IV, I'll share ideas and examples and offer some guidelines that I have found helpful in working with groups. It mainly boils down to listening and sharing with kindness and respect; and your groups will be supported by your own developing practice of everyday creativity.

As important as it is, and as simple as it is, opportunities for everyday creativity and everyday connection are less routine than they once were, so we have to be proactive about expressing and sharing ourselves. In the process, maybe we can improve the quality of our interactions.

The widespread isolation so many are feeling is a SOCIAL DISORDER. IT CAN BE HEALED! But you will need to take action. The simplest of actions:

- *go into yourself and take something of what you find out into the world*
  . . . .

- *go out into the world and bring something of what you find into yourself*
  . . . .

- *repeat...repeat...repeat...*
  . . . .

My Point and Mission

To summarize:

My point

    Creative expression is radically important.

    Anyone can do it.

    Giving form to the imaginal impulse is human nature.

    Making things is a way to participate in the world.

    Just let go and let it happen.

    When you're creatively engaged you can forget about yourself.

    This is when you really find connection.

    This is when you really find yourself.

My mission

to get people into a regular, healthy flow of creative expression in their daily lives;

to get people comfortable in sharing creative expression with others;

to get people into the settings that allow the sharing of creative expression.

Who am I to say?
Ok, you may be wondering what makes me so sure about all this. I'll tell you something of my background and how I got here, now, writing this book.

About Me
Creative engagement is the story of my life, really—at least, in one way of telling it. Looking back through the annals of time I see myself always gluing pieces of paper together or making cookies or whatnot—and talking it out the whole way! That's me. And I've learned an awful lot about myself and the world around me through the process.

Some of the things I've learned are

   - that most people are not this way

   - that many people say they would like to be this way

YET

   - are *incredibly resistant* to acting on the simple impulse to creative expression

BUT

   - if you can actually GET THEM to engage, the effect is, by their own accounts, **OVERWHELMINGLY POSITIVE**.

That's strange, isn't it? I thought so. And I've pursued this strangeness over decades: through my quirky passage to adulthood; through my education (BS Education; MA/PhD Mythological Studies/Depth Psychology); and through my work and play as teacher-artist-facilitator-counselor-friend-parent-writer-ponderer-and-perennial maker of things. In all honesty, I'm an expert on this topic.

But It's Not about Me!
When my kids were little I grappled with this issue: if my own kids get a rich and fabulous education, but precious few others can, what's the point? Even if I'm *only* concerned for my own kids' well-being, what kind of world will they live in? Can my own kids' great education sustain a healthy society where people can read each other both critically and compassionately; where people can think about current events in historical context; where people can have opinions that are not solely emotionally based; where people can communicate with each other calmly and candidly; where people can work together on existential problems? No. The answer is no.

Many people will say the value of an education is to get a job. Ok, that's not wrong; but to have a society where people can get along reasonably, everyone needs a "good education"; and it's clear that not everyone has been able to get one. I guess it's "fortunate," in our world of crumbling infrastructure, unequal opportunities, and chaotic change, that a "good education" does not have to come from school. We can help each other by sharing knowledge and ideas. It's easy, if we will only do it, but we will need to create the opportunities to do so.

> Education is the antidote to ignorance, which is simply "not knowing." Tucked away in our own silos we are ignorant of each other's experiences and realities. It's really up to us to bridge the gap. Educate and be educated.

Start a Mutual Aid Society
For all my thinking and research and experience, I believe that the heart, the kernel, the essential center of a "good education" is the ability to engage creatively with the world around you, and to share what you know with others. Over the years my convictions as to the importance of creative engagement and expression have only strengthened. Alarmingly, cultural awareness and opportunity seem to have diminished as my own awareness has grown.

I can try to sell you this idea of everyday creative engagement because it's for your own betterment — and it is. With a regular creative practice, you'll lead a more fulfilling life, be better able to more easily work through problems and bear difficulties, find meaning and rhythm and connection — I believe all of that is true — and I wish that for you.

But it isn't what I really care about — sorry...

What I really care about is how we, as a species, can heal the social wounds that we are suffering from, so we can stop destroying the world. We need to know how to connect with one another, to work together, to play together... and that healing won't come from you or me simply straightening out our personal shit and having better personal lives. It will come from communities - families - social groups that encourage the creative participation of individuals. And **THAT** will lead to you and me having better personal lives.

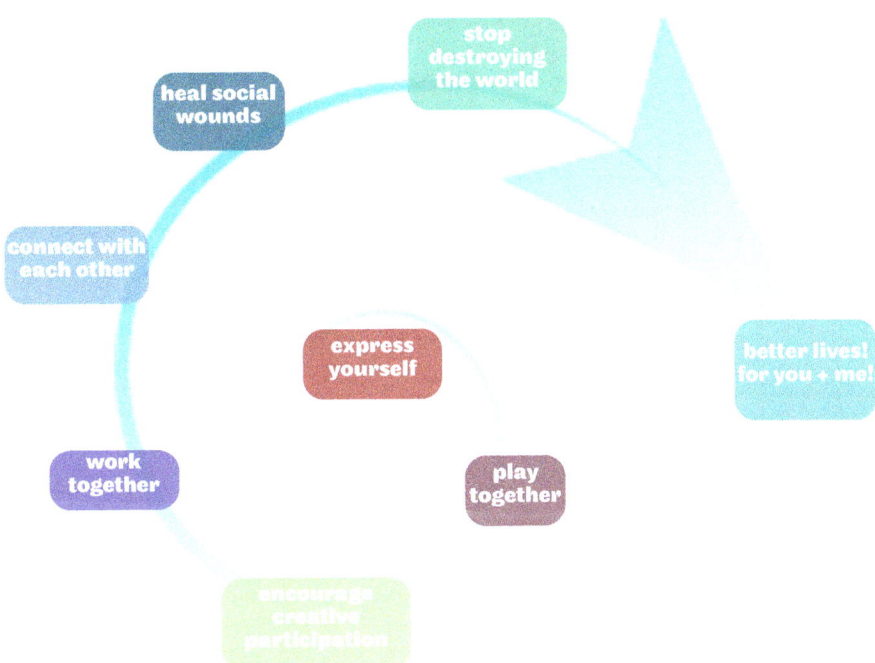

Maksim Shebeko - stock.adobe.com

Milling grain makes it digestible for humans, but dominant western culture took it too far, by choosing to screen out the most nutritious parts in order to achieve the "purity" of white flour.

We have subsequently discovered white flour to be largely devoid of nutrients, its widespread use implicated in poor health and disease. Now, we are wise to remember the value of all the parts (as indigenous cultures have done).

"Purity," whether in flour or in culture, is not necessarily desirable.

Experience Comes First

Experience is not rational. It is pre-rational (before rationality). It is trans-rational (beyond rationality).

It is the stuff of life, before it has been parsed, organized, rated, screened, labeled…

It is not less than or more primitive than rational thought. It is the very stuff of existence. We are ALWAYS immersed in it, though we may lose awareness of the fact.

To think rationally is to screen out all sorts of experience, abstracting (or extracting) what is most relevant to the task at hand. It's a very useful ability, but it's not the only tool in the tool chest. Extracting the essence and throwing the rest on the waste pile is bad practice. All of that "chaff" is not worthless.

Too much focus, too much refinement, too much purity has led us to dire straits, inner and outer. It's true of mental and physical habits (which are **NOT TRULY DISTINCT**). It's true of industrial practices, social structures, and spiritual beliefs.

Is there a remedy? Yep. If we remember, we can become more aware of experience in each moment.

Part II : Being Creative

Being Creative

First Show Up

Obvious? Yes. But it's the first thing you need to do to establish your everyday practice, and probably the easiest thing to avoid. Showing up is not hard to do — or is it the hardest to do? Lots of excuses can keep you from showing up: chief among them, 1) not finding time and 2) not knowing what to do once you arrive. Neither of these are good excuses. Read on.

You don't need to know what to do, so just throw that one out. Believe me. In fact, not knowing what to do is a perfect starting point, and I'll return to that idea. But getting around to showing up for yourself is trickier. You may indeed have a very busy schedule, yet you probably have time for this practice, and it's probably other more devious unconscious resistance strategies that convince you otherwise. I hope this chapter will help you work through that.

Another way of saying "Show up" is "Be present." It's a way of life. It won't take any more time than the time you have.

To be present is to notice. To perceive. Tune into the moment. Observe what is happening within you and around you. You may become aware of the air that you are breathing, in and out. The way it feels in your lungs. The way it feels on your skin. Moist or dry? Cool or warm? You may notice the weather, outside and in. What's happening in the sky? What noises do you hear? Human...machine...animal...elemental...What qualities describe your breath? What feelings do you notice? What do your eyes alight on? Is your stomach gurgling? What thoughts

Notice yourself.
And notice
beyond yourself.

and images are floating through your mind? You don't need to write all this down. Just notice, whatever it is you notice, in any moment.

Showing up is the first and most important step to this creative practice.

Noticing psyche in everything

Notice colors
— and sounds —
odors
— and feelings

Noticing the world around and within you, you realize you are never alone. I don't say this as a poem or a philosophy or a spiritual belief, although it is all of these. I say it as an experiential fact.

We are here in the world. The world is all around us, each of us, in every direction. The world is more than human.

This is you interacting with the world.

Expand your
senses

I find this understanding of reality heartening. If you were feeling lonely, well...you're not alone. You are here. Who and what else is here with you?

We feel alone when:

For your body
is
a giant sense
organ

- we are only noticing ourselves

and

- we are only counting "humans"

This is you
interacting with
the world.

To be sure, human-to-human relationships are important, and that's what Part IV is about. But/and we exist in a world full of beings and creatures and substances and wisps of unknowns. We can develop relationships wherever we are with whomever/whatever is around us. Another way of saying this is "participate."

Participation

To participate, first notice who else is present and what they are saying. Now, when considering the more than human world, you might not know "who" is present and you might not know "what" they are saying, so you have to begin with just listening: awareness. Participation begins with the sensory experience.

Include, rather than ignore, what you are unsure of or unable to define. Much is obscure when you enter unknown territory. Impressions do not at first seem meaningful, and foreign communication sounds at first like gibberish, but with time and practice, patterns of meaning emerge.

> "As we return to our senses, we gradually discover our sensory perceptions to be simply our part of a vast, interpenetrating web work of perceptions and sensations born by countless other bodies".
> (Abram 65).

By participation, I mean being present and phenomenologically engaged with inner and outer experience, not solely personal and not solely conscious, allowing awareness of both knowns and unknowns.

... you are never alone ... you are not isolated ...

anima mundi
noun
psyche continuous in all things; world spirit

participation
noun
the action of taking part in something

Join the Conversation

This process of everyday creativity is a conversation. A conversation begins with listening.

A conversation isn't all about you, but it definitely includes you. I'm sure you've been with someone who just keeps talking talking talking, not even pausing for breath. They are not noticing. They are not listening. Then there are the tight-lipped folks who don't contribute at all: maybe they're not interested, or maybe they think you're not interested. They are not sharing. Either way, with "talk too much" or "talk too little," it's not much of a conversation; but we can all be good conversationalists, and it pretty much starts with tuning in and paying attention.

Wait! Isn't this the section on personal creative practices? Yes!

I am not speaking only of human conversation. You must listen for more than words, inner and outer.

Who's here?
In the conversation of creative expression, many things outside of you have a say: ambient temperature, relative humidity, and the quality of light, for a start, may be important participants.

How about the materials you are working with? Wood? Wool? Pencil? Paper? Soil? Guitar strings? Whatever, whomever, they all have unique characteristics. They all contribute in specific ways. What are they bringing to the conversation?

What ideas and images are you working with, from, or toward? Where is your inspiration coming from? Something you read last night? The amazing feathers of a chicken? A song in your head? A tête-à-tête you overheard twenty-five years ago? The sunset? The breeze? The rainstorm? The news? The incredible fragrance coming from that patch of strawberries? The pain of existence? The sadness of loss? What loss? The slow burn of anger? At whom? Or what?

I could go on and on...It's not hard. What is hard is to think of anything that might possibly be considered a discrete, original idea; meaning, an idea that originates within you and you alone at a particular moment in time, like spontaneous generation. Hello: Spontaneous generation doesn't happen. I don't say that as an expression of futility! It's just to point out the obvious— that everything is connected, nothing stands in isolation, and ideas and images do not arise spontaneously out of your own mind without reference to anything else; nor could you ever possibly carry out a creative project of any type "on your own," without the participation of "others."

So, begin with being present. Notice the things beings materials influences elements ideas around you. To be a good conversationalist, listen. Feel the rhythm and the melody, and join in! You're a participant.

Being Creative *Join the Conversation* 51

Archetypes, intuition, and imagination
How they inform your everyday practice

About Archetypes

Archetypal images and patterns show up in all of your interactions and life processes, on every level from personal dreams to world mythology, in nature and in culture, in physical and in imaginal forms. Both universal and personal, these essential human principles give our lives structure. They're patterns of which you may or may not be aware. It's useful to learn to recognize them and include them in your conversations.

*... Sun ... Mother ... Child ... Tree ... Warrior ... Trickster ...
Archetypal patterns repeat across human experience,
finding unique form in each person's life*

A particular sort of metaphor, they are both universal (we all relate to the idea of Sun) and personal (we each have our own direct, particular experience of Sun). There are many *systems* of archetypes, too, like the 12 signs of the zodiac, the characters and events of any mythology, or the figures and potent symbols of Tarot. For example: the Empress, the Hermit, the Lovers, the Fool — each of these carries its own archetypal pattern. As they interact in combination, they form endless permutations.

There's no set list of archetypes nor, as far as we know, any definitive original source from which these patterns are generated. They are ideals informing common experiences that structure our lives. We each understand them in our own idiosyncratic ways, yet they form the basis for a common social understanding, helping us to relate to one another. For instance, though your mother isn't my mother, nonetheless when you talk about your mother, it orients me to the relationship you're describing, because I, too, have a mother.

We learn to read the archetypal patterns in the world and in our lives through observation. These patterns provide a sense of rhythm and structure. A study of tarot, astrology, or mythology will help attune you to the archetypal view, so those are great places to dig in and learn more. Increased awareness of the patterns allows you to navigate through your life more skillfully.

Archetypal patterns repeat across human experience

   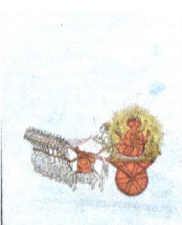   

Let's say you become aware of The Fool archetype showing up repeatedly in various forms, and you may wonder — am I too serious? do I need to be more foolish? more carefree?" Or perhaps "Oops! I see where I am being TOO foolish and ought to exercise more caution." You have to kind of "read the story" to figure out how to interpret it, because there is always more than one interpretation possible.

Maybe you become aware that you keep conjuring up the Negative Mother, someone like the Evil Stepmother who ought to protect you but is instead trying to poison you; so, in response you might begin to seek out more nurturing Mother figures to hang out with, while you learn to protect yourself against negative influences; and/or, you realize where your own "loving" behaviors are "toxic." As you see where imbalance and dysrhythmia lie in your life, you can leverage this understanding to make better choices, more centered on your values and goals.

Archetypal awareness leads to more satisfying engagement and interaction with the world; and by world, I mean both the human world and the more than human world: simply the world in which you live, inclusive of all beings, creatures, elements, and perceptions.

In your everyday creative practice, you can engage with these patterns in a deep, transformative way.

Explore
At different times in your life, one or another will take on greater importance, or "show up" more frequently in your experience. Different roles you find yourself playing will take on various archetypal qualities.

Remember — you are not an archetype! Humans are not archetypes! You are not "The Queen of Wands," nor "The Great Mother," for instance. You are not "Death" nor "The Saviour." You are not "Aries," even if you have five planets in Aries. It helps to call them "archetypal images" rather than "archetypes": that is, think of them as descriptive (adjectives), not definitive (nouns).

Sun images, l to r: Mural painting, Punta del Este (Vilaró); Mardi Gras Venezia (Gnuckx); Jonathan Borba; Four headed sun god, Sūrya (Company School); Fresco, St. John the Baptist Church, Kratovo, Macedonia; Weidenhäuser Straße in Marburg (Vincentz); The Sun (Munch); Ganjifa playing card; New Mexico Zia Earth And Sun (Lilje); Junkanoo 'off the shoulder' dancer costume (RealJunkanoo); "Jomfru Maria som gudmor/ The Lassie and Her Godmother" (Kittelsen); Daoudi Aissa; Fire mark for Compagnie du Soleil Societe ; Rajiv Bajaj.

Explore Archetypes In Your Life

What archetypal pattern is like my present behavior and fantasy?

Who am I like when I do and feel this way?

"Seeing through" archetypes

James Hillman uses the idea of "seeing through" archetypes (Re-Visioning Psychology), as they frame the way we understand the events of our lives.

Maybe you have "seen through" the perspective of Mother–or Teacher –or Warrior –or Poet... These are a few. You can probably think of many more yourself. Use this space to jot down those you think of:

Archetypal mood board

Use a notebook, the wall, or your computer–wherever seems best to you.

Choose one archetype to work with.

It might be one that is coming up for you a lot, in dreams, in your waking life, in the movies you feel like watching, in the roles you find yourself playing.

It may be one that you keep running into in a negative way, and you're wondering why, or looking for guidance on how to deal with it.

It could be one that you're simply curious about or drawn to in this moment.

It does not need to be a human form (but could be).

What is the archetype?

How would you describe?

List keywords that you associate. They don't have to agree with each other. Every archetype has many faces. For instance, "Mother" might include both "loving" and "terrifying"...

Think of examples of this archetype: from your life, from history, literature, film, myth, art, fairy tales...

Gather images. These can be from the internet, from your personal photos, you can sketch them... They do not need to be "literal," but any image that evokes this archetype for you.

Want to take it a step further? Imagine your own creative expression of this archetype and give it form...as story or poem or painting or collage...or any way you imagine!

About Intuition

To know intellectually is to know by reason. In contrast, intuition is knowing by non-rational means: a direct apprehension that simply comes to you, somehow, from somewhere.

Intuitions may seem to come from world or psyche, outside or inside, and may bring anything from nondescript "hunches" to elegant solutions for intellectual problems. For Jung, intuitions are unconscious material coming to light. They are commonly perceived through imagery, dreams, synchronous events, and bodily feelings; and they are often rich with metaphor or symbolic resonance, as if they are overflowing with meaning.

The symbol uses metaphor to unlock meaningful correspondences. One thing points to others. The wonder of metaphor is that it may be deeply true but not literally true, the way a story about a boy wizard teaches you how to use your power in the world, even if that boy only exists in story. An intuition may require contemplation to unwrap it, and it may shift in what it means to you over time.

IMPORTANT: the intuition is not always "right," yet is frequently bringing useful or pertinent information. If we pay attention, it can help us to a better understanding. Don't silence rational thought! But make sure to include intuition in the conversation.

Be respectful.

We can never be conscious of everything around us, within us, and between us, so try to cultivate an openness to new understanding, and a willingness to become aware of what is not yet known. These unknowns often first arise through intuitive ways of knowing.

An openness to intuition may redirect more destructive, unconscious expression. such as the unconscious projection of exaggerated fears, suspicions and animosity upon others.

I dreamt that i stepped out of my front door and fell off a cliff! Hmmm... it might mean i should not ever set foot out of my house again! hmmm...

hmmm...or it might mean to look around before I step out into that new opportunity... hmmm...or maybe i better think twice about that second mortgage...hmmm... a sudden shift in circumstances?

Intuitions may seem to arise without effort, but there are ways to encourage the intuitive flow. Chief among them is, again, simply to notice: if you are open and aware of the suggestions that come to you intuitively, your intuitive sense will strengthen. On the other hand, if you ignore the prompts of intuition, it may find more literal and possibly destructive expression, until you get the message.

Be conscious of your intuition, and be willing to develop it.

As we open to the intuition and allow ourselves to become more aware and conversant, the intuition in turn offers up rich imagery for us to explore and work with.

Cultivate an attitude of kindness,
respect and humility, inner and outer.
I mean:
be kind, respectful, and humble to yourself as well as to
others;
to ideas and images that come to you, to drawings and songs
that come out of you, and to all beings, real and pretend.
It's not to be complacent:
you don't have to like everything or everyone,
but conversations need us to be respectful and open-minded,
recognizing other viewpoints and de-centering ourselves
enough to understand that
no one is the most important person in the world;
no race, no culture, no religion, no species
is the most important.
There are plenty of times in your life when you do prioritize
your own needs and goals, but this practice isn't one of them.

image • imagination • imaginal: definition of terms

image
noun
a representation of a thing or idea; this might be a mental representation, a visible impression or appearance, a physical copy or imitation, a likeness. Image, as set forth by Henri Corbin in his "Mundus Imaginalis," refers to any apprehension of the imaginal realm, which is not only visual in nature.

imaginal
adjective
of or relating to the imagination; of or relating to a mental image.

imagination
noun
the power or capacity to form internal images or ideas of objects and situations not actually present to the senses, including remembered objects and situations, and those constructed by mentally combining or projecting images of previously experienced qualities, objects, and situations.

imaginary
adjective
existing only in the imagination, with the implication that it does not correspond to reality.

creativity
noun
the use of the imagination or original ideas, especially in the production of an artistic work.

About Imagination

What is imagination? We can only imagine... We can study it, of course, but no expert is in charge of it—thank heavens! Yet, what we understand and believe and imagine about the imagination has consequences for how we use it. In the dominant western view, imagination has been degraded, viewed as a manifestation of unreality, a function of the individual human mind, located in the sensible world within the human brain. This way of thinking has not always nor everywhere held sway.

The Islamic scholar, Henri Corbin, made a crucial contribution to the world of depth psychology with his 1964 paper on the *Mundus Imaginalis*. Islamic cosmology upholds the real existence of the imaginal realm as "the country of non-where," characterized *not* as internal subjective fantasy, but rather a "precise order of reality, which corresponds to a precise mode of perception" — that is, the imaginal realm is *real*, but it is "a place outside of all places," so it can't be found within our geographic reality. It's the converse, actually: the geographic reality exists within the imaginal realm. "The 'where' is in *it*." In this view, the imaginal realm exists in between sensible reality and the world of pure intelligences; the imaginative power is called upon to link sensory and intellectual perceptions. One reaches the *mundus imaginalis* by journeying inward until "[finding] oneself paradoxically on the outside" of material reality; or, by traveling from the outside to find oneself inside; in either case, it is the active imagination which accomplishes the transmutation.

To describe this order of reality, Corbin rejects the common usage of the word "imaginary" for its characteristic sense of unreality. "Imaginary" means "fictional"; but Islamic philosophy upholds "the validity of inspired imaginative visions, of cosmogonies and theogonies and above all the veracity of the spiritual meaning perceived in the imaginative information supplied by prophetic revelations." A right relation to such visionary experiences relies on a cosmological structure that recognizes the existence of multiple realms of experience, but in the current western cosmology, the sensible world is largely considered the *only real* world; and, though we drown in imagery, the image has been degraded by its reduction to a location within the sensible world. "The greater the success of this reduction, the more people lose their sense of the imaginal and the more they are condemned to producing nothing but fiction." In other words, if we believe the imagination is "nothing but fiction" then that is what we will get: an existential example of "use it or lose it."

This idea corresponds to an extent with Heidegger's sense of the "enframing," a perspective brought into the modern world by industrialization, in which every thing is ordered according to its usefulness. "Where this ordering holds sway, it drives out every other possibility of revealing." ("Question" 332) In this way of ordering and perceiving the world, what we can't count doesn't count. That is, when we quantify everything, order and rate it according to economic value, this framework structures our perceptions and does not allow alternate, more organic understandings. Think of how monoculture enforces a rigid agricultural framework, policed by pesticides, for the cause of maximum production, but at the expense of richly diverse and flourishing natural ecosystems. For efficiency's sake, industrial agriculture tries to control all variables and screen out any unknowns, while a more natural ecosystem is a place of discovery, always revealing new gifts, relationships and understandings. (Pests and problems, too, let's be honest).

The enframing obscures or ignores the mytho-poetic "coming into Being," that unexpected and mysterious arising of new form and meaning. The consequences are grave. We are threatened when we allow ourselves to be trapped inside the enframing, viewing world-as-resource only and renouncing other ways of knowing, withholding response to other questions and truths that call to us.

How do we free ourselves? We must imagine a way.

Don't use your imagination to imagine that the imagination is insignificant.

Heidegger uses Hölderlin's phrase, "the saving power," to denote that seed of possibility which might at any point burst forth into life and open another way of unfolding truth. The arts, says Heidegger, may best foster the saving power. (333-341)

The poetic imagination
Heidegger understands the poetic imagination to be dynamic and revelatory, non-human, disclosing itself to us from out of the unknown. Not something which dwells in place, not a function that is housed within the self, but free and nomadic.

Not you.

Not yours.

But the poet — aka you — serves a very important function. The poet stands ready to give form to the unknown as it reveals itself.

> **The poet gives the image form.**

> **The image is not only visual, and the poem is not only verbal. "Image" can refer to any type of mental representation. Our term "poem" extends from the word "poiesis" (Latin borrowed from Greek), meaning "creative production."**

Bachelard, scientist, philosopher, and poet, writes beautifully of the power of the poetic image to open worlds. The imagination is *sur-real*: "a power which forms images which surpass reality in order to change reality" (qtd. in Kearney, Poetics 101). Thus the imagination extends reality while retaining its commitment to reality; that is, the imagination builds upon what is already there. It's *"Yes, AND..."* The human plays a vital role in listening and responding to the voice of imagination: "Like demi-urges before the kneading trough, we structure the becoming of matter" (qtd. in Kearney, Poetics 107). Bachelard stresses the dynamic nature of the imagination; it is a conversation and a synthesis between self and other, between reality and possibility, a playful relationship that generates a spiraling movement, propelling us ahead of ourselves.

Communication about the imaginal depends upon the poetic image itself, which can be explored, considered, and described at length, but never fully defined. Rational language seeks to delineate meaning in precise terms, but this alone will not suffice. We cannot extract the meaning and then dispose of the image without being exclusionary and reductive. An image can be repeatedly revisited and seen in a new light. By nature, the image lends itself to multiple interpretations.

Expressive arts therapist and professor Shaun McNiff advocates "treating images as persons and dialoguing with them" (83). Like a person, the image cannot be reduced or defined, but is an ongoing source of meaning. Hillman tells us we "see through" images — they frame and color our understandings.

Note that, just as we must make some character judgments of persons we meet, we must discriminate amongst images and intuitions that come to us. We can be in relationship with them without abdicating our agency. We are not beholden. We must and do discriminate among all that issues from the imagination if we are to frame order out of chaos and decide on our way forward, but we are not unerringly equipped to sort "good" from "bad" or "higher" from "lower" in some absolute sense; not least of all because these qualifiers are always switching roles. Next time you look, you may see it differently. We are served by an attitude of humility regarding such judgments, remembering that the basest rocks may hold precious gems, the wise person often comes dressed as a fool, and the best stories are those that surprise us with unexpected revelations.

Use these ideas in your everyday creative practice.

Archetype, intuition, and imagination are big players in your everyday creative practice. Before exploring how they show up in the practices themselves, let's unpack the nature of expression, the importance of play, and things that can get in the way.

Expression

How to express yourself, and what is meant by expression, anyway? I'll clarify how I'm using my terms.

Creative Expression ≠ Art
    I'M NOT TALKING ABOUT ART AT ALL

This book is not an art class. Why am I saying it? I guess because so frequently in conversation, when I say I work with the creative process, people start talking about art (in fact, usually they rush to confess they're "not good at art").

The difference between creative expression and art:
Art-making is a form of creative expression that generally (but not always) begins with the intention to produce a finished work. The artist may not know just how the work will end up, but it is often conceived at the outset and carried out with the desire to give form to a particular vision, according to aesthetic principles. Often, the artist intends to demonstrate skill and finesse with chosen tools and media; and often, will expect the work to be judged according to cultural standards; and perhaps, to be marketable.

"Art" typically IS the end product—the thing that you make; and while you're making it, your focus or concern may be — How is it going to hold together when it's done? Will it be powerful? Beautiful? Worthy?

This book, though, is about engaging in the *process* of creativity, with emphasis on expression rather than art. This process is intentional (more about that to follow); but not the sort of intentions mentioned above.

art • aesthetic • create • expression: definition of terms

art
noun
the quality, production, expression, or realm, according to aesthetic principles, of what is beautiful, appealing, or of more than ordinary significance.

aesthetic
adjective
concerned with beauty or the appreciation of beauty; giving or designed to give pleasure through beauty; of pleasing appearance.
noun
a set of principles underlying and guiding the work of a particular artist or artistic movement.

create
verb
to cause to come into being, as something unique that would not naturally evolve or that is not made by ordinary processes.

creative
adjective
having the quality or power of creating.

expression
noun
the process of making known one's thoughts or feelings.

Free symbolic expression and expressive arts
Carl Rogers, the humanistic psychologist, promoted the idea of "free symbolic expression": whatever comes to you is ok to express symbolically. Psyche and imagination bring us all kinds of feelings and imagery, some of which might be disturbing or ridiculous, hideous, unfair, nonsensical — all manner of things that you wouldn't want to act on, *other than* through symbolic expression. In other circumstances you might need to hold these things back or push them away. Finding ways to express them symbolically allows you to explore, discover, and process, without causing harm.

Rogers' daughter, Natalie Rogers, was a great proponent of this practice, specifically using multi-modal expressive arts for exploration and healing. I was fortunate to study with her. Many of the techniques that I recommend come from her teaching.

> *I have an impulse and I follow it. I sense it and draw it out, with color, words, movement, sound, shape.... It doesn't matter if I know "what" it is. I can always follow the impulse creatively and symbolically (when I am in a safe space). That action is deeply rewarding to me. What I discover in the process often guides me in life choices, though sometimes it seems to be simply expression for its own sake.*

I invite you to feel this kind of freedom in your everyday creative practice.

If you have an impulse to write or draw something, to sing a few notes, to use a certain color... go ahead. You don't need to edit or judge or hold back or justify what you're bringing forth. Sometimes you can't know what is coming out until after it's out. And truthfully, sometimes even then, you don't know. The process itself, the actual making marks, saying words, finding rhythm, choosing colors, getting paint or clay on your hands — that *process* itself has value — it's reason enough. So this is an important distinction between creative expression and art.

What about artistry, craftsmanship and the deep, often difficult, and rewarding work of the artist in producing a work of art? There is great value to be found here. I, too, engage in this art-making. But it's important to recognize that these two goals—*creative expression* and *art-making* — are distinct, and though they work together, only one at a time can take priority. The *process* of free symbolic expression feeds the artist and non-artist alike; *BUT* the priority cannot be to simultaneously engage in open dialogue with the imaginal world and to make a fine work of art — even though one may sometimes lead to the other.

I'm championing a method that is improvisational, open and accepting of all symbolic expressive urges, within the safe container you establish for your practice. Through the process of free symbolic expression. You may indeed create some things that are powerful, beautiful, and worthy, or that inspire you to more intentional projects, but let that be a bonus (or an invitation). You may also create some things that are ugly, silly, even embarrassing... Good for you! That, too, is an expected part of the process. I encourage you simply to be present with the creative process, and to feel the freedom of following the impulse.

> *Symbolic expression provides the opportunity*
> *to explore themes that might be otherwise off-limits.*

Projects, Skill Building, and Messing Around
I differentiate between these three types of creative processes. They're all great and important, they support one another and seep into each other; but it's really helpful to know which one is your priority at the moment, because they each have different objectives. If you're not sure what your objective is, it's easy to be disappointed in the results!

Projects
You are oriented toward the goal, a finished thing that meets certain specifications. Make a list, make a plan, make a timeline: make important decisions at the outset.

Skill Building
You want to get better at a particular thing, like drawing hands, baking bread, or reading music. Take a class, buy a book, watch a how-to video: follow specific exercises to strengthen your skills.

Messing Around
You just want to jump into the creative fray. So just do! Follow your impulses. Get those juices flowing. Don't hold back. See what happens. Who knows where you will end up?

Creativity is a process of engaging with the unknown, always! To create is to bring forth something new, something that hasn't existed before. A regular practice of creative engagement allows us to work imaginatively with the unknowns in our lives, and so we get to know them a little better. They become less scary as we give them shape and definition. Sometimes they let us know about issues that need more attention.

The intuition often speaks through imagery, so, when you allow spontaneous content to reveal itself through your creative expression, you strengthen your intuitive voice. These imperfect and unresolved first renderings and iterations are rich with energy and meaning. They are like dreams; and, just like dreams, we can re-enter them, explore them, and dialogue with them. "Where does this lead? Show me...Tell me more..." Through such work, we encounter the alchemical active imagination.

"Active imagination" is Jung's term for working consciously with content that is arising from the unconscious ("Transcendent"). Through a state of reverie, unconscious material is encouraged to flow into awareness where it is expressed and observed but not judged by the conscious mind. This type of work lets us become aware of things we've been ignoring or repressing.

Jung stressed the importance of withholding critique or interpretation, as best as possible. Aesthetics and rational analysis almost inevitably butt in; it's very hard to turn them off completely, but the key is not to let them take the lead. Doing so will impede the flow of unconscious material.

Again, think of the image — or the expression of psyche — as a person — a being — alive — Therefore, be kind to it as you would to any other being. Relate to it with courtesy and curiosity. How do you feel towards it? Converse with it. Interact with it. What does it tell you or suggest to you? Let yourself be surprised by the unexpected. Let the unexpected unfold. Follow the not-knowing.

Honoring the creative process
Let the creative process be an end in itself. In its many permutations, the creative process provides the perfect means to wander freely between inner and outer. You are expanding the third.

Here is participation, here is flow. You can honor this practice by showing up regularly without the intention of producing something specific. Give yourself space and time, perhaps beginning by choosing some medium to mess around with, like paper and pencil, or vocalization, dance, paint, or clay: again, it could be anything you choose. I often refer to this as "messing around," but take this process of messing around seriously. Respect it. Be present. Don't fill it up with idle chatter. Don't be texting, listening to a podcast, posting on instagram ugh. And if nothing happens? Boring is good.

Establishing a safe space for your explorations and expression
You need a safe container for your practice sessions. At its most basic, the container is defined by the limits of space and time you set aside. I've said that everyday creativity is a state of mind, an approach to life that can unfold in any moment — true. AND ALSO, as a regular practice, it will be supported by defining the space and time you use. I've also said it's ok if you don't have a regular space and time — also true. AND ALSO, working towards a regular creative space and time to hold your non-judgmental open-ended practice of listening, expressing, and sharing, will be worthwhile, as you are able.

Privacy: This work is private. It doesn't have to be shared with anyone. As important as I believe sharing to be, I encourage you to honor your own privacy. Only share what feels good to share; and only when it feels right, with those you want to share with. (Opportunities to share can be rare; that's why I write about how to establish space for sharing creative experience). Let this practice be a safe place to hold your thoughts and feelings. Sometimes others won't understand, and sometimes you just don't want to share.

Physical space: if you are able to set up a regular spot in your home, great!... but not essential. Everyone will not have the same type of environment available and your situation may vary from day to day. Ideally, choose or create space that feels relaxing, inspiring, private, and free of distractions: a sanctuary where you can relax and focus. You will be most at ease where you feel at home and connected with yourself. This can be a work in progress.

Time limits: Limiting the time is very helpful in establishing a regular practice, particularly because this practice involves holding unstructured time open for whatever comes up, which may even be "nothing." Defining your beginning and ending times provides structure and allows more enjoyment of the time given.

If you encounter resistance (*"I don't have time for this...blah blah blah"*) you can counter that by saying "It's just for 10 minutes" or however long you will set aside. On the other hand, once I get started, sometimes I'll want to keep going for hours. This is a great feeling in the moment, but I notice that a really long session one day can lead to a pushback effect the next day– "nah...I'm not into it today...I did so much yesterday I can just skip today...I don't have time..." It does feel wonderful to really let go into the process and be able to spontaneously keep going if you feel like it. Just be aware that you may be more successful in keeping the rhythm of a regular practice going if you limit yourself to a particular length of time. You're the decider of how much time you have and how much to regularly set aside.

Inner space: Set your intention to be present and hold the space with love. Be kind and respectful to yourself. Tune into your experience without judgment. Be present. Be unattached. Be imperfect.

Simply follow these steps to prepare your inner space:

- *relax*
- *ground*
- *protect*

Relax by finding a comfortable position. Do some stretches if you like. Soften and deepen your breathing. Soften the edges of your mind. Let your thoughts and tensions float away.

Ground by bringing awareness to your body in your location. Feel the ground beneath you, the air around you, the skin of your body, as you gently breathe in and out.

Protect yourself by visualizing an aura of loving kindness around and within you. Affirmations are helpful, such as: "I am a radiant being, filled with light and love" (Shakti Gawain).

feel the ground. feel your skin. feel the air

Crafting a ritual: Any regular practice takes on ritual characteristics; you can emphasize this as desired. Make it mystical, sacred, theatrical—or minimal and basic. It's up to you how you want to play it. Your practice can be a sacred act of devotion, a ritual you develop in alignment with your beliefs. I would caution that if you make it too complicated, you may not be able to keep up with it. Effective rituals can be very simple indeed.

I endeavor always to give thanks for each interaction. Honor the engagement itself: the mystery that occurs as you let go into the experience. I choose to imbue my practice with a sacred quality because I find it to be so. You may or may not relate to it in this way, but meanwhile...

Creativity is ALWAYS an interaction with the unknown. It is not only you and *your* projections, *your* skill, *your* imagination; but you building bridges between what you know and what you don't know. Allowing the thoughts and perceptions that you might ordinarily block out is the ground of your participation with the world. Beginning with the meditative exploration of both inner and outer landscapes, imagery arises. The psyche might bring forth any combination of imagery, from a variety of sources, known and unknown; we can think of this imagery as communicative. This imagery may at first seem jumbly or chaotic. That's ok. Cohesion develops through the process of playing. Hands-on processes work together with the natural human propensity for narrative formation, and these images come more clearly into form. We are actively collaborating *with* them, turning them over with hands and mind, conversing with them, getting to know them better.

The creative process-as-participation is a conversation that requires both awareness and expression. The ego-self takes on the role of scribe rather than artist, listening and facilitating expression of the interaction between self and Other. In honestly being present in the creative process, one must be unattached to the outcome (or product or artwork or spiritual awakening!). If one is distracted by egoic concerns, such as how the expression reflects artistic skill, or what it means, or what others will think, or how they will judge it, or whether they will buy it, then communication between self and Other is sidelined. The playful nature is easy, fun, relaxing, in the moment. The profound experience is long lasting, far-reaching, reverberating.

> *If what's coming through you is NOT YOU*
>
> *but rather you giving form to psyche that wants expression,*
>
> *you do not have to take credit or blame for how fabulous or stupid it looks.*

> "Other" is anything other than my conscious identity as "Self."

What I "make" doesn't have to be good or beautiful
I don't even have to know what it is — before I start, while I'm working on it, or even after I finish – for the process to

- *help me work through and release feelings;*

- *dissipate anxiety or malaise;*

- *lead to discoveries;*

- *support a sense of meaningfulness.*

All of these benefits can increase exponentially when you engage in these creative processes together with others (see Part IV), so long as participants share these foundational understandings that I'm preaching.

But what if I want it to be? (good or beautiful)
Yes, because part of the joy of creativity is the joy of bringing something beautiful or useful or meaningful into existence. I fully subscribe to that. It's important to me, too. Who wants to just make gobbledy-gook all the time? I get it. I believe— *I KNOW—* that this sort of open-ended creative exploration as an everyday practice will, over time, support your artistic vision. Tuning in and responding to imaginal impulses gets you aligned with themes, artwork, and media you are most drawn to, and the regular practice helps you develop your skill set and your confidence.

When you have a vision in mind of something you want to create, it's a matter of intention. You're setting your mind toward a particular goal, and then making your creative choices to move in that particular direction. Of course, this is different from free and spontaneous expression where you have no attachment to outcome but are endeavoring to give voice to the "active imagination." With active imagination, the goal isn't to dive so deeply into the unconscious that you lose consciousness, but you *are* trying to *minimize* your conscious involvement in order to give voice to what's coming to you from the unconscious. Aesthetic principles and critical analysis will still show up, because they are part of consciousness. When you think about it, you have a whole continuum of control over your state of mind, and you're in charge of how much control you exert. You can blend openness with intention; you don't have to completely cede your conscious involvement with the process. A kind of craftsmanship comes with practice, where you can fine-tune this "blend"; this is a great strength in developing your artistic voice. The facility and confidence that comes with regular practice of everyday creativity can be applied to your intentional artistic projects. Just remember to continue your practice of open-ended expression, where expression is a manifestation of participation — that is, you as participant and you as witness, giving voice to the influences around and within you. If this practice is an honest opening to the unknown and exploration and conversation with what is found, then the goal cannot be to produce art and use it for ego gains. It is simply the wrong mindset with which to enter the process.

Watch out, ego! Don't be a troublemaker!
The obsession with the personal, "The Self," as if it is not intimately and infinitely connected to (even inhabited by) the rest of the world— this is at the heart of the crisis of western civilization in which we now find ourselves.

Self-absorption is the western disease. We are prone to becoming trapped in our own interiors because we are often unable to recognize our continuity with others and the world around us. Differentiation, definition, organization — yes, these are good, as long as we balance with awareness of the rest of reality.

Important points about expression:

- *be open and unattached*
- *allow the unknown*
- *process over product*
- *listen and wait*
- *be spacious*
- *entertain the ideas and choices that arise*
- *engage with the work: imaginal dialogue, creative visualization*
- *develop a ritual process*

Fear and Anxiety

FEARS

Just express yourself! Be free!
Throw off your clothes!

That's all well and good. It's a great sentiment, but it's not always so straightforward to do. In my experience, most people do have fear or self-consciousness about expressing themselves creatively — certainly in public, and often, even in private. It's not always that simple to just cast your armor aside. Not everyone feels that free, even if they wish they did. Self-consciousness isn't the only issue; for many people there may be real risks to such vulnerability. Social strictures against letting something wild and unknown come out of you are deep, very deep. That something may be potentially ugly, stupid, embarrassing, revealing, humiliating...You name it. If you have a fear, major or minor, of being revealed in this way, it may help you to know that:

1) so do most other people

2) this reflects societal and perhaps family repression

3) the most powerful way to constrain yourself from a satisfying creative practice is to make disparaging comments like: *"I'm just not creative" "I did it wrong" "Mine isn't any good" "This looks terrible."* So stop saying those things.

I'll talk more about fears engendered by the socio-political aspects of play and risk, but first I want to consider the personal nature of fear and repression.

Self-denigration is an expression of anxiety about "getting it right," or being seen as "imperfect"; and this is a consistent barrier to creative expression. Counter-productive phrases such as *"Mine looks stupid...I'm*

a lousy artist...I can't do this!" are better indicators of performance anxiety than of ability, yet they become self-fulfilling prophecies.

How to overcome?

Step 1: Create a safe container for your free expression: a space and time where you can work and play without being judged and criticized by others.

Step 2: Don't let *yourself* be mean. Just don't say those critical things to yourself. Stop it! Your safe container is not safe if you yourself are the attacker.

Sounds simple enough. But if you hear yourself thinking mean things about your own expressions, know that many, many people also think the same kinds of mean things about their own expressions. I do it myself, regularly — Me! and I wrote the book on Creative Expression! (this one). That mean judgey voice comes up for me *plenty*, and when I hear it — *'That looks stupid'* — I say — *'You're stupid! Shut up!'* And then I laugh and get back to work.

That sounds pretty juvenile—and it is. The adolescent banter in my head sounds a lot like my siblings and maybe I should try to respond with more maturity, but I must admit it makes me happy to give it sass. Shrug.

Sometimes, the voices in your head seem more intimidating or harder to ignore. The impact of self-inflicted internalized negative thinking patterns is huge. It is important to be aware of these inner voices, to get to know them and to come to terms with them. Widely referred to as "inner critics," these might typically be either protective or abusive in character (or sneakily, both), and you may choose either to befriend or dismiss them, but don't let them stand in your way. Personally, I avoid the term "inner critic," as I think the voices we encounter in our heads are myriad and more nuanced than to be lumped into one aspect; but otherwise, the advice is sound. As you observe your inner-inter-actions and enter into dialogue, you learn more about their various natures and how to deal with them. Just like living breathing people, you need to judge whether or not you want to entertain their opinions, and act accordingly. My strategy in the personal example above is simply to dismiss the voice. (And, it still shows up...)

Whatever you learn and however you decide to deal with this negative talk, the way to overcome that voice is to work through it. Just keep going. Don't give up on yourself. Be as kind to yourself as you would be to someone else: a child, for instance, because it's often the child in you who feels embarrassed and deficient and perhaps has done from a very young age. That's unfortunate, yet it's a common side effect in a culture that discourages playful creativity.

My undergraduate education degree required that I take a course called "Teaching Art." We, the teachers-in-training, engaged in a variety of art activities designed for children. Every member of our class, regardless of artistic disposition, reported therapeutic effects and, what's more, joy, generated by these activities. The exploratory, open-ended nature of "children's projects" relieved the pressure to produce something accomplished, or to be "a good artist." We engaged gleefully, playfully, and also deeply, in the process, and it was clear to me that this type of activity was not "just for kids." If we nurture our own natural playfulness, as well as our children's, we are better off.

"Fear of expression" is alleviated when perfect representation is not the goal. Is it possible that simply giving people explicit permission to experiment (and even, perhaps, to fail) could open the door to the joy of creative flow?

Permission Slip

I _____ give myself permission to
_____
_____
_____

You have permission to give yourself permission! Use as needed.

Working alone in my studio for hours...days...years... I discovered that I was so much more extraverted when alone than when with others. It made me laugh! "Um, wouldn't this work better the other way around?"

I thought it was funny and weird, a little twisted up; but now I realize it's probably common. It makes a lot of sense for a person to be more comfortable revealing themselves when no one else is looking; to have quirky, interesting, amusing or profound aspects of personality that they hide from others.

People who are "famous"— I know that's not the objective here—but people who are well-known performers are typically those who have, in some way, been able to open up or put aside that protective barrier that keeps others from seeing something true about them. They still need to protect themselves, but they let people know them, in **some** way. Fame isn't the objective here, but figuring out how to dismantle the barriers to authentic expression is. Some people have barriers so impenetrable that they are even unable to see and know themselves.

Me telling you this probably won't magically alleviate your fears. It takes practice: a systematic, simple practice, over time, in a place where you feel safe, will deconstruct the damaging beliefs that keep you from expressing yourself in the world. As you become more comfortable with your own expression in your own company, your confidence will naturally strengthen and you will find growing opportunities to express yourself with others.

ONE MORE TIME

And what's the point of strengthening your "playful creativity" muscles?

Playful activities

reduce anxiety,

promote joy, and

encourage communication of the imaginal.

Creative making builds intuitive awareness by giving form to ideas and inspirations. As you encourage yourself to play this way, you will naturally over time become more comfortable with sharing your playful nature.

Relieving anxiety

How can something that makes you so anxious relieve anxiety? The anxiety is what you feel when you're holding yourself back: it's the *thought* of it, and also the corresponding physical tightness of holding. The worrying over whether to express it. The relief is what you feel when you let go.

There was a guy who came to my expressive arts studio. He wanted to play with some materials and he was obviously anxious about it. I gave him paper and pastels and said, "Just put some colors on the paper. Just make some marks. Pick whatever colors you like. All the colors are valid. There's no way to do it wrong." This was very hard for him to do, just to pick up a color and make a mark with it. As he did, he said "I feel like I'm standing in front of you naked." I was surprised by the depth of his anxiety, and I think he was blown away by how easy and good it felt when he took the expressive action of making a mark. BTW he is a professional musician, so, very used to performing in front of others. Ease of expression in one realm doesn't necessarily translate to another, and often, accomplished artists have greater barriers to free expression.

I've noticed sometimes people become very squirmy when the directions are to do something very simple. Just do it. Stop fussing.

But you might wonder, why so much resistance to doing something simple, something that I want to do, that will make me feel better?

The many faces of resistance

There are many reasons (and combinations of reasons) behind resistance. Consider:

- *resistance as self-protection*
- *resistance as socio-political activism*
- *resistance as avoidance*
- *resistance as habit (everyday resistance)*

Resistance can perform a protective function (you want to resist an attacker, and you want to resist the dominant paradigm of disempowerment); or it can be a resistance to action or expression that you'd like to clear away, as when the remnants of a past trauma prevent you from moving forward. There are circum-

> **resistance**
> *noun*
> the refusal to accept or comply with something; the attempt to prevent something by action or argument

stances where we are well-served by strengthening the ability to resist; then again, sometimes resistance keeps us from the very things we need or desire. Sometimes the distinction is obvious, but not always. It can be tricky to suss out. In the wilds of the unconscious, these forms of resistance can be intertwined. When you have an aversion to someone or something, you may not be sure if that's your good instinct protecting you or some old psychic detritus getting in the way. Take your time in these instances. Test the waters a bit. Does your resistance make you feel stronger and empowered, or does it feel like an obstacle on your path? Pay attention and see if you can deconstruct what's happening. The work of this book helps you figure out how to move through the obstacles.

give it an image

How would you describe the quality of your resistance?

A terrified ball huddled up in the corner?

A raging beast?

A stony silent mountain?

A skittering mouse?

Give it an image.

You will be able to explore it and get to know it better.

The nature of resistance
The first step is to notice when you are resisting, because sometimes it happens unconsciously. Like every time you are about to sit down and write, oops! you think of something else you urgently need to do. "Wow! That plate should be in the dishwasher! Stat! Whoa, look at this dust!" Whaaat? Hmm...

Notice when you feel you'd like to do something, but somehow you just don't get around to it. Notice when something's been on your list for days- weeks- years but somehow you keep forgetting about it. These are the kinds of resistance we want to dismantle. Maybe you even find yourself consciously pushing to do a thing, but you just can't get yourself to budge.

When I used to smoke cigarettes, I somehow *always* needed another cigarette before I sat down to creative work. My husband said I was creating a smoke screen. Hmmm. Yep.

You can take steps to systematically work through these stuck places. Just remember, self-discipline is helpful; self-punishment is not. It's the difference between being firm and being mean. There's no good reason to be mean. Compassion is always in order.

Resistance is complicated, but I'd like to broadly differentiate between resistance that results from trauma and resistance that results from habitual inertia, though they may very well be related.

Trauma and avoidance
When you have experienced trauma (and we all have, to one degree or another) it is normal to avoid situations where you might retraumatize yourself—because it hurts. You just don't want to go there again.

There are many, many degrees of trauma, from toe-stubbing to the most heinous, horrific, unthinkable ordeal. Trauma is very personal and so is recovery. You may think you've moved past it, and then you discover another layer. There's no set timetable and no little book of exercises to magically heal whatever you've been through, although there are many insightful and useful approaches. Therapy can be beneficial and so can your own personal process. However we choose to deal with it, it's safe to say that we all have suffered trauma, and we all need to learn compassion for ourselves and for others as a result.

We can use methods of creative engagement to help ourselves and each other to move through past experience and into radical presence. I feel strongly about the importance of the social experience in healing trauma, and, in Part IV, we look at grassroots ways we can be there for each other. Meanwhile, as individuals dealing with our own personal experiences of trauma, we have tools to help us untangle the brambles protecting our creative vulnerability. Read on...

Loneliness and Addiction

It's easy to understand the relationship between trauma and addiction, as people seek means to numb recurrent memories and placate their interminable internal suffering.

The relationship between loneliness and addiction is less well-known. but no less significant, as author Johann Hari highlights in his book, *Chasing the Scream.* A supportive and stimulating community can obviate the desire for the numbing substance. The experience of trauma makes us lonely. Perhaps it is loneliness itself that we simply can't face.

The use of everyday creative expression for working out traumatic memory
A critique of analytical psychology is that the discipline approaches psyche as pathological: not a good starting point, for surely there is and can be such a thing as healthy psyche. It has been suggested that the field itself suffers from a pathology. Ok. There's a shadow side to everything.

Nonetheless, the gift of analytical psychology is in revealing to us the pathological places and moments in our lives past and present: that is, where and when we've been wounded or tangled. Finding them is the first step to healing them. In our everyday creative explorations, we discover many clues to suss out these spots and try to set them right.

"We cannot change anything until we accept it." Jung

In a practice of opening yourself up to express and observe those things you are less conscious of, wise psyche will naturally offer you what you most need to know. This is a correlate of the view that the body (and nature as a whole) is self-equilibrating. What comes to you through free symbolic expression may be something you've forgotten or neglected that needs to be processed in some way: though not necessarily linked to trauma, this certainly is one way traumatic memories come to light. When something is bothering you, it pushes to get out of your system. Toxins within? Maybe you throw up, or get a skin rash...or have a disturbing dream that sticks with you...or find that you keep sketching scenes from a particular fairy tale...or feel a lot of strong feelings as you engage in freeform improvisational painting or sculpting or music or movement.... The key is to give these feelings and clues an opportunity for expression, to notice them and work with them and see where they lead. Just as with throwing up, sometimes you need help to move through these things; but often, the act of expression together with self-care will bring the healing you need. You may find that your own gentle persistence with this process will release a lot of your resistance to creative expression. Stay present and be your own compassionate witness. Ask for help when you need it.

Microtrauma results from a repetitive injury over a long time. The term is generally used in reference to physical stresses to muscles, tendons, bones, and tissues, which may be small enough to seem insignificant in the moment, but over time can result in severe injury. Carpal tunnel syndrome is one example. Margaret Crastnopol has used the term to refer to cumulative psychic injury: tiny interpersonal aggressions that are hard to confront, because they're so subtle, or unimportant, or not worth mentioning, or...*I'm not even sure that really happened. Is it me? Am I imagining things? I'm probably making too much of this. I don't feel right bringing it up. I feel silly talking about it. I shouldn't make such a big deal about it. I should just forget about it....* but it continues, and it continues to bug me, so how can I forget it? As Crastnopol writes, psychoanalysis is a good setting to work through these type of issues which can insidiously have a real negative impact on your life. And guess what? Creative expression is another way to work with these issues.

You may have trouble to confront such interpersonal frictions and imbalances directly, when you're not really sure what's happening. You may not feel prepared to talk with the other person about it, and it's possible they have no awareness of the issue or would respond defensively. But you can certainly talk to yourself or your journal or your paintbox about it. Feeling anxious because you're not sure if it's "all in your head"? Poof! Forget that, because in this process of free symbolic expression you are simply feeling what you feel and expressing it. You do not need to verify, validate, defend, confess...and you don't need to share it! Just feel it and express it in whatever form it takes. The process may bring you the clarity you need to understand your feelings, and perhaps prepare you to communicate with the other about it. Or maybe the process is all you need to let go of the feelings. And if you happen to return to the same image or feeling over and over without a sense of movement or clarity — if you find something you want help with, then you can seek that help.

Trauma is often accompanied by feelings of shame — that the bad thing that happened to you is your fault — and because you're ashamed you seal it off from yourself and the world. You don't want others to know and you may not even want yourself to know, so you hide it away. Discovering those hidden places may help you realize you were never at fault to begin with. Opening up and absolving yourself from shame is a huge relief. At the same time, discovering old wounds may be triggering, so reach out for professional help when you need a hand.

Can you describe your clown?

Sometimes we wall off parts of ourselves because they aren't recognized by others as having worth. Maybe our parents tried to train those parts out of us. Maybe friends or bullies made fun of those parts. In the process of socialization, we learn to hide what we fear may be judged. In her book called *Animal Joy*, therapist Nuar Alsadir relates her experience of learning to clown, and the discovery and liberation that came in the process. Can you describe your clown?

Imagine your vulnerable self, the one you've hidden for fear of being judged; at least, you think it's hidden — only everyone can see it except you. Ever had that experience? Where you're sure you've disguised that most humiliating or unlovable thing about yourself, only to find that your skirt's tucked up in your underwear and you're trailing toilet paper when you come out of the bathroom? It really can be true that in the process of trying to hide, it is we ourselves who lose awareness of these shameful parts that ironically remain obvious to others.

A creative practice grounded in free symbolic expression helps you to recover your "hidden self." You may find a tenderness for your adorable bashful clown; you may even find that others will share your affection.

Until you make the unconscious conscious, it will direct your life and you will call it fate. —Jung

Bringing light to your dark spaces
Journeying into the unconscious depths, you shine light into places that are hidden: causes of sorrow, disappointment, and anxiety. By exploring these unconscious areas — bringing consciousness to them, that is — you bring awareness to your blindspots. It's a quest to answer the riddles of our lives. We search for what is missing in ourselves and in others. What we bring back, we can re-integrate into our lives; or perhaps, just let go.

This journey, though often difficult, can bring great rewards in relationships and in personal satisfaction. We gain skills as we navigate the journey repeatedly, straightening out confusions that have tripped us up. The insights gained are strengthening and preparatory for wherever you go next.

If resistance is a wall you've built to hide yourself from yourself, it's worth deconstructing. Maybe it takes some time to take it down and discover what's back there. It can be scary because you don't always know what you will find. Work consistently, patiently, and mindfully. You learn as you go along. Go step-by-step and appreciate your progress over time.

It is life that asks the questions...We are the ones who must answer. —Viktor Frankl (Yes, 33)

WHO ARE YOU?

WHERE ARE YOU HEADED?

WHAT DO YOU WANT TO DO?

WHY IS THAT BIRD STARING AT YOU?

Habitual resistance

SO MUCH RESISTANCE!!! So many causes.

I'm sitting at my computer writing, when I clearly want to go to my studio and paint — "nothing" is stopping me, yet somehow it's very hard to shift gears.

It's like being under a spell — and how hard it is to rouse myself out of it! I know I'm not alone in this experience of everyday resistance. Where does it come from and why is it so strong?

The demands of work. Entrainment to our socio-political structures. An educational system that shapes us in limiting ways. Uber powerful commercial interests. The super-highway within that leads directly from compulsive achievement to passive consumption. Cultural maps imposed on us that obscure alternate pathways.

Don't waste time! Maximize productivity! Stay focused on your work! (which is probably on the computer).

Ok, time for a break. Check your phone. Check your email. Check your insta.

Ahh, work day's over. Put on a movie. Text your friends. Surf. Scroll. Surf. Scroll.

Call it entrenchment, entrancement, obsession, addiction... Whatever you call it, it's mundane. When we are daily "under the spell," it can be super hard to overcome. Hard to make the extra effort to move from passivity to participation.

Don't neglect the body in your quest to re-member the body (by which I mean healing the body-mind split).

That microtrauma I mentioned —the physical kind? Well, you probably suffer from it, because you probably make your body hold certain postures for much long- long- longer than is good for it. You probably use certain muscles repeatedly while ignoring others that need attention. You probably override the internal messages you get, asking- telling- demanding that you get up and stretch and move. Probably, because this is so common in today's workaday, stay focused, get it done (on the computer) world—these behaviors are "normal" in the sense of average, but they are pathological.

So while you're working on reintegrating your lost inner life, remember to reintegrate your missing body experience as well. Getting your body moving is a fantastic way into the practices of everyday creativity. As you shift gears, remembering to stretch and move and walk around, you may find that your resistance to creative expression just falls away. Simple movements can work wonders. If you want to explore body awareness in greater depth, yoga and pilates are great disciplines for healing, and somatic therapies and integrative massage are highly recommended. And, oh yeah! Dance!

But at least take the first step! Before you say "I'm going to practice this for an hour every day for the rest of my life," just make movement easy and integral to your life, because it's the fluidity of practice that will best help you deconstruct your resistance. Once again, let's underscore the power of awareness. There is a relationship between inattention and overuse (abuse), and your own ability to make intentional changes in your life begins with awareness. If you can develop new habits to short-circuit your habits of entrenchment, then you are taking steps to liberate yourself.

- Make a habit of noticing when you've been doing one thing for too long.

- Make a habit of shifting gears.

- Make a habit of creative expression.

- First notice.

Overcome that inertia to do the simplest thing: to participate in your own life.

Practice shifting gears
get up and move around
make a silly face
let out a roar or a groan
dance with your dog
make a big colorful scribble,
listen to the rain
talk to the trees.

Actually, it IS scary and dangerous
There is risk in honest expression. On the personal level and on the socio-political level creative expression is radical and dangerous, because it is so very powerful. Having grown up in an atmosphere of freedom, it's easy for me to be glib about it, but expression can be dangerous both because you may be afraid of what will come out of you and because others may react adversely.

I see my work in this area as an act of resistance (the kind I want to strengthen) to a status quo that refuses to recognize my importance, your importance, and the brilliant power we can generate together when we connect through expressing our true thoughts and feelings. Ignoring and belittling are effective strategies for silencing and disempowering. Don't believe it! This work is radically liberating. It is ignored because it's powerful, not because it's silly. Remember *THAT* the next time somebody tries to devalue you or your opinion.

Everyday creative expression may be scary and dangerous, yet it is a playful process. A deeper look into the nature of play will address why limits and flexibility are both so important.

> *In modern physics it is very clear that the discoveries that later become utilized for our technological gains are generally made in the first place because a physicist lets his imagination go and discovers something simply for the joy of discovery. But this always runs the risk of radically upsetting our previously nicely worked-out theories, as it did when Einstein introduced his theory of relativity, and Heisenberg introduced his principle of indeterminacy.... The creativity of the spirit does and must threaten the structure and presuppositions of our rational, orderly society and way of life. (Rollo May 71)*

Play & Risk

Play = Risk
You may think I'm kidding around (wah, wah), but... Play is serious business. I kind of have a chip on my shoulder about it, basically because I've been trying to make this same point for 40 years. It gets devalued and brushed aside because play is cute, it's childish, it's nice, it's silly, it's fun, it's feminine, it reminds you of your mommy or your grandmother or your kindergarten teacher... Don't let that fool you.

Although play is fun, play is also risky. Play is revolutionary.

And, it's essential to your health and a healthy society.

Play as goofing around
But yes, also, play is kidding around. *"Doing whatever I feel like." "Goofing off." "Making things up as I go along."* Yep. And this also means discovering things for yourself, and expressing what *YOU* notice and think and feel, not what someone else tells you to notice and think and feel. Dangerous, indeed.

Wondering. Wandering. Exploring. Experimenting. Trying something just cause you feel like it, or because you want to see what happens. Aimlessness. Being silly. Or serious. Following the impulse. Pushing the limits.

Play as movement
Play is movement, by its most fundamental definition: freedom to move; or, as Salen and Zimmerman have described it, an active exploration of the relationship between freedom and limits.

Picture play as this oscillating movement, back and forth between pretend and real, back and forth between imagination and form. The leverage of the movement creates the space in between. In the space is freedom. The "work of play" is in maintaining openness to the creative experience. Stay with it.

Swinging on a swing set:
the higher you go, the higher you go

Play is pretend and it is real
As Winnicott tells us, "play is in fact neither a matter of inner psychic reality nor a matter of external reality"; rather, it occurs in an intermediate space which is created through the continuous "to and fro" between inner and outer, or between "real" and "pretend." Creative acts emerge out of this between-space.

The nature of play is dynamic, and the developing content is transformed through this dynamic process. What began as "pretend" may actually become "real," like when the vision of a chocolate sundae takes form as a tangible, melting, goopy dish of ice cream, or when a dream image becomes the basis for an invention. Often, though, playful fantasies may simply fade away and be forgotten, and that's ok, too.

> "It is in playing and only in playing that the individual child or adult is able to be creative and to use the whole personality, and it is only in being creative that the individual discovers the self."
> —Winnicott (72-73)

grok
neologism coined by Robert Heinlein meaning to understand intuitively

The absence of playful behaviors in adults is associated with a variety of mental pathologies and breakdowns. For me, it was the realization that many adults don't grok the significance of playful behaviors (for all ages!) that shifted my professional focus from working with kids to working with adults. If adults "get it" they'll pass it directly to their children, and be happy when schools incorporate playful learning into the curriculum.

IF THEY DON'T WE'RE ALL SCREWED!

That play is widely considered frivolous is evidence of a cultural tendency toward a true/false organization, a social preference for order and control, and a resistance to relaxation; the intermediate space of possibility is lacking. Yet, it is this liminal space of play that makes transformation possible. We pretty much all seek the experience of transformation, in one way or another. Change is life. Playful behavior is important for all.

Fear of the unknown inhibits play, as in, you won't try because you don't know how it will work out. Trust is needed to enter into play because play is risky: the outcome is unknown, or else it is not play. Where the outcome is already planned or determined, this is not play. For one who is not able to entertain the real (what is) and the pretend (what might be) simultaneously, playing is not possible. This would be a person who thinks in "black and white" or "true/false" terms. This could describe any of us, at times; but too much time spent in the reductive environment of "true/false" thinking is a sign of anxiety, a lack of the requisite trust needed to enter into the space of play.

> For the individual, when experience of the "between" is deficient, then one lives either in a fantasy world or a world too realistic. A meaningful sense of self comes about only through the experience of the ambiguous "between."

Play is destructive as well as creative. It has as much potential to disrupt as to emancipate. What Schechner calls "deep play" (based on the Hindu concept of maya-lila) where everything is in flux and anything may happen "is as terrifying as it is exciting, as blinding as it is beautiful" (42). The charming quality of playfulness that we associate with children and puppies has a more frightening aspect, as those who have raised children and puppies can attest. Fun can turn to fight in an instant. The euphoria of dizzy spinning can end with a crash. Thus, the importance of limits.

> In Hindu tradition, *lila* is the perpetual back-and-forth creative play between awareness and action that creates the kaleidoscopic expansion of the universe into a multitude of forms (Khanna 67); so, pretty important.

Magic circle as container
I've already described "the container" as the limiting safe space we hold for creative expression. The container mitigates the risk. The "magic circle" is another instance of this. Free of many of the rules and roles that govern everyday life, yet always defined by rules of its own, the "magic circle" is Huizinga's term for the (implicitly or explicitly) bounded space within which play-worlds exist (10). Entry requires the suspension of disbelief: one enters the circle with a willingness to accept the sometimes absurd limitations of the rules because of the pleasure of the game (Suits 38). In fact, when we acknowledge the absurdity of the many rules we follow daily in order to play "the game of life," then we must agree with Huizinga when he said, "We might call all society a game, if

---

Imagine a world with only T/F options:

THE EARTH IS ROUND, TRUE OR FALSE?

> HMM, WELL, TECHNICALLY IT'S IRREGULAR—WIDER AT THE EQUATOR AND FLATTER AT THE POLES.

ANSWER THE QUESTION, TRUE OR FALSE???

OK, NEXT QUESTION: KIDS LIKE CLOWNS, TRUE OR FALSE?

> UM, SOME DO BUT SOME ARE TERRIFIED…

I SAID, TRUE OR FALSE?!

THE WHOLE IS GREATER THAN THE SUM OF THE PARTS, TRUE OR FALSE?

> OH, MAN.

we bear in mind that this game is the living principle of all civilization." Civilization is built upon "the rules we agree on." (46-47, 100-101)

The protective limits of the magic circle create a ritual container to lessen the inherent riskiness of play. This is the nature of ritual, whereby rules provide the sense of order and formality meant to reduce the risk of the transformational experience; and, indeed, play is a transformational experience.

"To ritualize is to make a pathway through what would otherwise be uncharted territory." — Driver (16)

Only walk on the circle. DO NOT TOUCH THE GROUND!! If you touch the ground, you have to sit in the middle til the next person goes all the way around. You have to drop a pebble in each hole and it CAN"T BOUNCE OFF! If it bounces off, you're out. If you make it all the way around, then you will receive secret instructions for Phase II.

the magic circle

Ways Into Play

Embrace metaphor

Play is the expression of metaphor in action. Through play, we make connections between what we know and what we imagine. This process occurs naturally in human behavior, as we often see with children (when play is allowed).

In the hands of a child, a bunch of flowers can "become" a family of fairies, a bucket can "become" a hat, a pebble can "become" a car... The possibilities are endless. One thing is like another thing: that's metaphor. Playfully, we can pretend that one thing *is* another thing because, as Winnicott's work elaborates, the space of play is a transitional area in which "pretend" and "real" can co-exist; the nature of objects and events in this transitional area is ambiguous and one is not required to sort them. At the same time, play is not complete fantasy; it requires a recognition that "these actions in which we now engage do not denote what those actions for which they stand would denote" (Bateson 180). The child knows the pebble isn't "really" a car.

This paradox of metaphor (alike but different) is a crucial characteristic of play, and, as Winnicott stressed, a paradox not to be forced to resolution. Refusing to allow the space of play not only inhibits the extremely important function of the imagination in making the world meaningful. It also forces us to make claims of rationality about content that is neither true nor false, and it is linked with other problems of social adjustment and personal development.

In play, metaphorical construction makes free use of dreams, thoughts, ideas, and materials at hand, mixing it up to create something new: something which extends beyond itself. A make-believe conversation might expand into a costume drama. A dream vision might take form as a painting or song. An idea which begins in play can become real. This is the transformative nature of play.

Metaphor Play

Metaphor is integral to comedy, myth, symbol, magic, word play...human life... If metaphorical thinking doesn't come easily to you, the practices in this book will help stimulate your metaphor-capacitor. Here are a couple of ideas to play with.

Your body as a house: what is the house like? For instance: *Comfortable? Chilly? Neat as a pin? Luxurious? Ramshackle? Funky? Windows: Many or few? Open or closed? Curtains or no?*

No right or wrong answers, and the way you picture it or feel it may change from one time to another. Remember you're not describing your real house, you're pretending that your body is a house and letting go into that description. You do not need to rationalize the images that come up for you! In fact, doing so may keep your metaphor superficial and prevent deeper imagery from arising. Nonsense? Check! Remember it's play! No need to defend your answers. Explore in your mind or on paper, in words or images.

Stream of consciousness: Begin with one image in mind, say from a dream or whatever comes to mind. Write down all the things you think of that it reminds you of, that it is "like." Arrange like a mind map or a list.

Fairy tale: Begin with a fairy tale that attracts or interests you. List the characters, elements, and actions. How do they describe aspects of you? Or people and situations you've experienced? Let it be an open-ended exploration; that is, don't look for one-to-one correspondences, but similarities. Metaphors are alike and different, and always open to interpretation, so it's ok–even encouraged–to contradict yourself in this exercise!

Word play: Make a study of silly jokes, the kind little kids love, the kind dads make...You can find whole books full of them and tons of them on the internet. They are virtually all corny puns, funny because one word has two meanings, etc. Pick a couple and try drawing them as cartoons. It will stimulate your metaphorical understanding.

Act silly

I do. Sure, people think I'm doofy, and I am. So what? Breaks the tension. Screw 'em if they can't take a joke! In all honesty, I'm embarrassed when people don't "get" my silliness. Sometimes they do, sometimes they don't; and sometimes I keep my silliness under wraps; and, if I'm *really* being honest, sometimes my silliness really is dumb and annoying. Still, silliness will always have a home in me. I mean, thank god Mel Brooks wasn't shy! Where would we be then?

Silliness is a way into play. I have started presentations with being ridiculous and I have started art projects with intentional mistakes. I'm never afraid of the blank page! Sometimes it's the best place to get the crap out of the way and just to warm up, so use it for that. I teach imperfection and ego deconstruction so I try to walk my talk. It's a way to get going, and a way to set the tone: don't take yourself too seriously.

Being silly when you're by yourself can lead into more silliness when you're with others.

Be ambiguous—sometimes…

Allow yourself to just be, without labels, without plans, to not know or not be sure… Let one thing morph into another.

Most likely you have plenty of opportunities to be labeled, planned, organized, certain, intentional… or at least to try to be these things. It's pretty important (useful–expected–*essential*) in many circumstances to be able to present yourself in a certain way, say…professionally, authoritatively, responsibly, clearly, capably, intelligently… If you're not able to play the part, you could lose your job, get arrested, be institutionalized, lose friends… so of course it's important to respond to behavioral expectations, though we all sometimes miss the mark.

I'm not against it. Sometimes it's both necessary and helpful for smooth interactions, and it's super-valuable to know when and how to "act appropriately." Just sayin' it's not healthy or good for you or anyone to be that way constantly—always focused, always on task, always aiming to please or impress or be right. It's important to have time and space where you relax and wander and don't know.

Expand…allow yourself to be spacious…
You have room to move — to improvise — to play.

And here we are in the third

This spacious relaxed ambiguous area, aka "The Third," is the space of possibility, where we don't know if it's you or me, real or pretend, drive or daimon–and, most crucially, in this space, we don't try to resolve these questions into true/false or me/not me, but allow the unknown to remain ambiguous. We don't know everything!!! Allowing yourself to experience that can be a joy. This is a place of paradox and play, where conversation and communication flourish, and this is where imagination enters and ideas come into form.

Ok, where is that third space? I know it's around here somewhere...

Play Happens in the Third:
Play is movement that engages with the unknown and results in the creation of something new. The process of play encourages your intuitive grasp of less conscious material. Bring this stuff into the field of consciousness where you can work with it and transform it or let it go.

The Personal Third

Of course, as there is a between between everything, the expansion of the third can take place anywhere — within you, as well as in between you and others. Both are important. I'll talk more about the social third in Part IV.

Your Inner+Outer Between-ness

The goal of between-ness is two-fold:

- *to establish the transitional space and*
- *to move easily between inner and outer*

Inner+Outer continuity
There is an inner and an outer to everything, and obviously they're connected. Yet, for many people, inner and outer realities can *feel* disconnected.

As we grow up, we seek to discover and define ourselves as individuals. Just as importantly, we learn to bring ourselves in line with socio-cultural expectations, and part of that process is learning to repress our individual differences to some extent. It's not always easy to connect the dots between your individuality and social belonging. So as not to stand out or be socially alienated, we may instead become alienated from our selves.

In your creative expression and your intuitive sense, you may be coming up with things that no one else is doing, saying, thinking—and that feels weird, maybe. Perhaps you're reluctant to communicate or admit to your inner experience. But mainly, it's normal for your own personal views and preferences and ideas to be idiosyncratic, and it's important to have a safe space to express your uniqueness.

If, in the absence of such a safe space, you feel you must always hide your inner experience, then even your own internal communication between your "hidden self" and your "visible self" may be damaged. It's a terrible thing to become estranged not only from the world, but also from yourself. It is lonely and isolating when inner experience is disconnected from outer experience.

The solution, though, is not simply to dissolve the boundary between inner and outer, but rather to expand the space between. Like the skin on your body or the walls of your house, the boundary between private and public is a necessary protection. It's best to have a transitional space in between: just like a front porch or foyer is not as public as being out on the street, and not as private as being in your bedroom. Here, you may relax and share some of your inner experience with those you choose. Such a transitional territory between the inner you and the outer you facilitates your healthy relationship with yourself, a precursor to building healthy relationships with others.

Unfolding

We can expand the personal third, moving into that inner+outer between-ness.

Start by noticing all the betweens in your life. Not simply to fill them up, but to open them and appreciate the ease they bring. Feel the spaciousness. In that space is possibility, where you can wonder, wander.... By noticing the betweens, you give them space to exist. You expand them with imagination. Now, you are able to move through them and feel the spaciousness.

Unfolding Meditation

Imagine relaxation   Imagine space   Imagine what if
Allow space   Breathe into it
Space is freedom -- to move – to unfold -- to be

Unfold yourself, the way a leaf or a flower unfurls,
gracefully expanding, moving into a more spacious life.

In the transitional space between inner and outer,
we experience participation.

Journal or draw what you discover in the process.

> "According to feng shui, our life and destiny are closely interwoven with the workings of the universe and nature. All permutations, from cosmic to atomic, resonate within us. The force that links man and his surroundings is called ch'i (translated as human spirit, energy, or cosmic breath). There are different kinds of ch'i: a kind that circulates in the earth, a kind that circulates in the atmosphere, and a kind that moves within our own bodies. Each of us possesses ch'i. Ch'i carries our bodies. Yet its characteristics and the ways in which it moves us are different in each of us. Ch'i is the breath essential to maintaining physical, environmental, and emotional balance. The point of feng shui is to harness and enhance environmental ch'i to improve the flow of ch'i within our bodies, thus improving our life and destiny." Lin Yun, Foreword, *Interior Design with Feng Shui* x.

Look for areas in your life where you can add transitions, and let your transitions be spacious. A pause and a breath between activities. A cool glass of water and a gaze at the sky when you rise in the morning. A shift from going out shoes to coming home shoes (or bare feet, in my case). A moment for a mental/emotional shift from focused work to friendly conversation. An open window allowing flow of sound and breeze between inner and outer.

When we first bought our home, decades ago, it was pleasant in its half-wild, woodsy setting, but the inner-outer transitions were difficult, not smooth. Rickety, crowded entrances were not inviting. Windows were missing where I imagined looking through. It was too hard to get outside from inside and vice versa. The relationship between inner comforts and outer abundance was messy, dysfunctional. Years of renovations have smoothed those transitions so that inner+outer flow more easily. We expanded the third space in between our home and its surroundings; and shifting energy on one level creates a corresponding shift on another level. It's now not only more comfortable but more functional and supportive of our inner and outer lives. That's feng shui. And that is the magic of metaphor in action. As above, so below. As within, so without.

Likewise, over the years I've been renovating the third space between myself and other people. It is sometimes hard work to open it up. I don't always care to do it. Once upon a time, adolescent traumas left me feeling alienated, and I often avoided social interaction. I told myself, "don't bother expressing yourself because no one will understand what you are saying," and that's a very painful way to feel, as many people know; but of course, if you DON'T express yourself, *for sure* no one will understand you. I was mired in the swamp of futility.

Yet I found I was able to push myself in small ways, to take small steps—to speak a little more than I felt like, to share a little more than I was inclined to, to look for little openings, the way a weed finds a crack in a sidewalk, and then to encourage that growth and expansion. Leverage is real! I learned to notice the places that were shut down and look for ways to open them up.

I found clues in my languaging, like noticing when I hear myself speaking in absolutes: "This *always* happens!" or "This *never* happens!"— that might be how I feel, but these absolute terms are rarely accurate. Hyperbole tries to convince you it is real, reducing the fullness of experience to black and white. It's an example of a collapsed third, where feelings are assigned to one of two categories–true (always) or false (never) because the third (sometimes, maybe) option doesn't seem to exist. But it's there. Just remember it's there, and you can find a way in.

> DON'T BELIEVE YOUR OWN HYPERBOLE

Being fluid
Moving easily between inner and outer is a worthy goal —but how to accomplish it? Remember the physical: if it's movement you're seeking, then move! Practice fluidity. My cure is to use oscillating rhythm in my everyday practice, going back and forth between introverted activities (such as writing, or reverie, or imaginal dialogue) and extraverted activities (being physically active and engaging with the world around me). This creates space and fluid movement between my inner world and my outer world.

Focus is great, *in moderation*, but sticking with one type of activity for too long makes it harder to shift. When you sit at your desk for too long, you may balk at getting up to do something else. Your stiff hips may complain about the movement, and your mind may argue for finishing one more task, but it's the balking that points out the need to shift. Alternating movement between inner and outer activities is my habit: the regular rhythm keeps things flowing and rewires my tendency to balk at the shift. And I do still balk. It's a practice.

I know it's not easy, because you're up against the status quo. If you find such an idea challenging, yeah, it is. Small steps are probably the best way–maybe the only way–to get there.

Typology
Your own experience of inner+outer fluidity — that is, where you may get stuck and how to manage it — may differ according to your typology as well as your life experience. I'm referring specifically to Jungian typology, which was subsequently adapted into the widely popular Myers-Briggs typology; but I could just as easily be talking about astrology or enneagram or any other typing system.

In any of these systems, you identify a predilection to function best in a particular mode — say, introverted or extraverted. We commonly think of introversion and extraversion as how much you like to be alone and how much you

> **personality type**
> any category within a system of classification according to psychological characteristics and behavioral tendencies. There are many such systems.

like to be around other people, but it's not simply to do with other people. It describes whether your attention is more inclined to go inward or outward. We commonly have a slight preference for one or the other, but we all have both an introverted aspect and an extraverted aspect. Likewise, an intuitive person also has a sensing aspect, a thinker has feelings, an earthy person also has emotional sensitivity, et cetera.

Uh, Coach? I have a note...

"Please excuse Mary from gym class. She has a Taurus moon"

Pop culture encourages over-reliance on one's typology as a fixed, limiting thing, as if type is something rigid and unchanging: a definitive box, rather than a supportive structure. Typology is, first of all, theoretical: a conceptual model, it is never meant to hem you in, but to help you see yourself better; to know your strengths and also to learn to develop your weaker muscles, and to watch out for your blind spots. Use typology as a support, not an excuse to get out of growth.

Familiarity with your *inferior function* in Jungian typology can point the way to transformation. Your least developed areas are your own gateway to the unconscious. As always, take a look at what you've been ignoring.

To make best use of Jungian typology, start with the concept of individuation. As Jung conceives of the self, the totality of the individual consists of both conscious and unconscious material. Your consciousness is a mere island in the sea of unconsciousness, and Jung theorizes existence of both the personal and the collective unconscious (a pool within an ocean, kind of). The ego is the center of consciousness in the self, which emerges in childhood. The continuing healthy development of ego requires an ever-growing awareness of the larger, encompassing self (conscious and unconscious), including establishing and maintaining a communicative relationship with the larger self. This process of becoming aware of and integrating unconscious contents, as they press upward toward consciousness, is what Jung calls individuation. It is a process of growth, a process of owning parts of yourself that you had previously not recognized.

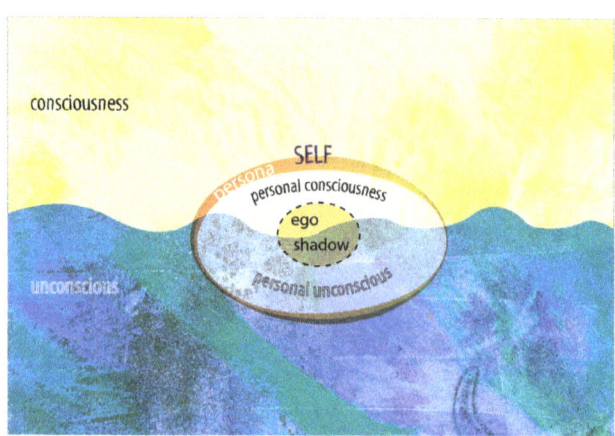

Jungian concept of self

The synthesizing of emerging unconscious material is a transformative process, one which is never complete, but continues unfolding in the healthy individual throughout life. This process is by nature compensatory, for the simple reason that what is unconscious is that which isn't conscious, and vice versa. It requires the individual to become aware of personal contradiction, which can be painful, difficult, and confusing; and it necessarily involves that least developed part of you. So, for instance, if you are generally extraverted, individuation involves looking into yourself, and if you are given to introversion, it involves looking out into the world.

To reiterate, your type describes that aspect of yourself which is most conscious, with which you identify most strongly, and with which you have the most facility. Your inferior function points to that aspect of yourself of which you have the least consciousness —and though it may be a blind spot, it's still there, still a part of you. Throughout your life, you can work toward wholeness by continually becoming more aware and integrating your less conscious aspects. Your type may continue to describe the strongest, most obvious aspect of your personality, but over time you can become more skillful in the use and expression of your less dominant functions as well (although we can never be in complete control of the unconscious: remember that, ego!). So really, whatever your type, establishing the habit of inner-outer fluidity will serve you in your process of individuation.

The insider-outsider dilemma
The western difficulty of reconciling "subjective" and "objective" perspectives has been duly noted in academia. Sometimes referred to as emic vs etic, the insider-outsider dilemma extends from the culturally perceived duality of inner self and outer self (or mind and body).

Literary scholar Roger Shattuck summarizes the predicament in his essay, "Knowledge Double Bound":

> *"Both common sense and the history of philosophy recognize two kinds, two tendencies of knowledge. We may approach, enter into, sympathize with, and unite with the thing known in order to attain subjective knowledge. Or we may stand outside, observe, anonymize, analyze, and ponder the thing known in order to attain objective knowledge. Subjective or empathetic knowledge causes us to lose a judicious perspective on the object; objective knowledge, in seeking to maintain that perspective, loses the bond of sympathy. We cannot know something by both means at the same time. The attempt to reconcile the two or to alternate between them leads to great mental stress."* (332)

There is a stress of trying to reconcile or alternate between inner and outer experience, yet that stress is exacerbated by this western academic/philosophic viewpoint that subject and object are split and must remain distinct from one another. I am suspicious. I think Shattuck is wrong when he says "We cannot know something by both means at the same time." I think that's the only way we can ever know anything.

It's hard to look in two directions at once, true. We don't have eyes in the back of our heads. But we do *have* backs of our heads, and life is not only about what we're looking at; we're immersed in life, always standing *somewhere* on the continuum between pure subjectivity and pure objectivity. We can move around, closer or further from one pole or the other, but we never truly inhabit either point. Can't be done, because those points, "subjectivity" and "objectivity," are concepts, ideals, abstractions; not real locations where a human can perch. Yeah, we identify insiders and outsiders, we recognize subjectivity and objectivity— *more* or *less* — and it's useful, but it's relative. And it's really helpful if we acknowledge that relativity instead of trying to overcome it — because if you're somewhere in between subjective and objective, then you have a relationship to both understandings; you have access to either; and you can practice a fluidity of movement between inner and outer perspectives.

Fluid narrative
What's real? That's debatable, isn't it? I mean, you may have a good answer to that question, and I may agree with you, but the nature of reality is multi-faceted and protean, and our opinions on it are always perspectival. It is a curious cultural fantasy that there could be one "true story" waiting to be told from real events; this fantasy stands in the way of recognizing our position as always both inside and outside —our position of always having a position. The "either/or" stance is inherent to the western view that *westerners* are the objective ones, while it's *"other cultures"* (especially those who practice participatory types of consciousness) who are the subjective ones.

Even a most objective narrative must assume a perspective. Even as we observe, we are embedded within the world through which we move, with all of our senses. Only by an act of imagination can you believe otherwise. We can navigate freely between observer and participant roles, as both positions are really always present as part of our experience. The continuum of inner-outer awareness is infinite. No matter how far in you go, or how far out, there always seems to be more. As a corollary, no matter where you are, you are always an insider in some ways and an outsider in others.

According to Hayden White, the notion "that real events could 'speak themselves' or be represented as 'telling their own story' " is a relatively modern stance, and a dubious one (3); for, as we know, events *happen* — they *occur* — but they don't tell a story. It is we who tell stories *about* them. We bring the narrative frame. There's a common expectation that an historical account must hold to facts alone, while at the same time providing a sense of plot and motivation, as well as analysis—well, that's an impossibility. Events do not come with narrative attached! Narrative must be constructed.

Narrative formation is always a creative process; and creativity, remember, occurs in between real and pretend, in between true and false. The narrative frame is, de facto, a perspective; therefore subjective, imparting meaning by providing context for (objective) events; so, "subjective" imagination and "objective" explanation are complementary, and we find both in all of our narratives, historical or otherwise (Kearney "Narrative" 73). The very idea of one without the other is a fallacy. Meaning comes, not from facts alone, but from facts "seen through" an archetypal frame or perspective. And, as we know: reframe the story, and understanding shifts.

Reframing our narratives

Note: this is not in support of "white washing" or "sweeping unpleasant things under the carpet." To the contrary, this practice starts from the point of acknowledging facts, and from there, trying to interpret them from a variety of positions.

There are many possible ways of telling any event. The practice of framing and reframing our personal narratives helps us to explore possibilities, encouraging a sense of fluidity. It can help with the integration of subjective and objective views. Personal narratives may change, almost with every re-telling, and I would say, "Let's hope so!" It is not just a matter of faulty memory, because from every new point in life, we see the past differently, and along the way, we gather new facts and insights.

Authoring Your Life

> **author, from the Latin auctor, literally "one who causes to grow," comes from the root augere, "to increase".**

"We are born into a storied world," as characters in family stories and traditions that are already underway, says Alan Parry. These stories give us structure, coherence, and often, comfort; yet, we can also feel trapped in roles that we fell into. This is what Parry calls "being lived by a story." When you feel "typecast," confined/defined by the interpretations of others, it's time to deconstruct and reframe. As Siri Husvedt puts it, it's your opportunity to "rewrite what has written you."

You can shift from being a character in a story to being the author of your life. Developing the ability to see yourself and others from new perspectives is a movement toward objectivity. By writing from a position outside of your "character," you create space, and space allows movement and change. Judith Barrington suggests shifting your narrative voice from first person to third person: actually writing about yourself as "she"/"he"/"they" rather than "I" (44-45). It's amazing how this practice detaches you from that one role that you were simply born into.

You are in charge of your own story. You have the authority to describe your experiences your way. You are the author of you.

> "Liberate the many stories that have been censored into oblivion by the tyranny of a single, dominant story."
> — Parry and Doan (27)

Stories Are Alive

In some oral traditions, stories are considered living beings. They want to be told; and because they are alive, they change. Some parts will grow or take on more importance, and some die off. Because you are a living being, your stories change. It's a sign of your own vitality and growth.

So many stories
Who are you? How many ways can you respond to that question? There are so many ways to tell your story, so many stories to tell. Now that you're the author, how would *you* describe your character? How many different characters have you played? *Child, parent, friend, partner, supervisor, worker, collaborator, contributor, organizer, dreamer, outsider, member, hero, villain, vixen, puritan, teacher, student, genius, goof, sneak, saint, tiger, dragon, mouse...*

There's a through-line, of course: all the various roles you've played are aspects of your one life. They're all you, but who you are is always evolving, and really, you look different in different lights. We all do. The point is not to promote "alternative facts," but to explore alternative views. Facts are stable, but the interpretations are fluid. The way you tell your own story is a naturally creative process of framing your experience to make it meaningful and descriptive of your life.

Honestly, you can try out alternative views without taking them to heart, simply for the experience of telling your life differently. Just like you might try on a mask, a costume, a new dress or haircut... How does it feel? Try on your personal stories with the intention to see old things from new angles. The change of perspective can be transformative. What do you learn about who you are and where you are going?

In the continual process of becoming, the narratives we craft define a trajectory from past to future. To successfully set such a course, we need to acknowledge what has already occurred and where we are now. Revisioning of the past helps to point us toward a desirable future, as we judge and order our actions in the present. By revisioning, I don't mean intentionally changing the facts, but understanding them in a new light as we learn and grow. So we forget some things, hide some things, maybe even swear to a few that never did happen. That's par. Again, I'm not saying "Anything goes, so go ahead and lie!" Rather, I'm stressing that the main threads of your life are more significant than a few misremembered details. As the human body is reconstituted over time, so are our memories and our understandings. We retell our stories, and, although they change, there are threads of continuity. Maybe I haven't seen you in forty years, but I still recognize you.

The personal sense of identity is woven into those threads, suspended between past and future selves. We are always building on what has already occurred, as we open to what might be. Self-creation through narrative is an ongoing process. Narrativizing orients us to the future, and its intentionality is instrumental in helping us "get there."

Who we are, and how we see ourselves, is always changing as we move through life. Moving fluidly through this wealth of changing perspectives keeps us healthy. So, tell your story over and over, as many times, in as many ways, as you like!

Narrative is a vehicle of change. Hop in!

Word magic

"Magic is the art of changing consciousness at will." - Dion Fortune

"The non-dual Kashmir Saivas view the process by which our daily reality is manifested from the infinite reality of Shiva as a 'sounding' forth...." Muller-Ortega, qtd. in Beck 168.

"In the beginning was the Word" - King James Bible.

What is the mechanism by which intention works? What is the magic that links word to deed? I cannot pretend to unveil the secret of this mystery; but on an obvious level, when you crystallize an intention into words, then you can easily hold it in your mind. Words are units of clarification. Each time you come to a relevant choice point, you are more aware that your decision will move you towards or away from your goal, and you can choose accordingly. If you haven't clarified your goals, then they can't guide you. You may instead be guided by unconscious wishes, or "luck" if there's such a thing, or simply by the wind.

> "If you think about it, the very best books are really just extremely long spells that turn you into a different person for the rest of your life."
>
> Jonathan Edward Durham

To reach a goal — *any* goal— a series of choices must be made, whether consciously or unconsciously. Making a choice always implies a simultaneous rejection of other options. The more clearly you can hold the objective in mind, the more straightforward will be your path to reaching it. A word is a most efficient container to hold the contraction of infinite possibility on the way to manifestation.

Using the magic of words
Life: it's all poetry. And I don't mean rhyme schemes. Poetry as in *poiesis*: using words (in this case) to give form to something formless. Think of poetry broadly, as a sensual experience. Choose and use words for how they feel rolling around in your mouth. Arrange them not according to rules or rhymes but because they sound right, according to how they best give voice to that image or sense that is seeking expression. Whisper...chant...intone...Name what is present. Feel the power of language vibrate your being.

Metaphor is magic
The oneness of inner and outer worlds is the foundation of magical thought. Ancient Egyptian culture, infused with magic and mystery on all levels, is relevant and helpful for understanding this philosophy. At the core of ancient Egyptian culture is a theory of symbolic unity, an understanding of a pervasive cosmic

order in all things. Art and artifacts were created in accordance with, and as representative of, a symbolic system for understanding life; as such, they are laden with mythological import. Mythological, magical meaning is intrinsic to Egyptian design.

This sense of all things being connected motivates the practice of sympathetic magic, wherein ritual use of symbolic speech and form is undertaken to sustain balance.

sympathetic magic using words, actions, or objects to influence symbolically corresponding events

There is an essential unity between word and the thought it represents, and this is the basis of word magic, which was widely practiced in ancient Egypt. Hieroglyphic script was believed to be very powerful magically, and so was used ritually, and with caution. The word *hieroglyph* means "sacred writing," and Egyptians believed that writing itself was a gift from the gods to humanity (from the mysterious unknown to the known reality; or, in depth psych terms, from the unconscious to consciousness). Hieroglyphs were thought to be potentially alive, and rituals encouraged the gods to inhabit statues, drawings and hieroglyphs (Pinch, Myth 15, 33). Wilkinson points out that statues, objects, art and architecture all functioned as hieroglyphs in three dimensions, their forms designed and placed in accordance with their symbolic meaning (148-169). Their location, both in the landscape and relative to one another, was conceived in such a way as to strengthen their magical efficacy.

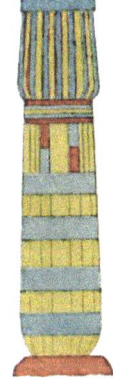

Hieroglyphics might take the form of sacred objects placed in the landscape, inviting the gods to linger. Image source nypl.org

Egyptians thought that names, in particular, hold magical power: "name is never a mere symbol," for a person's identity is "indissolubly linked, in mythic thinking, with his name" (Cassirer 49-50). This is true across cultures and remains true today. We may not practice word magic as the Egyptians did, yet no one wants their name to be sullied. There is power in a name, and there is power in words. We may speak about this power differently, and use it differently, but the relation is essentially unchanged by all the insights and theories that have arisen over the intervening eons. Words do things. Used intentionally, words guide us and help us to focus. We find that words spoken carelessly or unconsciously can prevent our success. Words are powerful, and the wise person uses them with care.

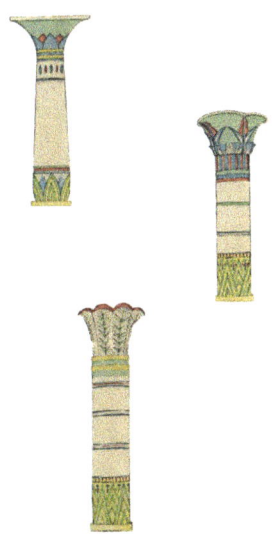

Egyptian columns. Henri Ernst. 1923

"Metaphors are means of doing things and not merely ways of saying things." —Jackson (138)

The philosophical argument for an underlying unity between word, thought, and image is based on the theory that language is rooted in metaphor as the conceptualization of experience. (See Cazeaux's exce;;ent argument.)

Language and thought are built upon metaphorical reference to physical experience, and communication is only possible through this reference to bodily sensation.

Lakoff and Johnson have shown that metaphor arises from the empirical ground of the body as an extension of neural processing, and research into neural structure supports this: we conceptualize subjective perceptions in terms of sensorimotor experience (Lakoff and Johnson 254-59). "In actuality we feel that no metaphor can ever be comprehended or even adequately represented independently of its experiential basis" (19). Metaphor is at the heart of our conceptual organization.

Metaphorical unity between image, thing, and name is found in every culture. Understanding the embodied nature of metaphor helps to explain how inner and outer experiences are directly related and can be used to catalyze transformation. Seeing connections between events that lack an obvious causal relationship has been called "magical thinking"; and indeed, the basis of magic is metaphorical correspondence. But in magic, too, the causal relationship exists—we just don't understand it or we can't see it. Perhaps by expanding the third space, in between true and false, we may access the missing causal connections.

Metaphor naturally serves as a link between the imaginal and the physical, mediating by virtue of its inherently open and ambiguous character. But it is not "just a metaphor," as in, merely a figure of speech used to describe one thing in terms of another. Metaphor, as the structure through which new meanings can unfold, is constitutive of reality.

Turning and turning, metaphor is the spiral dynamic which connects all and is there from the start.

Isis and the Name of Ra (Egyptian tradition)

The goddess Isis created a snake that bit her ancestor, the great and aging Sun god Ra. Ra suffered greatly from the venomous wound, which only Isis could cure. She promised to heal Ra only if he revealed to her his true name, given to him by his parents and hidden from all others as a protection from magical attacks. Now, however, he must make himself vulnerable to Isis in order to be healed; and, in fact, to protect his lineage, as she will pass his ancient magical name on to her son Horus.

In "The Effectiveness of Symbols," Lévi-Strauss describes the structure of a Cuna shamanistic cure for difficult childbirth.

The Cuna cure as described consists mainly, but not solely, of the shaman intoning directly to the laboring mother a song of his journey through the imaginal landscape of her body, where he restores her system to balance, with the help of spiritual or imaginal entities. The use of repetition and detailed descriptive language suggests similarities to practices such as hypnotic induction, guided meditation and creative visualization. Lévi-Strauss posits language as the essential mechanism of the cure, maintaining that "the shamanistic cure lies on the borderline between contemporary physical medicine and psychological therapies"—that is, between inner and outer.

Chinese Philosophy

In Chinese traditional philosophy the "symbolic correlations between the personal body and the body of the world" are based on a conception of one coextensive world organism characterized by mutual dependency, where "inner and outer worlds of experience [have] identical systems of physiology" (Jackson 127); this understanding infused ancient Chinese culture, and is still found in contemporary practices of Chinese medicine, Chi Gung, Feng Shui and I Ching. The human is not distinct from nature but a constituent of the larger container of the ecological system, or "whole." Our individual health and well-being is continuous with the world around us. Upon reflection, this view seems, not naïve, but quite simply and obviously the way things are.

It may be narrative, in song or poem, that provides entry to the hidden realms of consciousness accessed by shamanic and indigenous healers. It may be metaphor (culturally situated) that forms the bridge between intention and accomplishment. As the anthropologist Michael Jackson argues, metaphor reveals the essential unity between language and world.

"It is the inseparability of conceptual and bodily activity which explains why metaphors often mediate the forms of human illness" (Jackson 137)

Contemporary physical medicine, psychological therapies, and shamanistic cures *all* function *both* internally and externally. Perhaps language is a key link between consciousness and creativity, assisting with the process of forming and visualizing ideas in the imaginal realm in order to cause effects on the physical level.

Narrative has the power to cure or curse, as when Isis cures a snakebite ("Isis and the Name of Ra"); or in Levi-Strauss's account of a Cuna shamanistic cure ("The Effectiveness of Symbols"); or in a testimony given in a court of law; or when parents give or withhold their blessings. The verbal act of a promise, a command, a will, or a wager carries a cultural expectation that can be morally and legally binding. These, of course, may be accompanied by other consequential actions, but, all that aside, no one really wants to be cursed by their parents, and it feels good to receive blessings. Does it make a difference?

I think so! If you agree, remember to use your word magic!

From ancient Egypt to you,
here, now...
poetry begins with presence.

So
here, now...
can you name what you are feeling...
noticing...?

I solemnly swear to tell the truth, the whole truth, and nothing but the truth, so help me God.

OM

Hail Mary, full of grace, the Lord is with thee. Blessed art thou among women, and blessed is the fruit of thy womb, Jesus. Holy Mary, mother of God, pray for us sooners now, and at the hour of death.

Merry meet and merry part and merry meet again!

Yes please!

I swear on my mother's grave!

YOU WHO ARE YOU WHO ARE YOU WHO ARE YOU WHO ARE YOU

Open Sesame!

Best Wishes!

Blessed Be!

tat tvam asi

I am that I am

TAYATA OM ZIY Z ZIYA VISAYA VISAYA ZIYA PRAHINI SHATKARI SHATKARI PRABHA DAKARE

Remember, remember the sacredness of things running streams and dwellings the young within the nest, a heart for sacred fire, the holy flame of fire

Many Blessings

Show me what democracy looks like!
This is what democracy looks like!

Gesundheit!

Sarva Mangalam!

Sleep, sleep, in the calm of all calm, sleep, O sleep, in the guidance of all guidance, sleep, sleep, in the love of all loves, sleep, my dear one, in the Lord of life, sleep, my dear one, in the god of life.

The Lord bless you and keep you the Lord make his face shine upon you and be gracious to you; the Lord turn his face toward you and give you peace.

HAPPY BIRTHDAY!

WE SHALL OVERCOME,
WE SHALL OVERCOME,
WE SHALL OVERCOME, SOME DAY.
OH DEEP IN MY HEART
OVERCOME, SOME DAY.

See with our eyes, hear with our ears, breathe with our nose, touch with our hands, kiss with our lips, love with our hearts! That ... we ... may be at last joyful ... blessing of all that is, was, and shall be!

All we are saying

..., I thee wed
three ... three, so mote it be

Thank you!

a chance

May the road rise up to greet you
May the wind be ever at your back

2 - 4 - 6 - 8
Who do we appreciate

ABRACADABRA!

The People united, will never be defeated

I CHARGE YOU, TOOLS OF THE ELEMENTS, TO SWEEP MY HOUSE CLEAN OF ALL ILL AND PAIN. THIS IS MY WILL, SO MOTE IT BE!
BANISH EVIL AND NEGATIVITY; THIS IS MY WILL, SO MOTE IT BE

TSA LA TSA LA / CHI LE CHI LE / TSULU TSULU / KAMPA KAMPA / KALA KALA / KILI KILI / KULU KULU / MU NYATZA MU NYATZA / ATATA HA HASA MA / VIDHUNA SA YA PA RA SE NYEN

health, happiness, peace and prosperity

Alchemy and Transformation

Operations applied to materials affect transformation.

Mind-body

The western alchemical tradition grew out of an understanding of psyche and matter as one. The practice was born from the marriage of Greek thought and Egyptian magic, around the first century CE; the Chinese alchemical tradition based in Taoism is parallel in significant ways.

Alchemy was the precursor to modern chemistry, in which experiments are performed to effect changes on matter. The difference with alchemy is that inner or spiritual change is observed coincident with material change; this reflects an understanding that mind and matter are a continuity; cohesive, not discrete.

What would that be like, to experience mind and matter as one? That's probably what we *DO* experience, because probably they *ARE* one; but for most westerners, anyway, that unity is experienced below the threshold of consciousness. As beings in human bodies, we engage in experience via our sensory perceptions. "The body is our general means of having a world" said Merleau-Ponty (147). Our bodies *perceive* (through our available sensory receptors) and these perceptions are translated into *meaning*. ...*thought knowledge image word feeling*: all are *translations* of experience through our bodily perceptions. We can infer that all of our understandings are conditioned by the human apparatus. The world does not present itself already divided into categories of sight, sound, smell and so on. The division of sensory information into five senses (or more, depending on the cultural framework) is a process that takes place in the body, not before. We do not have the option to, let's say, *objectively* experience a flower, because a butterfly or a bee, of course, experiences a flower very differently from you, and both experiences are real, but neither is objectively "more accurate." As Kant argued, we are not privy to the pure, objective perception of qualities, because we, like any other embodied being, are limited by our perceptual apparatus and the shapes our perceptions can take for us.

So, let's say a thought is inspired by a perception, which is grounded in bodily experience. Our bodies sort and translate, but according to what system? Metaphor, says Cazeaux, is the system, the schema of our organization: *this* is like *that*. The very process of translating a sensory perception into a thought is metaphorical: *this* (perception) is *that* (thought).

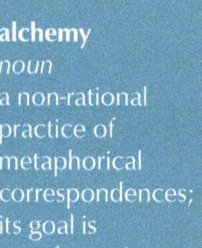

alchemy
noun
a non-rational practice of metaphorical correspondences; its goal is transformation.

Traditional alchemy comprises a wide variety of practices that can be summarized as the reduction of a substance to its essential elements, which are then rejoined into a new form. Generally, heat is applied to induce such transformations as calcination, sublimation, dissolution, coagulation, separation, conjunction, putrefaction, distillation, multiplication and tincture. These processes are directed toward synthesis, refinement and purification, but there is a cyclical quality to the practice (not a "one and done").

Transformation occurs within an enclosing vessel, such as an alembic or a crucible; accordingly, secrecy is an important theme, for the experience is mysterious and cannot be translated to the uninitiated. The alchemist is in intense relationship with the work. Through this deep involvement, complexity and nuance are revealed to the one who is absorbed in the process; these finer points will be lost on those who are not so deeply engaged. Some things, one knows only by doing.

The experimental process of alchemy follows the promptings of intuition, using the application of reason, in order to catalyze transformations that can be observed on all levels: inner and outer, in self and in matter.

We take in and process huge amounts of sensory data. Much of what we perceive and sort does not enter into consciousness at all; yet the experience is held in the memory below the threshold of consciousness. "Psychoid" is Jung's term to describe the pre-conscious level of experience where psyche and matter are undifferentiated.

> *The part of the unconscious which is designated as the subtle body becomes more and more identical with the functioning of the body, and therefore it grows darker and darker and ends in the utter darkness of matter; that aspect of the unconscious is exceedingly incomprehensible.... One must include not only the shadow — the psychological unconscious — but also the physiological unconscious, that so-called somatic unconscious which is the subtle body.... Somewhere our unconscious becomes material, because the body is the living unit, and our conscious and unconscious are embedded in it: they contact the body. Somewhere there is a place where the two ends meet and become interlocked. And that is the place [i.e. subtle body] where one cannot say whether it is matter or what one calls 'psyche.'*

(Jung Nietzsche 441)

If, in western culture, the mind-body split is coincident with the emergence of consciousness—or is, in fact, the very separation of consciousness from unconscious, and if, as Merleau-Ponty's work suggests, the body is the location of the split, then there is an experience deep within us of a participatory reality which is prior to the split. This experience would, according to Jung's theory, be pre-conscious. This describes the psychoid level, where psyche and matter are one, and which is implicated in synchronous acts.

If we live in a unified world, where mind and body are truly one, then metaphor is a way of remembering that unity. "As above, so below"—the magical metaphorical alchemical dictum — is simply a way of connecting with what we have consciously lost awareness of.

Synchronous experience can be understood through this frame of reference. Synchronicity is when two or more events are observed to coincide, and though not known to be causally linked, yet they are metaphorically linked.

Let's say I'm reading a book about a rare woodpecker when suddenly that rare woodpecker alights on a tree in front of me. That's synchronicity. Or, let's say I'm reading a letter from an old friend to whom I haven't spoken in twenty years; as

I'm reading it, my phone rings and—*whaaat?* It's that same friend! That's synchronicity.

In a world where mind and body (and you and I) are believed to be separate, or where mind is believed to be simply brain, fully contained within body, then synchronicities may appear to be impossible, or merely coincident; but when mind and body (and you and I) are understood as different aspects of one unified experience, and mind as a river extending beyond the sensible realms of the body, then synchronous experience makes more logical sense.

How does this relate to alchemy? Back to my old friend... Let's say the reason we haven't talked in twenty years is due to a misunderstanding that we never cleared up. I begin to work through what happened. Maybe I do some writing or painting or imaginal dialogue, and in the process, I come to a place of discovery where I see past events in a new light. In that moment, I acknowledge my errors of judgment and feel forgiveness of perceived slights, and am filled with love and affection for my old friend. *That's* alchemy, whether my old friend calls or not — But what if they DID call then —*whoa!*

Transform the inner and the outer will also be transformed; and vice versa. Many are the stories of shamans who create inner balance in order to bring balance into the world, via a rainstorm or a healing event or.... Perhaps you've heard of the 4000 meditators who focused together for six weeks on reducing violence in DC, with statistically significant results. If we practice being peace, our peacefulness can extend into the world to create change. Fortunately, it's not only bad moods and negative thinking that are contagious! But they definitely are, too. Your inner condition affects the world, just as the world affects your inner condition.

Alchemy in depth psychology

Jung rediscovered the ancient texts of alchemy and recognized their correspondence with the depth psychological approach. In the alchemical tradition, psyche and matter are one thing: simply the inner (or introverted) and outer (or extraverted) views of the same phenomena.

The vessel has the utmost importance in alchemical processes: it provides the limiting boundary and the space within that allows movement. Within the vessel one observes and experiences the mixing and

---

There's a common image of ancient alchemists as crazed magi consumed by the greedy desire to change lead into gold. Toxic substances like lead and mercury were often used, which could cause dementia and other maladies; and rediscovered texts are cryptic. Many certainly sound mad, to the uninitiated, at least. The moral and mental conditions of alchemists were varied, and so were the arcane goals of their various projects; but alchemy is always about transformation, and especially the "inner gold" that may be achieved via outer processes.

interaction of substances, the physical and the metaphysical. The alchemist's observations are both rational and non-rational. The vessel provides protection against being overcome by the contents—although vessels do break. There are explosions and accidents, and forces too powerful to be contained.

"The alchemist puts his reveries into experiments." Bachelard (75)

The Self can be seen as a vessel containing all the conflicting tendencies of the individual; failure of the vessel results in psychosis. The therapeutic relationship is also like a vessel. Within a protective barrier of confidentiality, one can safely share secrets and risk vulnerability, and explain things that might seem inexplicable —"crazy" — to an outside observer.

The vessel can also be the safe space or the ritual we create to hold creative work. Into this vessel goes the content flowing out of the unconscious: dream images, ideas, impulses, what have you...Because dreams come to us out of the unconscious, they often use the language of metaphor, and can tell us things we're not consciously aware of. Projecting imaginal contents into a vessel outside of the self can allow for better integration, by providing both detachment and perspective. The contained and externalized practice of symbolic expression allows psychic contents to be studied at a remove, reducing the pressure of contents otherwise held within, where they are more at risk of erupting forcefully through unconscious literal expression.

"It is in the process of affecting transformations that the human self is created and re-created." Greene (21)

The alchemy of making things
Regular creative engagement is a process of integrating, organizing, and clarifying your parts. Just as your home space can get messy and cluttered, so does your inner space, unless you apply yourself to straightening things out and figuring out what you want to do with stuff. Bringing order and clarity to your life is not "once and done" but an ongoing process.

The creative process is alchemical in nature, offering the opportunity to reunify inner and outer experience; that is, to heal the mind-body split. Your absorption in the process allows the fluid transition between inner and outer worlds. Just as in Islamic cosmology (also an alchemical tradition), the journey inward leads to the outer world, and the outer journey leads within.

The creative project is an alchemical vessel: a focal container into which the maker pours attention, and becomes absorbed in the making. Skills develop, discoveries are made, and matter reveals its secrets. Such experience provides access to dimensions of symbolic material which are unavailable through intellectual inquiry. Transformation happens in the process. This is alchemy.

Within the vessel of a project, psyche and matter are in participation, as ideas and feelings are in play with materials and elemental processes. In physical making, processes might include kneading, mixing, dyeing, cutting, heating, cooling, bathing, adhering, tempering, polishing, and so on. The process of creation can be exhilarating, but also difficult and uncomfortable, involving sacrifice and suffering. Failure happens and can be disheartening. Emergence of the new requires death of the old. Irritants and imperfections, both inner and outer, make their presence known. These may be released through processes of refinement and purification, but they may also be instrumental in accomplishing those operations, as when the irritant engenders the pearl. Coniunctio, "the sacred marriage," is generally considered the culmination of the alchemical process—that synthesis of contents which produces something totally new—the "gold" which Jung called the transcendent function. The experience of transforming matter catalyzes personal transformation—it is not "only" a metaphor.

Craftsmanship is a process of focused projection. It begins with following the thread of intuition, and attuning to psyche in the world, in materials, and in others. Engaging in the conversation between inner and outer, the hands are mediators: our wondrous and skillful digits, the tools of Hermes, mediate between image and abstraction, bringing idea into form. The transformational alchemical process takes time and requires work. It is more than thinking and imagining; it includes physical experience. Our relationship to the elements—earth, air, fire, water—through materials, forces, and processes, is illuminated. Alchemy is an experience of acting in concert with the world, aligning with the larger system that has held us and sustained us for as long as we can remember, and continues to sustain us even as we forget.

> The Hermetic dictum, "As above, so below," has been claimed as a secret teaching of an Egyptian sage or god, Hermes Trismegistus, although the Hermetica seems to have had its origins in the Greco-Roman period (332bce-395ce) (Pinch *Intro* 7). Nonetheless, it captures, in a nutshell, the essence of mythic thinking: the metaphor has magical power. Cassirer summarizes it this way: "Whoever has brought any part of a whole into his power has thereby acquired power, in the magical sense, over the whole itself" (92): pars pro toto.

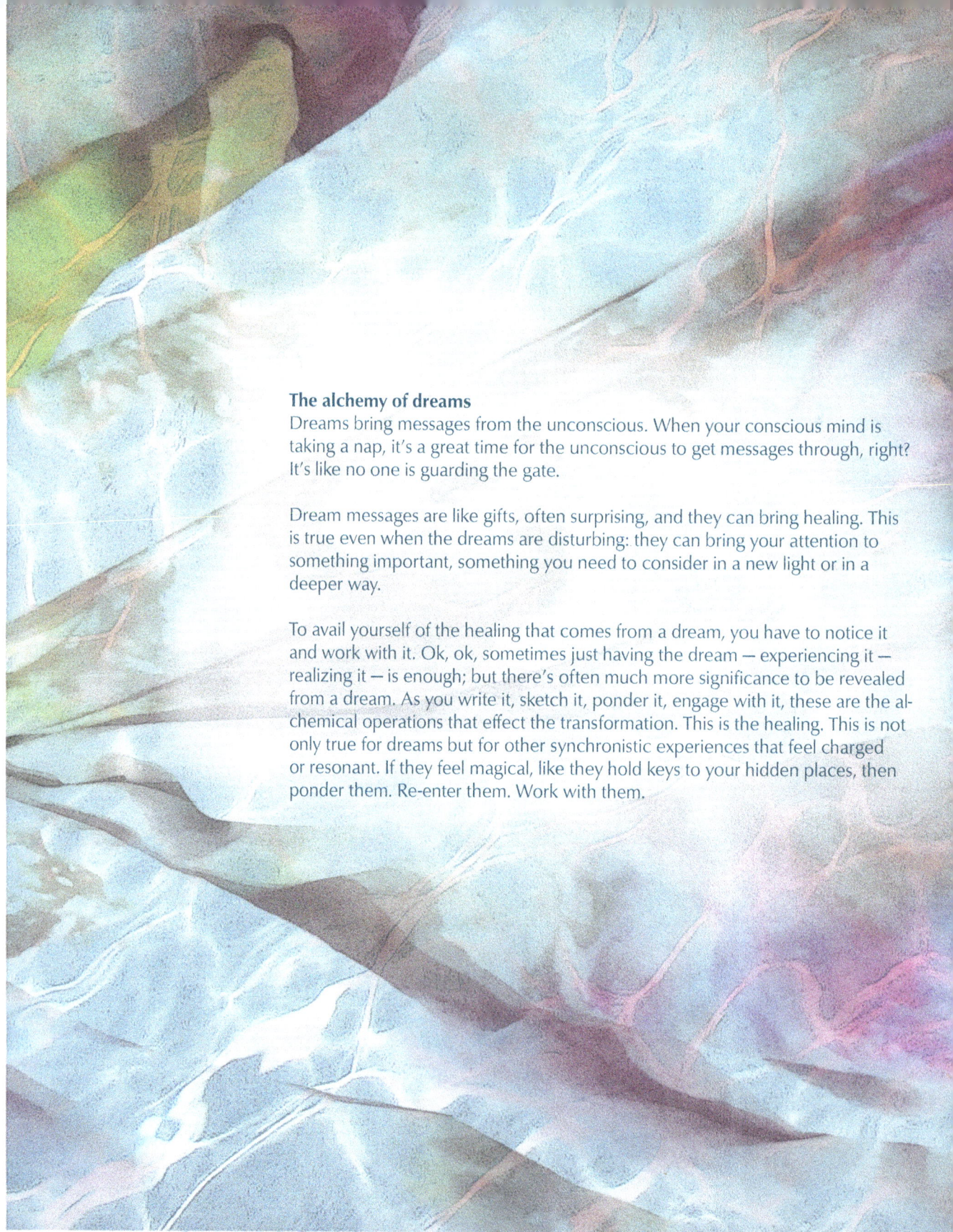

The alchemy of dreams

Dreams bring messages from the unconscious. When your conscious mind is taking a nap, it's a great time for the unconscious to get messages through, right? It's like no one is guarding the gate.

Dream messages are like gifts, often surprising, and they can bring healing. This is true even when the dreams are disturbing: they can bring your attention to something important, something you need to consider in a new light or in a deeper way.

To avail yourself of the healing that comes from a dream, you have to notice it and work with it. Ok, ok, sometimes just having the dream — experiencing it — realizing it — is enough; but there's often much more significance to be revealed from a dream. As you write it, sketch it, ponder it, engage with it, these are the alchemical operations that effect the transformation. This is the healing. This is not only true for dreams but for other synchronistic experiences that feel charged or resonant. If they feel magical, like they hold keys to your hidden places, then ponder them. Re-enter them. Work with them.

If you have trouble remembering your dreams...

Give yourself a prompt before bed: an intention to remember.

Give yourself a few moments to remember when you wake up. Don't jump right out of bed, don't immediately pick up your phone, but let yourself linger, if possible, and see what's floating around in your mind.

Keep a journal nearby. Jotting down even a couple of key words or images can be enough to keep the dream with you.

Fragments are fine! You may not remember a whole screenplay: often dreams don't come that way. One image may be very rich, and sometimes will unfold into something much more meaningful than it first appears.

If dreams don't come to you at night, you can go looking for them in your waking day, through daydreams and reverie.

More ideas for working with dreams are in the How-To Guide at the end of this chapter.

The alchemy of aging

Is aging an alchemical process? I've come to think of it that way. It's as if we spend the first half of life constructing the self and the second half deconstructing it. Or maybe we spend the first half covering our nakedness with inhibitions and masks, and the second half revealing what we had so cleverly disguised. A fool's game? For sure, AND ALSO I think something worthwhile is happening in this aging process of doing and undoing, covering up and then revealing. Maturity? Depth? Like wine, like cheese, we are always transforming. What if that's what life's all about?

"Aging is an extraordinary process whereby you become the person you always should have been." David Bowie

As alchemists in pursuit of gold, we explore our hidden realms, transforming wounds, hurts, disappointments, inner knots in the process, thereby becoming ourselves. Says Winnicott, "play serves the function of self revelation." So let's get to it!

Adapted from image by Shomixer - adobestock

Last Night As I Was Sleeping
ANTONIO MACHADO

Last night as I was sleeping,
I dreamt—marvelous error!—
that a spring was breaking
out in my heart.
I said: Along which secret aqueduct,
Oh water, are you coming to me,
water of a new life
that I have never drunk?

Last night as I was sleeping,
I dreamt—marvelous error!—
that I had a beehive
here inside my heart.
And the golden bees
were making white combs
and sweet honey
from my old failures.

Last night as I was sleeping,
I dreamt—marvelous error!—
that a fiery sun was giving
light inside my heart.
It was fiery because I felt
warmth as from a hearth,
and sun because it gave light
and brought tears to my eyes.

Last night as I slept,
I dreamt—marvelous error!—
that it was God I had
here inside my heart.

translated by Robert Bly

Your Everyday Practice

is the practice of tuning in, being present, and engaging creatively in the moment: Be open to improvisation. Allow things to happen that you hadn't planned. Give expression to images, impulses, intuitions, ideas that come to you.

TRUE STORY: Once when I was about 5, I painted bottom of my foot blue. My mother asked "why?" and I replied, "my foot fell asleep, so I painted it blue."

It does not mean that everyday you must produce a thing. Some days, sure! As you like it. But the practice itself doesn't ask that of you. This practice doesn't ask you to draw everyday, or write everyday, or sing everyday—this practice asks you to engage creatively everyday. It's a way of life, a way of recognizing that you are alive; allowing the vitality of the life force to move through you and connect you with the world, which is also alive. This awareness can bring you great joy, and a deepening sense of a meaningful life. Not constantly, ok? I'm not saying you'll be joyful in every moment! Maybe you will, I don't know about that. What I do know is that, in this practice, over time, you will find yourself following the trail of meaning and dipping into the well of joy.

START HERE >>> DO NOTHING...MAKE SPACE

Set the stage

Here are a few things you can do to lay the groundwork for your practice.

Boredom ... quietude ... messing around ... doing nothing
These prepare the ground for creative expression and the emergence of the intuitive experience. Creative engagement requires space and time.

Space and time simply aren't given in the average westerner's busy schedule. Economic and technological developments have led to increasingly superficial relationships with the physical world: less making, less doing, less physical connection. Many have come to view arts and crafts as spectator sports, and the creative space out of which these arise is given to other pursuits; yet many others are finding renewal through creativity. It takes a concerted effort to clear space and time for your expression, and when you do, the first thing you should do is — nothing...

Can you step outside of the pressure machine? Can you relax without letting the airwaves flood your consciousness?

Think of the phrase "free time"

"Free time." It used to happen regularly for me, anyway. Now, when every moment is tabulated, it's hard to conjure that type of openness. You may feel you don't have the time or space for an everyday creative practice—but opening up time and space is exactly what this practice can do for you. Just a moment... a few moments...can become expansive. Start by noticing your moments. Start with awareness.

<u>Pay</u> attention to how you "<u>spend</u>" your time. Or, better yet, put your wallet aside and inhabit the gift of your life. Watch its patterns and flow over the course of the day, and from one day to the next.

Privileges of Space and Time

Space and time are freely available to everyone — Except when they aren't.

Space and time are class privileges: upper caste advantages. How can my words speak to those whose every moment is controlled by others or concerned with survival? I don't have an answer.

May freedom come to all.

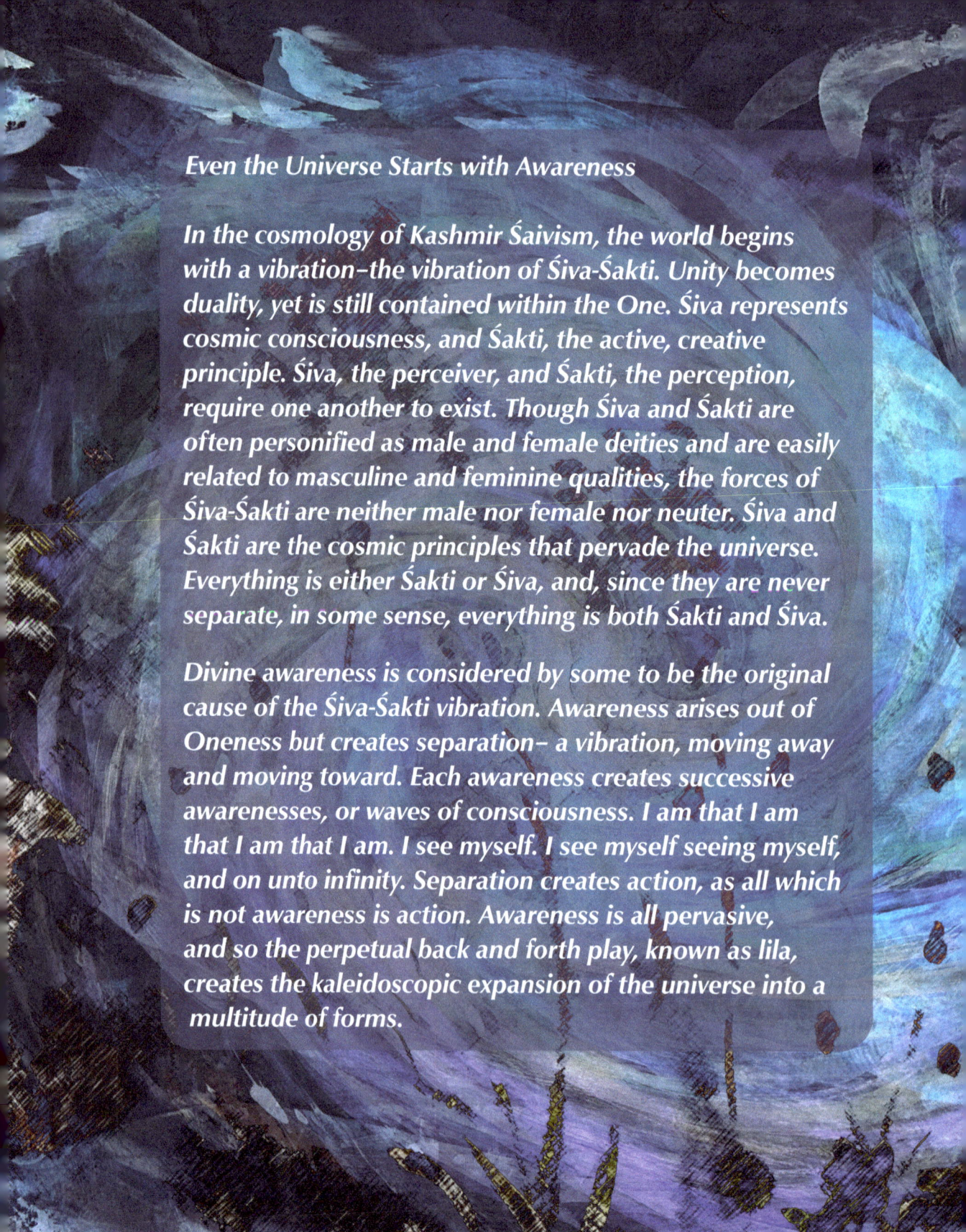

Even the Universe Starts with Awareness

In the cosmology of Kashmir Śaivism, the world begins with a vibration—the vibration of Śiva-Śakti. Unity becomes duality, yet is still contained within the One. Śiva represents cosmic consciousness, and Śakti, the active, creative principle. Śiva, the perceiver, and Śakti, the perception, require one another to exist. Though Śiva and Śakti are often personified as male and female deities and are easily related to masculine and feminine qualities, the forces of Śiva-Śakti are neither male nor female nor neuter. Śiva and Śakti are the cosmic principles that pervade the universe. Everything is either Śakti or Śiva, and, since they are never separate, in some sense, everything is both Śakti and Śiva.

Divine awareness is considered by some to be the original cause of the Śiva-Śakti vibration. Awareness arises out of Oneness but creates separation— a vibration, moving away and moving toward. Each awareness creates successive awarenesses, or waves of consciousness. I am that I am that I am that I am. I see myself. I see myself seeing myself, and on unto infinity. Separation creates action, as all which is not awareness is action. Awareness is all pervasive, and so the perpetual back and forth play, known as lila, creates the kaleidoscopic expansion of the universe into a multitude of forms.

Nurture a relaxed and quiet atmosphere
A calm setting is conducive for your creative explorations. What if that's exactly what you don't have? Look for ways, times and places you can find or encourage calm.

"When things change inside you, things change around you." —Unknown

"Do not let the behavior of others destroy your inner peace." —Dalai Lama

"Inner peace begins the moment you choose not to allow another person or event to control your emotions."—Pema Chodron

"Peace is not the absence of conflict, but the ability to cope with it." — Mahatma Gandhi

"Peace is not just the absence of conflict; peace is the creation of an environment where all can flourish regardless of race, color, creed, religion, gender, class, caste or any other social markers of difference." — Nelson Mandela

"Peace comes from within. Do not seek it without." —Buddha

"If you cannot find peace within yourself, you will never find it anywhere else."— Marvin Gaye

Practice peace. Remember, It's a practice.

Daydream
Were you raised to believe that daydreaming is a waste of time? Curses! Nothing could be further from the truth. Daydreaming, which we can also call reverie, is the floaty ground of inspiration. Tune into your own personal streaming media station.

Create the Container
Clarify the limits of time and space that will work for you. It's just a matter of knowing where you are and how much time you have and how much protection feels safe and comfortable. This is different according to who you are and what you're up to. This doesn't have to be the same time or space or activity everyday.

If you're cooking, you can think of the container as the pot you use and the kitchen where you're working; but it's also how much time you have, and it may be a sort of control of who is wandering in and out of the space while you're using it. It's setting the limits of what feels ok to you.

If you're playing a game, it's the magic circle created by the rules of the game and entering into the game itself.

If you're casting a spell, it's the circle of protection you cast around you and the way you ground yourself when you begin and when you finish.

If you're painting a picture, it's the space and time that will work for you, hold you, provide a feeling of safety. Is it ok with you if people walk by and look over your shoulder and comment? For some people, that's fine; for some, "Aieeee!" Just know what will be ok for you and take steps to establish those boundaries before you begin.

More about setting up space for particular activities in the How-To Guide.

Openings: Find them - Make them - Enter them
I'm talking about finding your way into the third, that dreamy in-between space. Entering the third can be like coming to a dance—maybe one you didn't even know was going on. Once you find it, there it is, opening up before you. You enter and you feel the rhythm and you join the dance.

How do you find the openings? Where is the way in? The THIRD chapter is all about ways into the THIRD, but, if you just begin... if you just practice a bit each day... being present, noticing, exploring, imagining...you will find your own pathways into this wonderful, magical space of possibility.

Imagine you are swimming, and feeling the water move against
your skin, and what's the water, and what's your skin?
Enter into that feeling of ambiguity... beyond you and me...
You are in the third!

NOW... You're here. And as you tune in, remember:

Creativity is always a conversation: Listen...
and then sing your way in!

Explore and experiment

You feel the impulse to express. What do you do? Your answers will vary from one time to the next, but noticing the voices and inspirations and dreamy images that come to you is where the practice begins. Follow that road. Find ways to engage in that conversation—which is sometimes with your self, and sometimes with others; and you may not always know the difference—which is FINE! What you are noticing is the *flow* of expression, the *flow* of conversation, the *flow* of participation. *And letting it flow.*

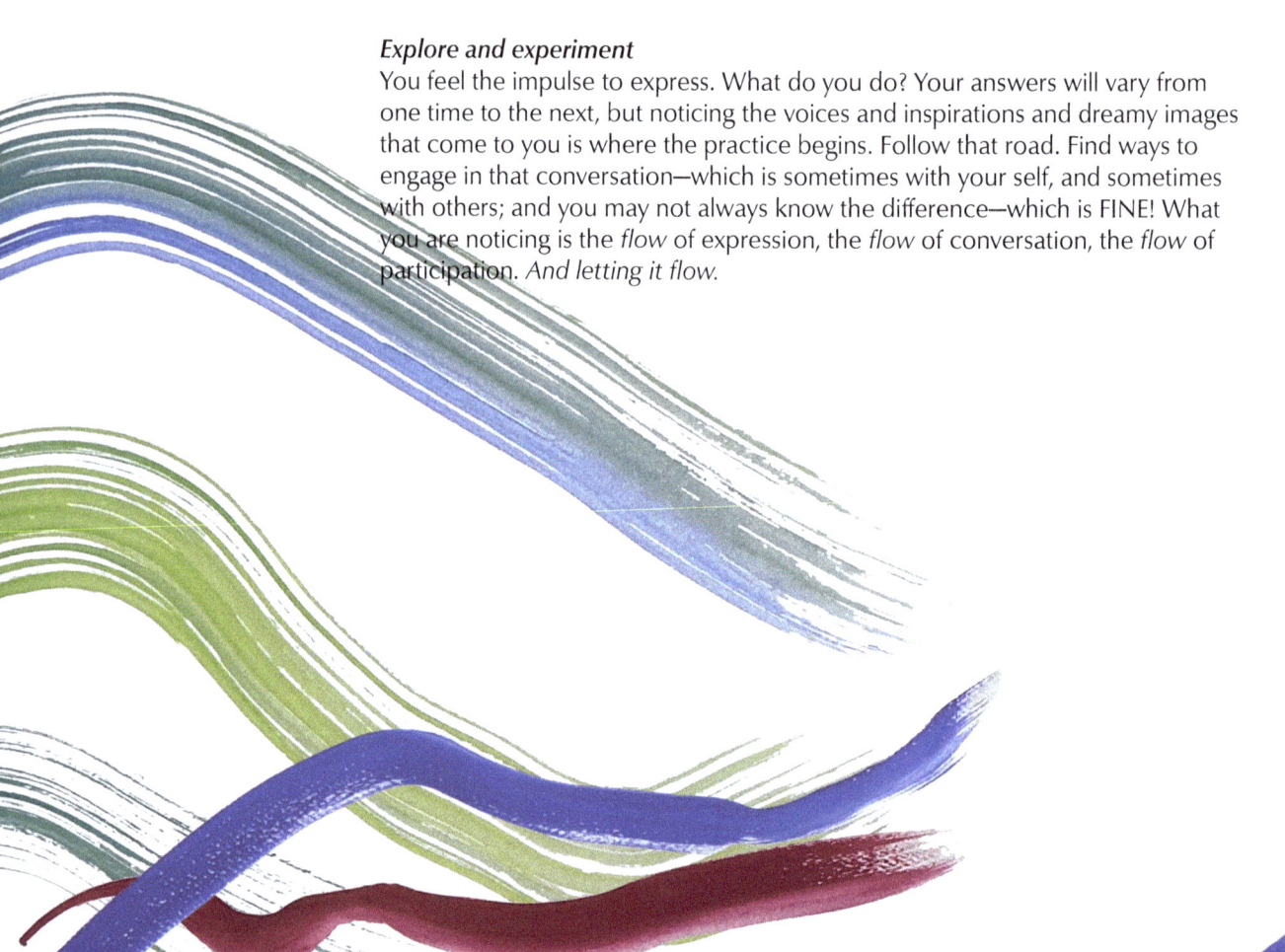

THINGS TO REMEMBER

Commit to yourself.

Show up.

Relax boundaries.

Explore.

Let mysteries be mysterious.

PRACTICES: THE HOW-TO GUIDE

Here are my favorite practices for everyday creativity. Each activity offers introductory suggestions. In keeping with the spirit of the book, my intent is to inspire you to explore, rather than to provide comprehensive instructions. If something strikes your fancy, take a leap and seek further resources. Dip in - poke around - mix and match - experiment as desired. Make up your own favorites!

Confession: I obsessed about the order of these activities: "This has to go before that — But that one definitely belongs next to that one…No, wait, this one should come right after…" Aargh! It doesn't matter AT ALL! Whatever order you like! They all flow into one another. Just start with awareness and follow your curiosity.

Activities

Awareness   131

Relaxation   132

Reverie   136

Creative Visualization   138

Imaginal Dialogue   144

Journaling   148

Open Studio   152

Themes for Exploration   163

Chance and Divination   166

Archetypal Exploration   168

Dream into Form   170

Re-Framing Narrative   172

Be Dramatic   174

The Theatrical Frame   176

Mixed Media Memoir   177

Ritual Craft   179

Awareness

The first step to any of these practices is always…tuning in. It is simple, very important, extremely effective—and oh so easy to overlook. Everything else is optional…**Do not skip this step!! It may seem too simple, but without it you will never get where you're trying to go.**

Take a moment, a few moments, a few calm breaths to gather your attention into this here, this now, this present, this moment.

> Sit quietly.
> Notice your body.
> Notice your surroundings.
> Notice your skin.
> Notice your breath.
> Notice through all your senses.
>
> Notice…

The practice of presence: this is the place to begin, and also the place to return to as you wrap up any activity. Where are you? Where are your edges? What else is around? Use my words or your own or anyone else's words. Or no words at all. Just remember the practice.

Relaxation

Practicing relaxation is beneficial entry into any of the activities that follow. Depending on how much time you can allow:

- Simply relax by calming the breath, calming the mind, slowing down, letting go… A few gentle stretches and a comfortable position are helpful to releasing tension.

- Use the progressive relaxation technique for a deeper experience. This familiar hypnosis technique is often used in hatha yoga practice together with Savasana, the corpse pose (lie flat on your back and play dead). It is wonderfully relaxing. Use it whenever you like.

- For any technique, your own preferences are important. If any of the suggestions are uncomfortable, replace with images and suggestions that are to your liking. Just stay with the spirit of the activity.

Simple Relaxation:

Breathe…Tune in…Be aware of your surroundings, your breathing, your body in your space…Let your breath calm and nourish you…If your mind is racing, slow it down…If you're feeling stress, let it go…let it go…let it go…If you're feeling sad…anxious…worried… let it go…Just breathe it out…and breathe in calm…Just be…

Progressive relaxation:

Find a comfortable position in a quiet place. Lie on the floor on your back, if it works for you, or whatever alternative you prefer. You'll be scanning your body, briefly tensing and then releasing each muscle group, as you let yourself relax and deepen.

Let your eyes close. Let your breathing slow and soften. Let your body relax.

Tense your muscles as you breathe in. Relax and let go as you breathe out. Give a little more time to areas that ask for it. Let your body parts shift slightly as you go, easing the relaxation. Let the earth hold you.

Bring your attention to your feet. Wiggle your toes, rotate your ankles, releasing tension and letting your feet relax.

Move up to your calves, breathing in and out, tense and let go, letting them spread relaxed and heavy onto the floor.

Let your knees be comfortable. Let your knees let go.

Bring your attention to your thighs. Let go of all the tension they are holding, as they relax into the floor.

Move up into your pelvis and hips, releasing any tension or discomfort, sinking and spreading, feeling relaxation spread through your body.

Let your torso feel heavy against the floor. Imagine your body as a sandbag. Fill each part with sand to rest heavily on the floor.

Relaxing your lower back, let it rest comfortably. Feel your body spread out.

Let your internal organs rest. Breathe out any tension, and breathe in calm.

Move up gradually to your waist… your ribs… your heart … your lungs… breathing in comfort, breathing out stress.

Move up through your upper chest and then into your shoulders. Let them relax and let go of whatever they've been carrying.

Take as long as you like for each area, using your breath and your intention to release, relax, let go.

Feel into your upper arms, elbows, letting go, into your forearms, wrists, hands, fingers…Let your arms rest heavy on the floor. Let your hands, fingers relax, let go…

Bring your attention to your neck, and then up into your skull. Letting go…letting go…

Feel your scalp relaxing, letting go, and…

Then moving to your forehead and letting your forehead muscles relax, letting your eyes and eyelids relax, your ears and nose, your jaw and tongue, your mouth, your lips, your chin, your neck…and so on, breathing out tension, breathing in calm as you go…

And move back through your body from head to toe, noticing those areas that would like a little more love, and breathing out tension, breathing in calm as you go. When you have come all the way back down to your toes, breathe deeply into your body and breathe fully out, releasing tension and allowing your body to feel relaxed and heavy, sinking into the floor.

To go deeper…

Imagine that you are on a wonderfully heavy soft pillow, floating slowly and comfortably into a special wonderful blissful place…

And counting slowly backwards from 10, and breathing gently and relaxing, and beginning with 10--9--8, and breathing deeply with each count, and letting yourself relax more and more deeply…and as you reach 1, letting go and relaxing into this wonderfully blissful soft and pleasant space.

And when you're ready to return to your normal waking reality, bring your attention to the edges of your skin…Feel the ground beneath you… Feel the air around you… And taking deep revitalizing breaths, and counting yourself up from 1 to 10 at your own pace, with each step feeling yourself more alive, more awake, more revitalized and ready to return to your day.

Notes:

Enhance the effects of progressive relaxation with some stretching or yoga beforehand.

Add meditative music of your choice.

Record these words or something similar; then lie back and listen to as you relax. (Remember to speak slowly and calmly.)

The more you practice, the easier you'll find it to drop into a relaxed state without a lot of preparation. Still, the progressive relaxation is valuable for those times when you want the deeper experience.

Use the relaxation process as you like to access imaginal space for the following activities.

Reverie

Aka, day dreaming…Reverie is a blissful state of mind, when your mind is diffuse and given to wandering…. Does it come easily to you or elude you? Reverie is like floating. To float, you need to let go…

From a place of relaxation…a quiet mind…in an easy chair…on a lazy walk…your mind floats…follow the path of your thoughts…your memories…one floats into another…you ride with the breeze…on the clouds…birds singing…the reflection on the stream…taking you where it will…

Just let go of focus and notice what imagery arises for you. Follow along. Be transported. Let it unfurl like a waking dream.

Let your mind wander. Like a leaf on the breeze…or floating downstream…a trickle of water down the windowpane…clouds in the sky…wisps in the sand…a song or a scent carries you…

When you are ready to return to your waking reality, bring your attention to your breathing, your skin, the ground beneath you. Are there are images or inspirations that you wish to remember or work with creatively? Take the time now to make notes, sketches, or whatever method you choose to bring them with you into your waking reality. Note that, just as in dreamwork, these images may grow, deepen, and evolve as you work with them.

If you are coming to this from a focused or hyper-alert state of mind, give yourself the space to transition, to soften, unclench, stretch…rest and relax…you are not chasing thoughts but simply flowing along with them…soften focus…let go let go let go…

Find the places and postures that will take you there…

Practice in the pool, the stream, the bath…or simply imagine yourself into the pool, the stream, the bath…

Practice on your feet. Wander as you wonder…

Lie back and watch the sky…

Listen to the music of the world all around you…

Expand your senses…

Creative Visualization

This is a great practice for strengthening your imaginal muscles. Like reverie, only more intentional, it's a simple technique that really improves the more you do it. To create the life you want, start here!

Use this process to imagine anything. Try it when you have a notion of a dream or goal but you don't know how to get there or how to make it happen or even where to begin: Begin with the image you have, whatever you know or sense about it. Imagine yourself into that dream. Feel what it feels like. Notice the details. Expand the dream and get to know it in detail.

Creative Visualization is the foundational technique for Imaginal Dialogue. Begin with relaxation, and then move into the visualization process.

Your visualization does not need to be "visual" in nature. It might be more of a "feeling" or "sensing" than a "seeing."

Practice in the way that works for you.

Use creative visualization to:

- **strengthen** your ability to visualize

- **clarify** your vision of specific things or feelings

- **"set the stage"** for the active imagination process

Strengthening:

Practice helps to strengthen your ability to imagine through any of the senses. Imagine any of the following examples with as much sensory detail and feeling as you can:

- *sight*: a child's face, the sunset, a skyscraper
- *sound:* bells ringing, your mother's voice, a speeding car
- *touch:* soft fur, sandpaper, slime
- *smell:* baking bread, fresh flowers, sweat, pine sap
- *taste:* lemon juice, cinnamon, hot pepper, tears
- *movement:* running down the sidewalk, wading in the ocean, dancing at a party

You get the idea. Practice sensory visualization using any of your own examples.

*See Pierro Ferrucci's sensory visions in **What We May Be** 30-34.

Clarifying Specific Outcomes:

Creative visualization is often used to visualize specific desirable things, ideas, or outcomes and move toward these goals by holding the images/intentions in mind. I don't know what matters to you, so I can't write the script —but you can! Choose a prompt that fits your intention, and then develop the scene that will visualize the outcome you desire. Phrase your prompt in the present tense as if you have already achieved the outcome. This becomes an affirmation.

Drop into relaxation and begin with the prompt.

Here are some examples:

> I am confident, graceful, witty…
>
> I am calm and clear…
>
> I am on a perfect adventure…
>
> I am achieving my most cherished dream…

So, for example, let's say you choose to work toward the goal of "I am confident." Where and how would you like to feel confident? On stage, giving a speech? Performing an original piece of music? Presenting an important piece of work? Enjoying a party for a certain occasion? Or just socializing in general? Or doing your work in the world. Or being yourself, everyday. Imagine yourself into the scene, being the way you'd like to be, with all the details you can dream up.

What are you wearing, how are you feeling, what is the scene, who else is there…What if you have trouble as you visualize? Say you feel very nervous — then take it down a notch. Imagine something a little less stressful. Keep breathing calmly and smoothly and let yourself find the good feelings you're looking for. You may identify specific things that make you nervous. Those are good clues that you can follow up! Oh, your shoes aren't comfortable, maybe you want to try a different type of shoe. Or you don't like the way your voice sounds. Maybe you want a voice coach. Sometimes clues let you easily adapt, sometimes they point to a mystery about yourself you can delve into for more information.

What if you want to imagine the perfect adventure, but you're just not sure what that is? What if your dream is unclear? That is the perfect time to try a few different things.

> How do I feel when I imagine climbing a mountain?
>
> How do I feel when I imagine myself in a sailboat?
>
> How do I feel when I'm in a strange city? What would I like that to feel like?
>
> I'm moving into my dreamhouse. What does it look like? How do I feel opening the front door? What is the neighborhood like?

Try out different scenarios — as wild and as varied as you like! Change as desired. The more you do, the better idea you'll have of what you're seeking. And make notes as you go along!

Visualize World Peace
A tall order, but what would it look like, actually? Explore your Utopian Vision, or perhaps simply a small step toward a grand dream.

Visualize Whirled Peas
A simpler task, and good for a laugh.

Setting the Stage:

Use creative visualization to "set the stage" for active imagination. Envision yourself into a particular setting. Once "there," let go… Observe what arises out of the intuitive unconscious. Use this technique to set up for Imaginal Dialogue. Here's an example that I like. Adjust any details as desired, or make up your own.

Secret Garden

Begin with relaxation. As your breathing softens into a restful flow, let your eyes gently close. With each breath, you deepen further into a blissful relaxation. Now you are approaching a most magical space. Imagine yourself walking along a beautiful lush path. Each step brings you closer to a wondrous place, which you cannot quite see as the path gently curves, but you sense you are almost there. You hear birds singing and the air is filled with a delightful fragrance. A stream sparkles with crystal clear water. You dip your fingers, your toes, to feel the refreshing flow. Bringing your hand to your lips you drink a few drops of this magical water and feel it refreshing, cleansing, and enlivening your whole self. As you take a few more steps, you now see that you are about to enter the most wondrous garden of your imagination. Know that you are perfectly safe and that nothing can harm you here. Pause for a moment to take it in. What do you see? Hear? Feel about this place? Use your whole self to notice. What is growing here? Now allow yourself to explore this special place. You are free to go where you like, touching. smelling, listening, lingering as desired.

You may feel inspired to enter into conversation. Perhaps with a plant, an insect, or another being of any sort that you encounter here.

Continue your experience for as long as you like. When you're ready to return to your normal waking reality, bring your attention to the edges of your skin… Feel the ground beneath you… Feel the air around you… And taking deep revitalizing breaths, open your eyes, feeling awake, revitalized and ready to return to your day.

What special places would you like to explore? A soft, pink cloud full of love? An underwater mermaid's lair? A primordial forest? Dream it up!

Shakti Gawain wrote her book on **Creative Visualization** *in 1978 and it remains a great resource --highly recommended! Full of exercises and useful info. She leans toward using visualization to manifest particular goals and delves more deeply into an understanding of how consciousness works.*

Imaginal Dialogue

Imaginal dialogue is a particular type of visualization, used to have a conversation with anyone or anything that you dream up.

You may begin with the intention of dialoguing with someone/something particular; or, you may take yourself into the receptive state and then ask for guidance or information on an issue. At the risk of stating the obvious, it's imaginal, so… you can do whatever you like.

If you have had a dream with a compelling or curious image, you can return to it, dialogue with it and see if you can discover more about it.

I've had many imaginal conversations with deceased loved ones, old friends, people who bug me; my five-year-old self; a beautiful ancient stone found in my path. Many times I've asked for imaginal guidance on an issue that is challenging me. Does that make me crazy? No (but thanks for asking). You can have imaginal conversations with full awareness that they are qualitatively different from face-to-face conversations with people who are physically present, and they can be quite fruitful: sometimes inspiring, sometimes instructive, sometimes healing or helping you to work through challenges.

This practice enriches your life, deepening your relationship to an ever-present source of personally meaningful content, and reminding you that it's never just you.

Tips:

- It's helpful to keep track in your journal. You may not realize the significance until later. Really. Sometimes, like a dream, you think you'll remember but you don't. Take notes as you dialogue, or wait til you're done, but keep track.

- Enter into this imaginal dialogue as a conversation with "an other," not a script you are writing. Let it unfold in the moment. If you seek help or guidance or insight on a particular issue, bring openness to the response you receive.

- The conversation may be non-verbal, just as images may be non-visual. Your imaginal interactions may take any form.

- It doesn't necessarily have to feel like you're talking to God or the Great Spirit, who's going to reveal the essence of your life to you. I mean, be respectful in any case, but it could be like speed dating, or maybe a meet and greet.

- Don't worry if it sounds dumb sometimes. You don't have to share it with anyone.

Example Script

Take a deep breath and relax, close your eyes if you like, ground, protect. Breathe and deepen…

If there's a theme an issue a question an interest a concern arising for you, become more aware of that now, holding it in your mind. If not, that's ok.

It may be that something new or surprising comes to mind, something different than what you had been thinking about… just hold this sense of theme in your mind for a moment.

And if nothing particular is coming up for you, that's ok, too…just relax and notice what you are feeling.

And you're breathing…

And in your mind, begin a conversation.

And if you were to say something in this moment, what would it be?

And if you were to ask a question now, what would it be?

And you may become aware of a kind of presence—don't be concerned about what's imagination or real, it doesn't matter. And let your sense of the presence become stronger, more clear… What do you notice? Perhaps a few physical characteristics? What do you feel, see, smell, hear…

Does the presence have anything to say to you? Listen. Perhaps the conversation picks up and continues easily.

Do you have a question you'd like to ask? If so, ask it now and listen or observe the response. The response may be non-verbal

What do you understand or feel about the presence or this conversation? What power does this presence have?

And as you're ready to wrap up and return to your normal waking state, you may want to thank the presence for the conversation.

And remembering that if you didn't feel a a sense of presence that you may be open to conversing with such a sense of presence at another time.

And as you're ready now to move back into waking reality, becoming conscious of your breath, your skin, the feel of the air on your skin, the edges of your body, noticing gravity and your body and your presence in this place. And as you're ready, opening your eyes and taking a moment to consider what you've observed or experienced during this visualization.

Write or sketch out the points you want to remember.

There are so many ways you can use this technique to work through challenges or find helpful insight. It is especially useful when working with subpersonalities. Here's one brief example:

Say you are arguing with yourself about a decision. Give the different sides of the argument to different characters, which are subpersonalities or aspects of self. You can give each a name if you like, and visualize their characteristics. Now let them talk it out, while you listen. This can really help you to clarify what the issues are, while giving you a detached perspective to take it all in.

Again, I recommend Piero Ferrucci's book, What We May Be, as a practical guide to psychosynthesis, which is the work of Roberto Assagioli. Internal Family Systems is another more recent but similar therapeutic approach used to dialogue with inner aspects.

Journaling

There are so many, many ways of journaling, of course! If you have a practice already, you may want to keep doing what you're doing. But read my thoughts about it, anyway.

Journaling is my lifelong practice. Even as a little kid, I was scrapbooking pictures and drawings and scribbles and pretend writing. I recommend it, because:

- it helps you to clear your mind
- it's a process of discovery

Things come out in the writing /sketching that you didn't realize were there. Some of them, you are happy to get off your chest! Journaling about them helps you to release them. Good riddance! And you know, feel free to rip it up, paint it black, burn it…as desired. *And also…*

Some discoveries are priceless treasures. They will enrich your life and understanding. You may not even realize their value until after you've journalled them.

It can be illuminating to look back over your journals. Especially to see:

- themes and patterns that you've been revisiting for weeks, months, years
- how you've grown and changed and reached important goals that you forgot about
- great inspiring ideas that got buried along the way and are now ripe for the picking

My Favorite Tips:

Make it easy. Use whatever kind of journal you're most comfortable with. A spiral bound notebook is one of my favorites, and so is a sketchbook with blank pages. Just don't make it too precious. Forget strict rules about what can or can't go in it, or how it looks! Perfectionism is deadly to the process.

Write by hand. Journaling by hand is the best way to go. Relax and express yourself in non-linear fashion. Write sideways. Draw arrows. Color outside the lines. Underline with passion. Use a variety of media. Let your hands make OTHER kinds of marks and motions. And this I swear is true: you will say different things when you write by hand than when you write by keystroke. Hand-writing helps you to voice the myriad impulses and ideas within you, all clamoring for expression! See what happens!

Date your entries. Simple enough. Dates will help you to easily cross-reference events and dreams over the long arc.

Practice Inner+Outer journaling. Track your inner thoughts and feelings alongside your outer events and observations, and something wonderful happens. As you move back and forth, you notice connections and relationships you might have overlooked. You will naturally find the space in between inner and outer expanding.

Write something everyday. What you write, and how much or how little--that's up to you! Personally, I avoid rules that will turn me away from the practice.

Things to journal about:

What did I wake up thinking about, wondering about, singing about, imagining?

What did I notice today?

What conversation did I overhear?

How did I move, think, speak?

What did I read today?

What events happened today? (might be a snowstorm, a political event, a party, a long car drive, an earache, an argument

What memories come to mind?

What's on the grocery list? Just write something. It doesn't have to be art! And who's to say a grocery list isn't an art form, anyway!

What art form would I most like to engage in right now?

What image would I draw? What song would I sing?

Further suggestions:

Take some time every week or two to review what you've written. *Simply scan over your entries so that you have a sense or an image of what's transpired. What's been most significant? What's been most troublesome? What terrain have you encountered? Where are you moving? Where are you stuck? Where have you found common ground with others? Where have you recognized your singularity? What themes are arising? If the review inspires you to make notes or express more deeply about anything, great!*

Let your journaling support you, not restrict you. *Journaling can feel like another heavy habit to carry along if you give yourself a lot of rules, but it doesn't have to be. Stick with* **One Simple Rule: write something everyday.** *But what you write, and how much or how little--that's up to you. When you see the interaction of what you think, feel, and do, your understanding of the events and relationships in your life is bound to grow!*

Sticky Notes are your friends! *For stream-of-consciousness journaling, when ideas and images are swirling all around, don't stress about putting them in order or writing complete sentences: just get them down. One per post-it. You'll figure out how they are related later. Move them around as desired.*

Open Studio

Make yourself a special place and time where play is sacred. I used to offer an Open Studio where people could come in, help themselves to supplies, and do their thing. That was fun. You can easily create something similar in your world.
Use creative visualization to imagine just how-where-when you would like it to be!

One of the most important things I learned from Natalie Rogers is the value of multi-modal expression. Most of us have a particular form of expression that we gravitate to, that we enjoy more, or that comes more easily—*Which is great, AND ALSO:* It's so very much worth exploring other forms, the ones you've never tried or that you know nothing about, the ones that intrigue you and even the ones that scare you or make you uncomfortable. Different things will be expressed. You will learn things from singing that you will never discover from drawing. Sculpting puts you in touch with your body and materials in a different way than dance will. Poetry will tell a story differently than will prose.

Perhaps most important of all, those unfamiliar forms are the ones where you have the least control and your naive, unpolished self has a chance to express. Giving up control is a good way to open up to your less conscious aspects, so have your favorites AND ALSO mess around with the less familiar. Remember, you don't have to "get good" at it —Just express!

For any of these processes, you may start with a theme in mind or a technique you'd like to explore. *Orrrr,* it's always great to just begin—pick something up and go! Feel free to dialogue with your work and materials in the process.

I've shared a few ideas and suggestions for each practice, just to get you started. You'll no doubt have lots of ideas of your own. There are not a lot of directions, because…just experiment! For more guidance, the internet is usually close at hand. I've suggested some excellent resources, as well.

Principles of Design

I know I said this practice of everyday creativity is exploratory and improvisational, and it is. Still, common design elements and principles are helpful scaffolding in exploring whatever medium you choose. Think about these concepts as a way to move your explorations forward. There are volumes written about any of them, if you want to learn more; but you can also just pick one or two words from the list and consider them as you express yourself.

balance	unity	variety	contrast
emphasis	rhythm	pattern	proportion
dominance	space	edges	movement
value	texture	shape	tone
color	line	size	proximity
direction	symmetry	harmony	form

Visual Arts:

Gather supplies. If you have a place where they can live, ready and waiting for you on a shelf or table, that's great. Or stock a small suitcase that you can tuck away and then easily get your hands on and take with you wherever you go.

Things I like to keep on hand:

paints/inks	assorted papers	glue
pencils/colored pencils	tissue paper	tape
craypas/pastels	substrates for collage	scissors
brushes	straight-edge	acrylic medium

These are my preferences, but the possibilities are endless. Please follow your personal preferences, and also experiment with new stuff.

Here are a few simple ideas to get going. Any of these may take off into a new direction…

Color Palette

Explore color. Choose one medium and experiment with placing colors next to each other, mixing colors, blending colors with black and/or white. Create color palettes of 3-5 colors that you like together. There's no such thing as an ugly color—really! But I do find some combinations that I love and some that rub me the wrong way. And sometimes my opinion changes. Different colors evoke different feelings in you on different days. What are you gravitating to right now? *You could make a journal just for color exploration —swatches and palettes.

Mark Making

Experiment and explore with simply making marks. Try a variety of pencils, pens, brushes on whatever paper or substrate you like. This is important to recognizing that the tools and materials are part of the conversation: they all have something to say. Try thick thin bold dainty curvy straight…Vary your pressure…try shading from light to dark. Build up marks on top of each other with cross-hatching, scribbles or simply varying the distances between the marks.

Paper

Paper is a world unto itself. Compare cutting it vs. tearing it, into either precise or serendipitous shapes. See how different colors, patterns, and textures of paper interact as you arrange and rearrange. Glue them together or glue them down to a substrate as you like; or you can always just move them around, fold them, play with them, and leave it at that. It's all play; no one says you have to end up with a finished product.

Mixing Media

Simply, putting together whatever you feel like. I like to glue down various papers onto a board, let them dry, and then paint and draw over them. One thing about mixing media is learning how they interact, which changes according to what order you do things in. Some glues may not accept drawing or paint on top, for instance. I often use matte medium to adhere papers where possible: it's an acrylic medium that's meant to allow you to work on top of it. Watercolor needs absorbent paper, and you can vary effects by working onto wet or dry paper; vary the intensity of the pigment by how much moisture you add. Different brushes make different marks. So, too, will your finger or a stick. Acrylic paint works on many more surfaces than watercolor and gives a different effect (but note: acrylic = plastic). Some of the beautiful photos that come out of print magazines have a coating that you can't draw on, but a light coat of matte medium can change that. The point is, just experiment and see what works. You're playing, and it doesn't need to result in an archival artwork. You'll find that some things won't work as you had anticipated, which is a great way to learn about the materials and should not be interpreted as a personal failure.

Sculpture:

The most tactile. You can sculpt with so many things: metal, stone, paper, clay, concrete, soil, sand, glass, ice, wax, fiber, bread dough, marzipan… Each material brings its own character to the process. Some take more preparation, more tools, and more knowledge or skill than others.

Clay

Get some clay from somewhere—maybe dig it out of your backyard or get a hunk from a friend who's a potter, or, of course, buy a bag from a ceramics supply store — but you may just want a small amount to play with. Clay has to be kept damp to be pliable (except for plasticine), but in that "space of pliability" there's a lot of room for more moisture or less moisture. You may enjoy just squeezing it and smushing it in between your hands, like playing with mud (it is, in fact, playing with mud, which, like I said, you may find in your yard); and for this spa treatment it might be pretty wet. If you want to work it into a form, it needs less moisture. Add more clay or more water to get the mix that feels just right to you. If you want to take a break and come back to it, cover with plastic. If you're done, you can let it air harden. Clay (like mud) can be messy, so attend to your space and clothes before you get going.

Paper clay is another fun sculpting medium — much less messy! Get it at a crafts store, or make your own with some toilet paper and glue. Find recipes online.

There are a million types of clay, and they all have different characteristics. Just like people, you get to know the ones you like to hang out with.

Environmental sculpture

Sculpt outside with the leaves, twigs, icicles, stones that you find in your environment. These are typically going to be temporary installations: enjoy them while they last. Look up Andy Goldsworthy to be amazed and inspired!

Or: Use your environment as the site of your installation, adding whatever materials inspire you (but do give a thought to other creatures and how your choices may effect them). Maybe fabric hangings or prayer flags. (Check out the work of Christo and Jeanne Claude) Maybe an altar or offerings. Maybe bells or bowls. Or, build a sculpture with concrete. Or earth.

Found Objects

What do you do with all the interesting objects you find? Collect them! Notice and appreciate them. Simply hold them and contemplate them. Display them by themselves or assembled and arranged with other objects they'd like to hang out with. Or, take a form and glue things to it. Isn't it interesting what you choose to treasure?

Bread sculpture

Use a nice stiff dough recipe. Build it on the cookie sheet. It will lie flat. Dab on water with your finger to stick pieces together. Make it freeform and abstract, or make a wreath, a lion, a tree, or make anything. Add your choice of embellishents, sweet or savory. A yeast dough will lose some definition as it rises. Just have fun with it.

Voice:

You are the instrument. Let sounds come through you. It feels SO GOOD! Experiment with all kinds of vocal sound. Vary the pitch, the volume, the intensity, the emotion. Open up that fifth chakra and give yourself a voice in the world.

Breathe…Sigh…Moan…Groan…Tone…Chant…Cry…Shout…Scream…Whisper…Sing…Pray

Feel the vibration in your chest in your throat in your skull in the air around you

Talk to yourself
to your dog and cat
to your paper and pencil

Sing songs you love

Sing whatever melodies come through you

Sing how you feel, with words or no words

Sing one note long and true, Let it vibrate through you. Let it ring out.

Let sounds come out when you do things, feel things, imagine things

Remember, it doesn't need to be beautiful, catchy, or harmonious. Just make the sounds that you feel.

There's a common expectation that sounds are for communicating between humans. When you diverge from that, people may react awkwardly or with judgment. Of course if you scream someone will ask if you're ok--you would hope, right? Look for ways, times, and places where you can free your voice. *Group vocal activities are awesome. More info in the Group Practices Guide.

Movement:

Our bodies are made to move! They are our vehicles, for expression, for action. Tune into your body, the way you inhabit it, and the way that you use it. Sadly, some of us have been acculturated to take up as little room as possible. Let your self fully inhabit your body, and let your body fully inhabit your space. And really, take as much space as you need. Give your body room to move and explore, and see what you discover.

- Express what your body wants to in this moment, whatever you are feeling

- Stretch fully into your body in the morning… or middday … or in the evening

- Feel yoursel into forgotten body parts

- Explore unusual ways of moving

- Move into an unexplored space. The space is your canvas. Fill it with your movement. Or move sparingly. Use rhythm, shape, repetition, contrast

- Open. How many ways can you OPEN with movement?

- Close. Close. Close.

- Open…close…open…close

- Respond to a sound… an image… a song with movement

- Move with rhythm. Can you move arrhythmically? It's harder than you might think.

- Interact with your shadow

- Move with caution move with abandon move with energy move with stealth

Move with purpose move with the wind

Reach creep pace jump stomp storm flow

Move as slowly and quietly as you can.

Music and Sound

Expand beyond your voice to making sounds with your whole body, and with objects, materials, and musical instruments in the world around you.

As always, begin with noticing.

With hands and feet notice the sounds of different surfaces and materials around you.

tap…swish…smooth…scratch…rub…knock…bang…kick…stomp…slide…swoosh…pluck…pick…click…cluck…clang…clack…

Try with your eyes closed.

Try in a small room. Try in the large outdoors.

Listen to the sounds of nature and play along. What can you add to the mix?

Listen for rhythms— of insects, of rain, of machinery… Improvise around the rhythm.

What sounds will harminize or blend with the sounds already happening?

And if it is silent? Listen to the silence. What do you hear? What music will you make into the silence?

Word Magic

Here I am thinking, not of narrative (which comes along in a few pages) but of words as they are used in poetry, in chants, in spells, in prayers and affirmations, as potent vessels of intention.

Affirmations: Words of Intention

Use the power of intention to craft a mantra or affirmation that you can easily hold in your mind and repeat to yourself as needed to stay on course. Whatever is simple, concise, and meaningful to you. Years ago, I settled on the phrase, "Clear, kind and strong" to keep me centered and bring me back to myself when I get off-balance. Some people like to choose a "word of the year" to define a theme or area of focus.

Prayers and Blessings

Words which help you through hard times, or words that protect your loved ones. There are many existing prayers and blessings that are beautiful and powerful. And/or, create your own. Prayers and blessings are simply getting very clear on what it is you need or want, and asking for it. Who are you asking? Does it matter? If it matters to you, ask whomever you like. If you can do it with beauty, so that your words flow into the wind, so much the better. But then again, really just make it heartfelt.

Chants:

Affirmations, prayers, poetry— all can become chants when we speak them aloud, repeatedly and rhythmically. They are used at rallies and games to focus the energy of the crowd on a specific point. You can use them yourself for the same purpose. Whether you whisper, sing, or shout, find the words you want to chant about. Like, "All we are saying… is give peace a chance!"

Magic Spells:

Is a magic spell different than a chant, a blessing, an affirmation? Not necessarily. It may be different in the ritual aspect you bring to it. Magic spells might be accompanied by symbolic actions and elemental assistance, but it does come down to "the art of changing consciousness at will," in Dion Fortune's words. What do you seek? Put it into concise words, and charge these words with your power. I use Starhawk's credo of strengthening "power within," not "power over." I do not condone seeking power over another. For more on crafting ritual, see that section coming up.

Poetry:

What makes a poem? I've often wondered... It's an evocative creation whose form has meaning beyond defined terms. It seems to me to be something that just "is born," though I know many poets labor long and hard to give birth. It is certainly an art form that you can develop. Here I would suggest something simple, like Magnetic Poetry, a game which consists of a box full of words. You pick out a few, "randomly," and see what evocative, powerful, or funny phrases you can come up with

Hieroglyphs:

When we put word and image together, it is magic indeed. Explore ways of integrating the two. Not just writing a description of the image, not just illustrating the text. How can you fuse the two together such that the whole is greater than the parts?

Find the words, phrases, poems and prayers that are meaningful to you, and gather them together.

I recommend any of Starhawk's books, but here, especially The Spiral Dance. I also recommend the book, Poetry as Spellcasting, by Tamiko Beyer, Destiny Hemphill, and Lisbeth White.

Themes for Exploration

Begin with a theme in mind, an image or idea that's timely for you in some way; then let go into it and see what happens. Not a particular project, mind you, but an area of exploration. Use whatever medium calls you. Here are some suggestions.

Opening to the the unknown:

Begin with meditative attunement to opening and the gestures of opening: open eyes, open arms, open jaw, open heart… Enter into the experience of not knowing, whatever that means for you. Perhaps you are deep in the ocean, breathing through gills. Or hurtling through space, exploding and collapsing… You are a newborn, taking a first breath, first light…Or crawling into a dark and mysterious cave:…Or in a marketplace where everyone is speaking a language you've never heard…So much is unknown in this life. What does it feel like to be surrounded, immersed in not knowing? Visualize the experience and express what you are feeling, sensing, noticing, through your medium of choice.

Balance

Begin with meditative attunement to the feeling of balance. What does it feel like to be in balance? To be out of balance? To lose your balance? To regain your balance. Visualize the sense, the feeling of balance. Balance as movement. Balance as stillness. An object in balance. A relationship in balance. A system in balance. A moment. A repose. A goal. An outcome. A dance. What images or ideas come to mind? Give them expression.

Growth

The growth of a plant, roots pushing down, tendrils emerging, seeking the light, reaching…The growth of an infant, from the most vulnerable invisible speck into bones and flesh and determination…The growth of a city…The growth of a plan…Undesirable things grow as well: disease, animosity, desertification… Contemplate growth in the way that interests you and express what comes to you.

Decay

Tune in to the process, the imagery of decay. Where do you notice it inside… outside…In your body, in your home, in your compost pile, in your city or town, in your leaf rot, in your history… It's a natural, necessary part of the cycle of life. Explore the imagery and see where it leads. Express as desired.

Ambiguity

The way a thing becomes another thing or is not what it seems or what you thought it was or contains its opposite or is fluid or is indescribable or impossible to pin down…. Explore ambiguity through your medium of choice.

Perspective

Begin with contemplating where you are in relation to other things, other people, or someone or something in particular, or an idea. Think of perspective as a spatial relationship, a geometric relationship, an interpretive stance… but it does imply a relationship, one that shifts with movement. So explore how your perspective shifts as you move or change your stance, literally…imaginally… mentally…. How does your perspective affect your experience? How does your experience affect your perspective? How would you like to express this?

Seasonal

Like "Harvest" in the fall, or "New Life" in the spring, tune into the season around you, where you are right now. What are the feelings of this season? See if you can push away the noise and clutter of marketing campaigns. What is happening in your local ecosystem, in your local ecopsyche? In your dreams? In your bodily senses?

Dog

Pet dogs, play with dogs, draw dogs, write about dogs, photograph dogs, move like a dog, imagine life as a dog, invent a dog. Dog puppet.

Encyclopedia

Make your own. Where would you start? Maybe it's completely made up. Or maybe you have or would like to have encyclopedic knowledge on a certain subject. Gather together all you know about it. Do some research. If you find an old encyclopedia in a thrift store, you can use it as the base for an altered book. Or you can tear out pages to use in a collage. Or you can open at random and create something based on what you find.

You can think deeply about any of these themes — and that's great, we're thinking beings — AND ALSO enter into the experience of the theme somatically. Just put yourself into it, imaginally or literally, and feel and notice and express what comes up.

Of course "Themes" are endless. Follow the suggestions above as far as they interest you, or follow your own interests. The theme could be Cows. Discomfort. Home. Loss. Gold. Melting. Just stay with what's alive for you.

Chance and Divination

Opening up to "Other" influences is an art, a skill, a practice both ancient and contemporary that takes many forms and has many uses. Especially helpful when you feel "stuck" creatively: look outside of yourself for direction or inspiration.

Whole books and lifetimes are spent on learning to read oracles, following the serendipitous turn, and training yourself to notice synchronous events. But expert or not, you can use systems of chance and divination to guide your creative decisions. The possibilities are endless.

Is it chance? Is it spirit? Is it your subconscious? For this practice, I suggest you not worry about that, just go with it. Be amused or be amazed!

Y/N/M

Take three small rectangles of paper, roughly same size and color. Write "Y" on one, "N" on the second, and "M" on the third (Yes/No/Maybe). Fold in half so you can't see the writing, ask the choice you are deliberating, toss the papers around in your hand, and pick one. That's your decision — go with it. "Write? draw?" "Go outside? stay inside?" "Turn left? Turn right?" "Add more red?" "Is this finished?"

I use this all the time because I can get stuck on decision making. I know most of the time the choice is inconsequential; this helps me to get out of the anxiety swamp. If the answer I pick makes me unhappy, then I do what I like. It just helps me to move through indecision.

Roll of the die

Similar to above, you can assign different choices or ideas to the numbers on the die (or simply "Odd" or "Even"). Ask your question and roll the die.

Flaneurie

A flaneur/flaneuse is one who wanders around with no particular aim, a curious observer. You can practice the art of flaneurie in your hometown, your backyard, or a more exotic locale. Let your whims guide you, or toss a coin for "Left" or "Right." Seek inspiration to write or draw or sing or dance about. ALSO the process of flaneurie is creative enagagement in itself.

Color choice

Make squares of paper with a different color on each. Mix them up in a bowl or pile. Close your eyes and choose two or three. Use these colors as the basis for your expression. You could do the same with musical notes, kitchen spices, etc.

Tarot inspiration

Shuffle deck and draw a card. Use the symbolism of the card for your inspiration. Or, using creative visualization, enter into the scene yourself and see where it leads you. Or, use the colors or images of the illustration to create something new. Draw additional cards to expand the story.

Explore the wonderful wild world of tarot and oracle decks. Look into the work of John Cage and the process of "chance operations." Delve into the surrealists. See the work of Walter Benjamin for more on becoming a flaneur .

Archetypal Exploration

You've pulled the Queen of Pentacles for three readings in a row…or…You keep noticing little Sun symbols everywhere you go…or…Why is everyone suddenly talking about the Orphan? When you notice a certain archetypal presence recurring, it's time to dive in!

In your everyday creative practice, you can engage with these patterns in a deep, transformative way. First of all, use the practices already discussed: creative visualization, imaginal dialogue, journaling, to learn more about these characters and how they relate to you.

The defining feature of an archetype is that it has broad cultural as well as personal significance, so research and conversation are great complements to your creative and imaginal explorations. Search in texts, online, around your house and in the world for instances of the symbol you are engaging with. It will really enrich your understanding. When you're drawn to a particular archetype, stay with it as long as it has resonance for you. That might mean one afternoon, or it might mean years.

A few ways you might work with Archetypal Themes:

- Paint a picture
- Write a story, a song, a poem
- Create a costume for yourself.
- Craft a ritual

Symbol dictionaries are useful, as long as you always remember that it's your personal response to any symbol that bears the most importance for you. My beloved professor Walter Odajnyk suggested making your own symbol dictionary; this would be an amazing project to undertake. Start today! Start anywhere!

Astrology and tarot are systems of archetypal relationships; the study and practice of either (both!) will enrich your understanding tenfold of how archetypes operate in our lives. The same is true for any mythological system. The study of mythology will show you how archetypal images take form and interact. Once you start seeing them, you will see them everywhere: in film, in literature, in the art museum, at the coffee shop, in your dreams… I should not neglect to mention the study of depth psychology, James Hillman, in particular.

Check the suggestions on pages 54-55, "Explore Archetypes In Your Life."

Dream into Form

Dreams: inspiring, haunting, guiding, confusing…They are a natural source of subject matter for creative explorations. But how to evoke the ethereal in the material? Here are some thoughts.

I think dreams visit us from the imaginal realm, and like other imaginalia, they may be looking for forms to inhabit while they are here. I got this idea when studying about Egyptian art, where sacred forms were constructed to house the gods. So think about being visited by your dreams and, for this purpose, notice which ones might stick with you for a while.

It's perfectly great if you wake from a dream and are inspired to immediately create something, and you just do, with no need for thought, planning or "dream work." That's "livin' the dream," so to speak. And then again, if there is a dream that stays with you, and you want to respond creatively but aren't sure how, here are some ideas to help you get into it.

> First, get to know the dream. Beginning with a dream in mind, relax into reverie. What images has the dream brought to you? What feelings did it leave you with? Can you re-enter the dream and explore the images up close? Make some notes or sketches in whatever way will help you in getting to know the dream better. Keep track of the creative ideas that come up while you're getting to know your dream.
>
> As Hillman taught, don't get caught up in what it means or might mean— don't intellectualize it, but rather, stick with the image. You can expand your experience of the image into waking life by mapping associations, that is, things that the things in the dream make you think of. For instance if I dreamt of a spinning orb, my associations would include a crystal ball, soap bubbles, marbles…

No right answers, but what comes up for you? Or what do you find in the world that you associate with the dream, like artworks or places or music. Use metaphor to riff on resonant symbols and expressions.

Before you decide on the form, you might start with wondering, what does the dream want? Imagine what type of form would support the dream. Where does this dream want to live, or visit?

Does it inspire a drawing or painting? A sculpture? A dance? A dinner party? A work of music? A pattern?

What colors? What vibe? What size? What shape? What texture?

And of course, you decide how much time you will give this project, and that will help with other decisions. Dreams being non-rational, don't be too surprised if the boundaries blur, or if what you thought you were doing turns into something else. Dream on!

Re-Framing Narrative

"Tell all the truth but tell it slant" Emily Dickinson

It's your story. Tell it your way.

Who are you?

1. What are the facts? Make a list — brief or thorough, but stick to the facts. It will be dry.

2. What roles have you played/do you play/do you imagine yourself playing? Again, this is a list (mother, daughter, sister, boss) to show how many different perspectives you have. Some of these may well be opposed to one another (sinner/saint, liar/sage, lover/enemy).

3. Introduce yourself in 100 words. We are often asked to do exactly this, but, looking just at the facts of your life and the various roles you've played, obviously, you could never say everything in 100 words! So what do you choose to say? Experiment, for fun, with several versions, each one true but different from the others: funny, serious, absurd, businesslike, heartfelt, poignant, glib… You can use any of these voices to tell your story. There is not one right or real one, though some may feel they come closer to expressing your truth.

Apply this same process to reframe stories from your life. Starting with an event, list the facts, then the characters, each with their own point-of-view. How many different versions of this story can you tell? If you have seen yourself as a hero, try telling the story as a villain, or vice versa. If you have seen yourself as a victim, retell the story from a place of power. If you were a child in the story, can you tell it from your mother's perspective? The point is to relax that part of you that insists, "This is exactly what happened--no two ways about it!"

Try telling it from the third person, switching your personal pronouns from "I" to "he/she/they." How much space can you create?

*Go fantastic! Translate your personal narratives into the world of make-believe. Again, use the facts and characters to structure the story, but revise into myth, fairy tale, sci-fi, comix, gothic horror—whatever you like. I'm not suggesting you use this on your resume (Tell us a little about yourself. I was born into a family of ghouls…) but getting playful with your stories is fun, and can reveal profound symbolic truths.

Great books include Story Revisions by Alan Parry and Robert Doan; and Writing the Memoir by Judith Barrington.

Be Dramatic

This might seem better suited to Group Practices, for the dramatic arts are performative, and that implies more than one person. But here, think about you as the actor.

When you *inter-act* with the world, communication goes beyond the words you choose to say. The way you say them also has meaning. Your tone, your appearance, your stance, your actions all carry meaning. In our society of selfies and social media, I am loathe to make anyone feel more self-conscious or compelled to fit into a certain role or costume, but it's helpful to be aware of the persona you project. We may strive to be authentic, yet we are still actors in the world! Generally we do not go forth naked, for good reason. It's good to be vulnerable, but not everywhere, all the time. We wear our masks and our costumes. We "carry ourselves" in various ways.

Think about:

- Masks: What's the persona or role you are playing?
- Costumes: How does what you wear support or contrast with your role?
- Actions: What message is conveyed by your actions?
- Script: How do your words align or conflict with what you hope to communicate?

We can think about these in broad terms, relating to our professional, social, and personal selves, and we don't want to overthink it really. There are often conflicts and quirks, and that's part of being human. It can be helpful, though, to step back and analyze these aspects when you feel that your message is misinterpreted and you don't know why.

For fun, explore these different aspects of your dramatic self. Try on different outfits: what makes you feel comfortable, uncomfortable, powerful, shy, bold… Try wild make-up. Try no make-up. Try a wig or a new hairstyle. Experiment with the way you walk into a room. Stride. Slump. This angle, that angle. Take a line, any line: something you feel like saying to somebody, or something you would never say, or a favorite line from a movie ("What a dump") and say it as many ways, with as much or as little feeling as you can.

Who you are is fluid and changeable-but not invisible. Let yourself explore your many facets. What do you want to show to the world?

Erving Goffman's work is illuminating on the many ways that we present ourselves and frame our actions in the world.

Check out Cindy Sherman's work: it's all about re-imaging herself.

The Theatrical Frame

The way you choose to frame anything — a story, a photograph, an event—has everything to do with what will be communicated to the viewer. This activity is geared toward object groupings, or the creation of a scene, a vignette, a shadow-box.

A shadowbox is an efficient little world: it won't hold very much. What will you choose to put in? What will you leave out? It could be like a poem made of objects. It could be a vignette from a story, one that you know or one that the scene suggests. It doesn't need to make sense; it just needs to satisfy you.

The variables:

- the image or scene: can you picture how it will look or what it portrays?
- the size and shape: big? tiny? square? round? shallow? deep?
- the containing box: are you building it or is it something you've found?
- the materials or objects: what goes in the box? found or constructed?
- the vibe: what feeling do you hope to convey?

Decide on these in whatever order works. Maybe you're clear on one thing and fuzzy about another. Start with what you know and figure out the rest as you go along. Sometimes trial and error is most helpful.

You can extend this idea to other media. With a photograph, a painting, a musical exploration: what will fall inside the frame? What will lie outside?

Look into the marvelous work of Joseph Cornell. And also the world of dollhouses and miniatures.

Mixed Media Memoir

It's a form of auto-biography (Art-o-biography?): put paint, print and photo together with journaling and creative reverie to create a visual memoir.

This is another way of telling your story: through visual art. you could do a thousand self-portraits, each one different. Certainly, you can "do it straight": that is, sketch or paint a representational image of yourself with reference to a mirror or photograph—and you could do a thousand of *these*, each one different.

Here are a few more approaches to try:

> On a mirror: actually paint onto the mirror. paint your eyes or whole face
>
> On a photocopy: paint over top. Start with a thin/translucent layer of white paint or gesso so you can see what's underneath but also feel more free to change it.
>
> Collage yourself: begin with a sketch or a photocopy and a variety of pleasing papers. Tear or cut shapes to glue on top. Add paint or drawing as desired.
>
> Framing and reframing: portrait and memoir try to capture something essential about a person, which necessarily means clearing away of the non-essential. Essential or non-essential will change from project to project. Think about what essential features--visible or not -- you would like to capture in your self portrait? Use framing and composition to support that choice. Is the feature your nose? Or is it your work with animals? Or a stormy mood? You may want to be very close-up, or you may want to include more of a scene.

From a story: Use stories you've generated from reframing your narratives or begin with a brief response to "tell me about yourself" and make a self-portrait to go along with. It might be any role or aspect. It may be realistic, abstract, fantastical, comical…Use reference material as needed to sketch first.

Subpersonalities: explore your various inner selves and imagine them into portrait form. This might be your inner child or inner critic, or any other aspect of self you can bring forward. Think of the characters you may have found through imaginal dialogue. Is there a witch? A professor? A monster? A wacky goofball? Only you can say…

Wander through portrait galleries online and in real life to be wowed by the variety of approaches people have taken to portraiture. Get inspired!

Ritual Craft

Rituals fulfill the human need to create forms that help us move safely through transitions. If the object is to change and change is inherently risky, then rituals are the containers we create to mitigate the risk.

Rituals are not necessarily spiritual or religious, but times of transformation are when we might feel the energy of the mysterious unknown most acutely. Because we don't know just what is happening or what will happen as we change, we create forms to hold energy and protect ourselves.

Often, rituals are traditions handed down to us, but ritual crafting is a creative enterprise. Rituals can be designed according to your need, your intention, and what you find meaningful, and they can be honed over time as you learn what works or feels best for you.

Ritual is intentional, not improvisational, but you could create ritual as a structure to hold your improvisation. For instance, before beginning a creative practice, clear the space, arrange the materials, and turn off the phone.

Design a ritual that is meaningful to you:

- Intention: Who or what is this for? What is the purpose? What is the mood? (Games and funerals are both rituals, but with very different intentions.)

- Planning: Choose appropriate symbols, metaphorical actions, time, and space space. It may be simple or complex. Use imagination, intuition, and related mythology to suggest meaningful symbols and shape for this ritual.

- Manifestation: A simple ritual might follow this form: opening; intention; action; blessing; closure; grounding. There might be an exchange, in the form of sacrifice, gift, or offering, given in gratitude for the safe accomplishment of purpose.

For many rituals, especially when working with imaginal dialogue, creative visualization, or divination techniques, I follow this practice: begin with a relaxing breath; ground by feeling my energy drop deeply into my body and into the ground; and protect myself by visualizing white light surrounding me. (Shorthand: relax, deepen, and protect.) And, to close, a deep breath, a moment of silent presence, and an expression of gratitude.

Here are a couple of simple rituals:
Light a candle and focus your intention. Imagine a circle of white light around your home or an infusion of pink love energy for a dear one.

Find water, immerse yourself. let the water hold and caress you. Let it cleanse you. Let it revitalize you. Be grateful.

Here's a potential outline for a more involved ritual:

Planning and Preparation	Potential Ritual Objects:
Cleansing the space	earth, air, fire, water, candle,
Creating sacred space	smudge, essential oil, stone,
Beginning: Welcoming	crystal, salt, plant, flowers,
Declaration of intention	colors, fabric, thread,
Invocation of energies	animal symbols, music,
Offering	chant, sound, movement,
Ending: Blessing, closure	dance, words, poetry, prayer
Grounding: Food, drink	

Use these guidelines to craft ritual structures throughout your life, for big events and daily ones.

Robbie Davis-Floyd lists these points as "Characteristics of Ritual": use of symbolism, embeddedness in a belief system, rhythmic repetition and redundancy, use of specific tools and technologies, ritual framing, a sense of order and formality, an atmosphere of inviolability, an aspect of performance, and, often, a playful dimension (260-262).

Victor Turner and Tom Driver also write about ritual from the viewpoint of cultural anthropology. Starhawk is a great resource for learning about ritual practice.

Rituals are especially important in group work. Find more in the Group Practices Guide.

Part III : Being In Between

Being In Between

Ah, here we are... in between the personal and the social.

Just between you and me... There's a "between" between everything. We have the option of stepping into the third space of possibility in any moment. It's a handy trick, knowing how to expand the third; but it's more than a gimmick. For our purposes here, 'expanding the third' is a process and practice we can cultivate to explore possibility, enhance our creative interactions, and, oh, help the world toward a healthier, more pleasant and balanced condition.

This chapter moves into this playful, intuitive domain, including more about my methods and some best practices for finding your way around the liminal realm.

Navigating the Third

The third is characterized by ambiguity, so it's helpful to understand:

- *The nature of the third space:* what you are getting into
- *Best practices:* how to "behave"
- *Tips and techniques:* how to "explore"

First up, preparing for the experience.

Where's the boundary? Know where you are.
Be aware that you are entering the third. Ok, you always are. maybe. you always might be, you never know… That's the spirit!

As I've been saying, the third and thirdness are always available to you, and the ability to soften, relax, and entertain possibilities is a practice that can be useful throughout the day in so many ways; and so, you might find yourself in the third at any time, intentionally or unexpectedly. It's a more dreamy, open-minded, unattached state-of-mind than your "normal everyday" consciousness. You can drift into it unawares, but it's useful to recognize when you are experiencing the ambiguity of the third and exercise some control over it, because there are definitely times when you'd prefer to be more firmly anchored, grounded, and decisive: perhaps when you're signing a contract, or taking an exam, or applying for a job.

When it comes to intentionally expanding and entering the third as a practice, to relax and feel comfortable exploring and experimenting creatively and intuitively, it's helpful to have a clear sense of the container and its boundaries.

Containing the third
It almost sounds counter-intuitive, and maybe it is? I mean, do you have to plan to be playful? Are you going to schedule it? That sounds wrong. Well, thirdness is always a mix of things, including contrariness. In the third we encourage fluidity and morphing and relaxed boundaries, which you might do at any time, spontaneously. But/and, in order to comfortably let go and explore the realm of the third safely, you want to be able to recognize the functional distinction between yourself and someone else, between solid ground and marvelous fantasy. The way to relax safely and comfortably, as a *practice*, is to establish a container.

In my work facilitating creative groups, some participants have asked me, how is this — listening to imaginary voices and allowing yourself to experience fantasies— different from psychosis? The difference is that you *know* the difference. You are in charge, by your awareness of being "in between" and your ability to return to your "normal." The difference is that you recognize the distinction between your dream/play space and your waking reality. The difference is in your perspective, your ability to reflect on your experiences in the third — just as you can be wholly caught up in the experience of watching a movie, and still know it's a movie.

Most people are not at risk of getting "lost at sea" — that is, opening up the floodgates to the unconscious and getting swept away from the ground of consciousness. For most people, the bigger challenge is to loosen up your conscious control enough to test the waters.

The container marks the safe boundary you establish, which allows you to relinquish control within that container, holding the relation between structure and freedom: the structure helps you feel free to let go into the experience. Everyone has their own comfort level with this. I've worked with vets who have a very different sense than I do of what's safe and what may be overwhelming. I've worked with women who have suffered traumatically from the invasion of their private spaces. Find what works for you and honor your boundaries.

When you establish a container, you're setting the parameters of what's OK. The boundaries are set by you and this allows you to relax and participate in whatever comes up, even if it's surprising! You won't feel threatened or endangered if you enter into it with clarity of expectation; and if something does feel too uncomfortable, you are able to say "no," because you know your limits. You can get back to solid ground when you need to. Practice self-care.

It's like a hypnotic trance: unexpected events can transpire, surprising information can become known, but only so far as you are willing to experience it. You can "snap out of it" at will.

Swimming in a swimming pool is a non-scary thing for me.

I can easily lie on my back, close my eyes, and float around the pool without worry. I know that's not true for everyone, but I'm comfortable with it. Swimming in the ocean, though—that IS scary for me! I can wade, sure, but it's very hard for me to relax enough to swim or float. I'm always checking on whether I'm being carried out to sea, and is that seaweed or a sea monster brushing against my leg? Obviously many people love ocean swimming. For some, the presence of a lifeguard creates the safe space. For others, no lifeguard is necessary. shrug.

There's a documentary called "Waterman" about the amazing Hawai'ian surfer Duke Kahanamoku. An incredibly strong swimmer, he was at home in the ocean in ways that I could only ever dream about. He was able to dive into the roughest waters and make his way safely back to shore, saving drowning victims all the way. Amazing. But I'd be more at home than him at navigating the streets of West Philly or the Atlanta airport. You need to know your own limits.

Elements of a good container:

- the space you are using
- the time you are using
- the limits you set

Crossing boundaries: entering the third

Do I sometimes —or often— find myself unexpectedly in the third? Oh yes! Often! For better and for worse. It's normal, and simply helpful to recognize that you have wandered into more playful or unclear circumstances: for instance:

- a situation becomes ambiguous or surreal

- things aren't going as expected

- there's a strong emotional vibe or intuition

- a serious discussion suddenly turns hilarious

- an interaction is unclear

- I feel like I'm dreaming

- deja vu

As I notice these qualities I can judge whether I'm comfortable to let it unfold or whether I prefer to move myself to solid ground. But for now, in this chapter, we're talking about intentionally entering the third for the sake of creative adventure.

Theatrical director William Ball embraces the intuitive voice of the actors with whom he works. While the first ideas which come out may be odd or quirky, Ball feels the key is to keep saying yes.

"We say yes to every creative idea... we do not say yes to everything for virtue's sake. We say yes because we understand that to do so is the practical way of sending a message to the intuition that every creative idea will be valued, respected and used; and when the intuition gets that message often enough, it will send us its most perfect and its most pure creative ideas. That is why... saying yes to everything is the most creative technique an artist can employ."
(Ball 18)

Getting there:
It's a simple thing, but it's a subtle thing. Just follow the wisps and curiosities and expression without worrying about what it is, what it looks like, what it's about, what it means.

This is where the subtlety comes in, I think — because, at first, the idea of just following the curiosity is enchanting and attractive, even exciting, and sometimes a grand adventure or charming interaction will unfold; but the reality is that it may not, and often **DOESN'T**, lead you right into some super-cool creation or exciting/scary revelation/interaction. It may just feel like nothing's happening. This can make people feel like either they're doing it wrong or that I don't know what I'm talking about. Ahem.

Nothing's Happening

KJJUNGGGHHH

When you hear yourself saying, "Nothing's happening..." the very next moment is often the significant resounding moment where everything changes

it's like —"No, I don't feel anything" ...and then suddenly—

KJJUNGGGHHH

"This creative/imaginal experience is going nowhere"... and then suddenly...

KJJUNGGGHHH

I am encouraging you to follow your curiosity and to *stay with it,* despite:

- the feeling that nothing is happening,

- the images/ideas/expressions that seem boring not special

- the sense that you have no idea what you're doing– or I have no idea what I'm talking about

- the voice in your head that says "This is stupid!"

IMPORTANT: if you want to end up with a creation that looks-sounds-feels a particular way, guaranteed to be impressive or delicious, then do some skill-building and follow a recipe—and there's nothing wrong with that! It's very satisfying. I love a good recipe. Get yourself an art journaling book that shows you what it's going to look like when you're finished and then shows you how to get there.

And if you want to explore the wilds — and the agonies and ecstasies — and the doldrums and the insecurities — starting from your own experience, in your own place and time, then this is the guidebook for you.

Nothing's Happening
And, also, it sometimes happens that...*nothing's happening...really*. That's ok, too. That's part of life and the creative process. An important part, actually. Just feel what you feel, notice what you notice, and stay with it. It's a PRACTICE.

How do straight lines turn into curves and spheres? With string art, it's a matter of perception. As the construction builds, shapes and patterns are revealed that were not visible a moment before– you just have to keep at it!

Meditation on Exploring the Third

You are in one world and you are in other worlds.

You do not leave one world to visit the other.

You shift your attention. You shift your intention.

Intention will guide you.

Attention will give you clues, information, that which you are seeking or that which you need to know.

You might close your eyes or darken the room to help you bring your attention to other realms. Quiet and relaxed, you see - hear - notice what you ordinarily would not in your daily waking world.

Do not push. Do not direct. Relax and attune.

The world is rich and full of many beings. Expand your ability to perceive and communicate. It begins with listening and attention.

Remember that in the third shapes and forms shift, as they are in a state of becoming, one into another and the next.

As you seek to "extract treasures" from this oceanic realm for use in the material waking reality remember

1. to be respectful and grateful, not greedy

2. to allow shape shifting, not becoming too attached to the forms, although they are helpful in the moment

3. to keep moving: be fluid, in this fluid realm

There are many beautiful forms which humans have cocreated. Simply remember that all that comes into form will also, sooner or later, disintegrate. That may feel sad, but it is not tragic. It is simply the way of all things. To be a part of the flow of life, you must allow change, evolution, shifting, and transformation. All is transforming. You, too.

Let it be simple. Leave your husks behind.

* You do not need to act on information you receive. Observe it, note it, contemplate it, and consider it. You may also decide that it is worthy of taking action.

metaphor
noun
a thing regarded as symbolic of something else

Metaphor is the essential bridge that mediates the "in-between" area of the third.

Etymologically, "metaphor" derives from the Greek *metapherein* "transfer, carry over" (meta "over, across" + pherein "to carry, bear). Like a bridge holding tension between two distinct yet similar terms or objects, metaphor is the translation of one thing in terms of another.

Recognizing a metaphor when you see it
Do you know one when you see one?

If you ask me, everything's a metaphor. Everything is like something else, but different. Everything can be interpreted in more than one way, on more than one level. Everything is a bridge to something else. Everything is in relationship. And, as already discussed, there is a philosophical, phenomenological basis to assert that, for humans, our perceptions are organized according to a schema of metaphor. All language is metaphorical. All communication is dependent on metaphor. It's all a translation.

This capacity to metaphorize, to see and understand one thing in terms of another, is none other than mythmaking in action.

Humans are mythmakers. We all do it, and we do it all the time. We do it without even realizing it. It is a fundamental quality of humanness.

Mythmaking: it's not a fault to fix nor a weakness to be overcome. The fault lies in not recognizing that you live in mythic territory. The fault lies in not understanding the presence and action of metaphorical relations, even as we are steeped in them. *This* is the weakness to be overcome.

Myth stew

So try to take a step outside of your myth stew for a moment (which you really can't do–but try anyway) to consider that perhaps we can *only, ever and always,* understand one thing in terms of another.

We feel things directly.

We experience things directly.

But when it comes to understanding, communicating, thinking about... *anything...*

making meaning = making metaphor = making myth

Metaphor is a translator of one thing to another: a connector that builds meaning by building bridges. The wonder of any metaphor is the way it always, by definition, means more than one thing.

> *If one thing reminds you of another thing...*
> *If a dream image connects to*
> *your feeling about an event in your life...*
> *If a song brings you unexpectedly to tears...*
>
> *...notice what's happening*
> *...listen to your language*
> *...follow the image where it leads*

The drive to find and make meaning can guide us through the most dire circumstances, while those lacking such a drive may lose their way. Psychologist and holocaust survivor Viktor Frankl articulates this in his compelling book, Man's Search for Meaning.

Metaphor often reveals itself in word play and punning, so the practice of writing about or otherwise expressing these experiences can be very helpful in bringing metaphorical correspondences into awareness. You might not notice the double entendre at first...and then it dawns on you!

Humans ALWAYS want to know:

'WHAT DOES IT MEAN?'

They just can't stop. The very idea that 'when THIS THING happens, it means THAT THING' is Metaphorical consciousness. aka mythmaking. Thank you very much

Yeah, but then they go, 'WOULDN'T IT BE COOLER IF WE COULD BE LIKE COMPUTERS AND ONLY SPEAK IN FACTS?' Doh.

Where's my feet?

"C'mon! This way!"

"Um...not sure..."

Letting the geni out of the bottle

In your creative explorations, you may come across things that intrigue you and entice you. Physical things, memories, scribbles in your journal...things can hold a concentration of meaning. When you open them up they expand...Be ready!

I can count on this to happen when I'm sorting through things that have been stuffed away: a project I was excited about, that somehow got pushed aside, suddenly brings on the excitement I had once felt; an old journal sweeps me back in time to a vivid memory I had forgotten...

Whoosh! The geni is out of the bottle.

The geni is very powerful. The geni has been trapped inside your things for eons since you tucked them away and kind of forgot about them. When you bring those wonderful precious treasures out into the light, you feel the release of power and the energy and the potential that has been trapped inside, waiting for you for so long.

As you feel the power and excitement and expansiveness of possibility at this point: remember, the geni is not necessarily in love with humans, nor beholden to you for all time, yet will grant a limited number of your wishes; so be clear and choose carefully.

> *meaning, you may feel very enthusiastic but you don't have to follow every idea to fruition, and you can't.

Where are your genies stashed away? Mine are in my notebooks and in my toys in the attic and in my old projects, and they certainly inhabit unexpected places as well. They are very powerful, so, as best I can, I like to be ready to open the bottle before I do. Of course, if you have read enough fairy tales, you know it doesn't always happen according to plan...

I THINK YOU SHOULD ADMIT THAT YOU JUST WROTE "FARTY TALES" BY MISTAKE

It's not all good times

Lest you think I am suggesting that this journey into thirdness will take you on a permanent high, to rest on fleecy clouds amidst vibrant rainbows...A fairy tale adventure where only good things happen? I've never seen a fairy tale like that. This practice of noticing, observing, being present, finding expression... It can be full of surprises. Along with gifts and treasures, there will be difficulties and frustrations. Because, you're human, right? And, the imaginal life is real life, too.

It has been duly noted that (white) Americans don't want to see or deal with pain, discomfort, dirt, bad smells; that we want the highs without the lows, the ultimates without the dulls, the bliss without the rot. Well, wake up! It ain't like that; and when we try to make it like that, we are simply shoveling all the trash and toxicity under the rug to be dealt with by someone else or at a later time. Uh, time's up.

Suffering is part of the human condition. To be present with your suffering and the suffering of others is a valuable learning. I've found that the suffering I experience is relieved by my willingness to be with it, feel it, witness it, express it, and, by neither fighting it nor clinging to it, let it pass or transform. This is *Zen 101*.

Awareness of your own pain, letting it out and giving it voice can be a healing balm, even if there's no one else around. If you have the opportunity to express your difficult feelings into a group who listens compassionately, the healing is strong. NOTE: It's worth pausing before you share with others to ask yourself: do you have a sense that this is an appropriate container for your feelings?

It can be very hard to find appropriate opportunities to share about your difficult experiences with others. Online generally doesn't provide the proper intimacy nor mindful presence nor safety. Even with best intentions, it's hard for others to know the tenor of your feelings; they want to show they care but then they are worried about you because they fear this might be a cry for help, when maybe it's just a cry. Or, they really don't know you, so they wonder, why are you sharing all this personal stuff on a grand stage? Or, they are trolls.

That's why I advocate for developing your own group opportunities for sharing. Opening space for expression of tender matters (which need not only be verbal) is a step toward integrating: your parts with you, and you with others. You may find that others have had similar experiences or feelings, and you may find that others care about you when you thought that no one did; and you may find a sense of relief in not having to pretend, or to only give voice to certain kinds of feelings.

Just start
Where to begin? Anywhere. When you sit down to do a jigsaw puzzle, you don't wait till you know where all the pieces go before you start. You start with the first pieces you find that fit together, and go on from there. It's the same with imaginal exploration and creative expression.

Rando

*well that was really random... Or wait?
Was that imaginal dialog? Pay attention
to tangential thoughts and images.
Notice the path that takes you there.
Don't automatically brush away the little
unrelated bits that pop into your mind.
Sometimes they are perfect symbolic gems
that are <u>precisely</u> relevant to whatever
you are working on or thinking about, but
useful <u>only if you notice them</u>.*

Engaging with multitudes of imaginal others
There are countless imaginal others you might engage with — as many as you can imagine! Even more! — and these beings can be full of nuance and dimension. Just like everyone you've ever known. They do not all need to be considered as "guides" or "helpful spirits."

Guidelines: Best Practices for Being In-Between

Here's a list of guidelines to being in-between. Is this too much fuss? Nah. To stay with the watery metaphors, it depends how deep you want to go. Use your common sense. Divers follow a safety checklist. When you're ready to take a deep dive into the imaginal realm, check this list.

Establish the container. Clear beginnings and endings. Limits of time and space.

Ground yourself. Feel your connection to the earth, Feel your skin, which surrounds you and protects you, the interface between you and the world, which breathes, allowing the flow of air and water, regulating temperature, noticing sensations...Feel your breath, in and out, softening, gentle... Feel the rhythms of your body, connecting you with the world around. Feel your vitality, the life force that flows through you... And note these three things:

    • **Self-protection:** Know and honor your limits. You may like to visualize a glowing, protective light all around you. You may like to use a simple prayer or intention that you find meaningful and centering ("I am a channel of white light" or "Ommmm"). You may like to visualize a cord (a guideline, after all) that connects you to your waking reality. If you feel you have ventured too far, just follow the cord back to where you started.

    • **Intention**: Clarify your intention before you begin: it may simply be to explore, or perhaps you seek a certain type of interaction ("I ask for guidance from helpful spirits on [x] topic").

    • **Attitude**: Let kindness and respect be your attitude.

Open and enter. Soften deepen relax

Tune in. Notice listen observe

Interact. Engage in whatever way you are called

Give thanks. Always express appreciation for your encounters and the gifts they bring. It's common courtesy.

Guidelines:

Establish a container

Ground yourself

Open and Enter

Tune in

Interact

Give thanks

Leave/Close

Debrief/Ground

Leave the liminal space and close the session. End with a clear sense that you are leaving the expanded liminal space and returning to a more normal waking reality. Notice your skin. Notice your breath. Notice the ground beneath you.

Debrief. What happened? It's good to spend some time processing. Think about your experience. Make some notes or sketches. If you have gained insights, jot them down. If there are images or ideas that are particularly strong or resonant for you, take note! You may want to return to them. It's not that you need to "figure everything out" or capture every detail of your experience; but contemplating and continuing to work with whatever came up for you *is* translating the imaginal experience into your waking reality. It's valuable. Admire it, kiss it, and then watch it swim away.

A fairy went a'marketing—She bought a little fish;
She put it in a crystal bowl
Upon a golden dish.

An hour she sat in wonderment
And watched its silver gleam,
And then she gently took it up
And slipped it in a stream.

Rose Fyleman

ANGELES ARRIEN: The Four-Fold Way

The great Angeles Arrien offered The Four-Fold Way, drawn from her research into indigenous traditions, as an approach to living with integrity. Easy to memorize, you can apply these basic tenets in all arenas of your life, for the greater good of all concerned.

1. *Show up or choose to be present. Being present allows us to access the human resources of power, presence, and communication. This is the way of the Warrior.*

2. *Pay attention to what has heart and meaning. Paying attention opens us to the human resources of love, gratitude, acknowledgment, and validation. This is the way of the Healer.*

3. *Tell the truth without blame or judgment. Nonjudgmental truthfulness maintains our authenticity and develops our inner vision and intuition. This is the way of the Visionary.*

4. *Be open to outcome, not attached to outcome. Openness and non-attachment helps us recover the human resources of wisdom and objectivity. This is the way of the Teacher.*

On Imaginal Guidance

Intro
Here is some guidance on Imaginal Guidance. But people have a lot of different beliefs. There's no reason you should take my word for anything! In the spirit of disclosure, let me tell you where I'm coming from:

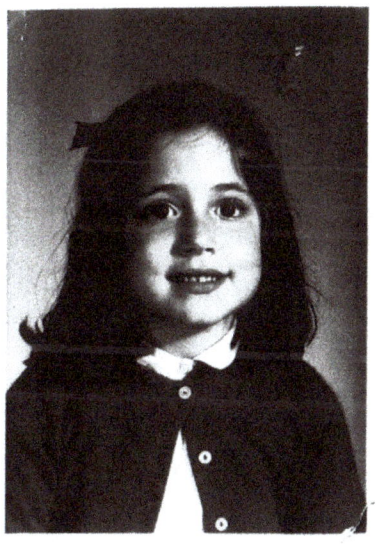

Little Mary

mary is agnostic. Having studied and participated in many spiritual-religious traditions and practices as insider AND outsider [raised as an Episcopalian, descended from Quaker and Celtic and German ancestors (with maybe a pinch of Rom? fingers crossed), playing with fairies, dabbling in wicca, embracing neo-feminist spirituality and then pantheism, practising yoga and meditation, becoming advanced reader of astrology, tarot, and other methods of oracle, following Buddhist teachings, studying religious thought in college and later earning my doctorate in world mythologies and depth psychology, finding my own path of creative expression intertwined with all of the above], I believe that anything is possible and nothing is for certain. I am guided by my moral compass and ethical concerns, my observations, my heart, my family traditions, my faith that there is more than I know, my ability to reason, and the knowledge I have gained over this and possibly other lifetimes.

Consciousness changes everyday: my consciousness, and the larger consciousness of which it is a part. So I have to take it as a matter of course, each day, that what I thought was true may no longer be true. This is a core belief for me, and it applies to everything. My more deeply held beliefs are less likely to be challenged by whatever happens today.

Deeper beliefs and truths that guide me, in my inner+outer life and in all the spaces in-between:

> One World
>
> Love is the answer.
>
> Be kind
>
> Follow the Fourfold Way:
>   Show up
>   Pay attention
>   Tell the truth
>   Be unattached to outcome
>
> Clean up your own shit, as best you can
>
> Use your gifts
>
> You don't know everything

Does this list hold true for you? If not, what is on your list of deeply held beliefs?

A "UNISEX" T-SHIRT IS ACTUALLY A MAN'S T-SHIRT BTW

A note on gods and gender:

Some deities were conceived as non-gendered in their cultures of origin, later becoming male through translation into the gendered language of a patriarchal culture.

We see everything through the lens of our own cultural biases, unless we take active steps to put aside that lens.

When deities from other times and places are described in 21st century English, it's a translation. We always see through the mythic lens of our own times and places. We can only approximate our understanding of other ways. Language and culture shape understanding. I wish we had more pronoun options in the English language.

I often avoid using the terms "spiritual" and "supernatural," because in my own cultural experience both are chock full of loaded assumptions about the nature of reality — assumptions I feel pretty iffy about. Maybe it's a matter of semantics rather than ontology, but for sure language shapes our understanding of reality. To move beyond errors in our thinking we must shift the language we use.

"Spiritual" can mean all sorts of things, but it often implies something separate from the material, and "supernatural" is defined as being "above nature." Those meanings are misaligned with the way I generally understand the nature of reality.

But I do not deny the numinous (or "spiritual") experience. Heaven forbid! My belief is that the spiritual flows freely with the material, and that <u>nature</u> includes kaleidoscopic multitudes beyond what we see and know; so that what is often called "super-natural" (beyond = super) is the mysterious infinite abiding spirit of Nature itself. I also choose not to refer to Nature by a gendered pronoun. "Nature" includes all of us, and more.

I recognize that my statements of belief shift and change and I acknowledge that much I don't know exists, beyond what I've stated here. For instance, I imagine that consciousness, along with many mysterious unknowns, exists beyond the earthly realm. Would that then be "supernatural"? Because when I invoke Nature, I'm mainly referring to Earthly Nature. Are the starry skies Nature too? I guess... Or... ?

I just don't know...

You may agree with these ideas or not — I'm just letting you know more about what beliefs underlie my thinking. What words do you find problematic? Do you have alternate phrasing that you prefer?

I say "Thank God!" and similar all the time, and I'm not intending a male "God the Father," (except, kind of, like it or not, because I was raised in the Episcopal church where God is definitely conceived of as God the Father. Anyway...) In many traditions, there is One Source which is not gendered or qualified in any way, but from which all specific deities descend. Some people prefer to call out to Goddess than God -- for many reasons! It's a matter of belief and a personal choice, but also part of the discussion is that, although God is not necessarily a gendered term, yet in western culture, God has overwhelmingly been conceived of as male, so when we invoke the Goddess, we are bringing some balance. I keep an altar to the Goddess and pray to the Goddess, and also I use the term "God" not only because it is the way I was raised but also in the attempt to reclaim it as a non-gendered term. I was once a bartender. Sometimes people would search for a more feminine term, but we used to say, "Tender has no gender." By the same token, I like to say, "God has no gender." Doesn't rhyme, so, not as cute. Nonetheless...

GOD HAS NO BOD?

mana:
noun
a generalized, diffuse force or power, which may be concentrated in objects or people

numinous:
noun
mysterious, awe-inspiring, filled with a sense of divinity

Is a strawberry better experienced by listing its constituent chemicals?

No. That describes it, too, but ***direct experience is life***, the source of vitality and inspiration. It's what I would call "participation," and it's available to any of us in any moment.

Evolution of numinous energy: A Theory
On Guides and Gods: One view

From mana to daimon to god to concept
Durkheim described *mana* as "an anonymous and diffused force," fluid, pervasive and impersonal. The term originated in Austronesian cultures, but the experience of the presence of unseen, undefined power is cross-cultural. Most of us can relate to that feeling.

In her research into Greek religion, Harrison asserted that a god-form originates in the direct experience of mana, not at first conceived/perceived as a separate being or Other, but developing over time into the idea of a god, associated with certain characteristics and powers. In this understanding, the sacred experience comes first, inspiring the *notion* of gods; only subsequently can individual gods become known as bearers of sacred powers.

The daimon, found cross-culturally, is an early form of divinity, arising locally, in place, through the direct experience of mana. Daimons are commonly given plant and animal forms, naturally carrying symbolically related characteristics and powers. The snake or serpent, for example, is a daimon recognized in many cultures as a symbol of immortality and fertility. Shedding its skin, the snake is associated with transformation and the renewal of life. Its phallic shape is linked with fertility. In ancient Greece, house snakes and holy snakes were recognized as genii loci, or protective spirits of the place. Guardians of tree, well, and spring, snakes appear frequently in Greek myth and artifact in association with prophecy and divination (431). Like sinuous tree roots, snakes travel both above and below ground, and thus between worlds. As well and spring bear precious gifts of water and oracle from some mysterious underground source, the snake, also, is believed to carry messages between worlds.

Less distinct than a god, the daimon typically performs a specific function: daimon of luck, daimon of initiation, daimon of fertility, etc. Gods with names and titles and complex family relations are subsequent developments. The Olympian gods (Zeus, Hera, & co) in comparison to daimons, are more idealized, more completely formed, more differentiated and more detached from humanity. Harrison says it's the human story-telling instinct that has honed their divine personalities (47).

Hermes was one such fertility daimon who evolved into an Olympian god. He was there before the Olympian gods came along: "He was really there from the beginning as daimon or 'luck' of the place or the situation, there long before the gods who made him their 'messenger.' " This exemplifies how religious culture evolved from direct experience to practices and beliefs defined by social convention. Historically, the philosophy of rationalism (that truth is to be found through intellect rather than experience) developed alongside.

Rationality is great. We use it all the time, obviously, and it's really central to finding fair agreement. My experience and your experience may differ, so a rational discussion can help us to establish a common ground to build upon. 1+1=2, right?

But if we assert that truth is *only* to be found through reason, or that reason is superior to other ways of knowing, we've gone too far. It's like saying the answer to life is 42 (as Douglas Adams revealed in *Hitchhiker's Guide to the Galaxy*).

From genii loci to centralized and legislated gods.

In the western world, the notion of divinity has become more abstract over time, "told" through memory and doctrine, rather than "felt" through energetic presence. Gods have become centralized and remote, untethered from place and experience; yet weirdly, they have simultaneously been literalized, as people attempt to substantiate claims of historical origins. As religious experience is politicized, genii loci are subsumed by larger, more powerful figures. Corporatized, really. Nothing better exemplifies this pattern of divine reduction toward monotheism than the burgeoning influence of Christianity over the centuries.

Images, idols, icons, and direct experience

The early Christian world was a syncretic mix of Hebrew, Greek and Egyptian influences. These different traditions came together like "Stone Soup," and if you've ever won-

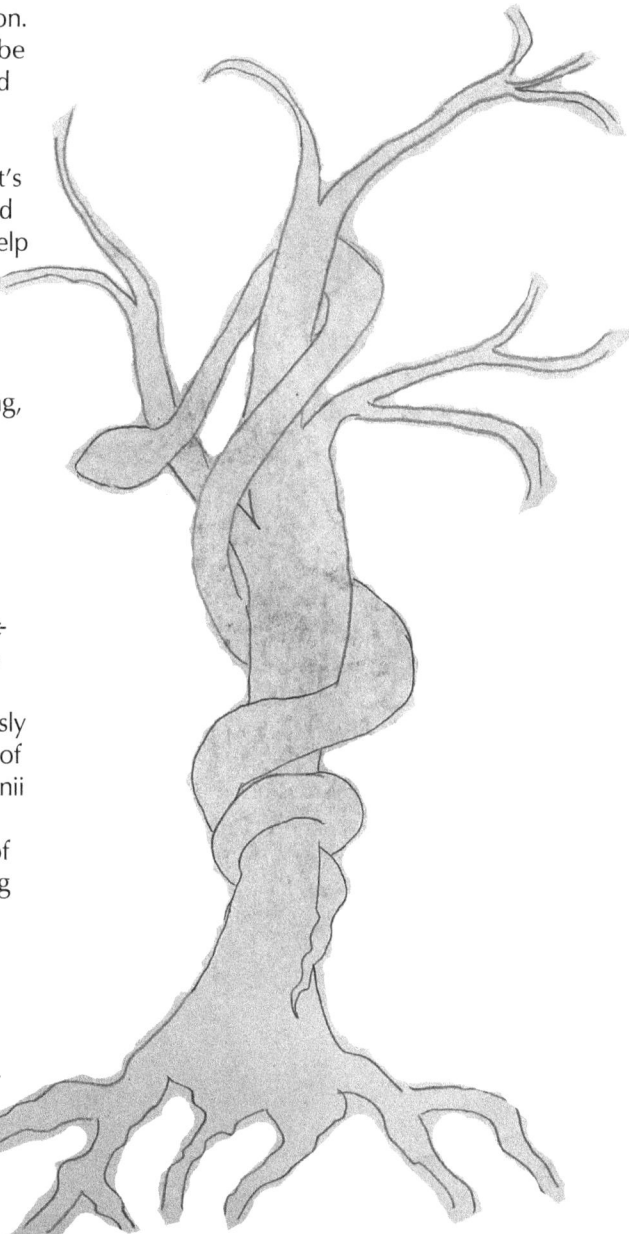

From *The Gift* by Lewis Hyde (67-68):

"The task of setting free one's gifts was a recognized labor in the ancient world. The Romans called a person's tutelar spirit his **genius**. In Greece it was called a **daemon**. Ancient authors tell us that Socrates, for example, had a **daemon** who would speak up when he was about to do something that did not accord with his true nature. It was believed that each man had his **idios daemon**, his personal spirit which could be cultivated and developed. Apuleius, the Roman author of **The Golden Ass**, wrote a treatise on the **daemon/genius**, and one of the things he says is that in Rome it was the custom on one's birthday to offer a sacrifice to one's own **genius**. A man didn't just receive gifts on his birthday, he would also give something to his guiding spirit. Respected in this way the **genius** made one "genial" – sexually potent, artistically creative, and spiritually fertile.

According to Apuleius, if a man cultivated his **genius** through such a sacrifice, it would become a **lar**, a protective household God, when he died. But if a man ignored his **genius**, it became a **larva** or a **lemur** when he died, a troublesome, restless spook that preys on the living. The **genius** or **daemon** comes to us at birth. It carries with it the fullness of our undeveloped powers. These are offered to us as we grow, and we choose whether or not to accept, which means we choose whether or not to labor in its service. For again, the **genius** has need of us. As with the elves, the spirit that brings us our gifts finds its eventual freedom only through our sacrifice, and those who do not reciprocate the gift of their **genius** will leave it in bondage when they die.

An abiding sense of gratitude moves a person to labor in the service of his **daemon**. The opposite is properly called narcissism. The narcissist feels his gifts come from himself. He works to display himself, not to suffer change. An age in which no one sacrifices to his **genius** or **daemon** is an age of narcissism. The "cult of genius" which we have seen in this century has nothing to do with the ancient cult. The public adoration of **genius** turns men and women into celebrities and cuts off all commerce with the guardian spirits. We should not speak of another's **genius**; this is a private affair. The celebrity trades on his gifts, he does not sacrifice to them. And without that sacrifice, without the return gift, the spirit cannot be set free. In an age of narcissism the centers of culture are populated with **larvae** and **lemures**, the spooks of unfulfilled **genii**."

dered about conflicting narratives in the Bible, this can help you understand why it's so: the Bible wasn't sat down and written like a novel, or divinely downloaded into one original document. Rather, it's a compilation of many differing versions of the tales of its origin. Likewise, the Christian stance on icons, idols, and images was not always one thing (still isn't, really) but has been carved out over the millennia.

Idolatry was a part of Judaic tradition prior to the Babylonian exile (c. 598 -538 bce). Before this period of exile, Jews kept idols: household gods that they revered. Around the time of the exile, as Jews were forced to leave their homeland, the Ten Commandments were codified and the first books of the Hebrew Bible were collected and written down. At this point, idolatry was forbidden by the second of the Ten Commandments.

However, icons and images were still revered in Egyptian and Greek traditions, and iconography became widespread in Christian practice as gentiles joined the faith: so, sacred icons and images were being stirred around in the pot of early Christian practices, but not without dispute.

The controversy between imagism and iconoclasm came to a head during the Byzantine Iconoclasm, comprising two periods in the 8th-9th century Byzantine Empire when the use of religious images and icons was banned. At the Nicaean Council of 787 CE, a policy decision was made allowing images to be *venerated* (honored) but not *adored* (worshipped); thereby ruling that no divine power resided within the images themselves but that images served only to point to the heavenly divine:

> "They were not presences or presentation, but representation, illustration and allegories to remind the faithful of abstract theological figuration" (Hillman, Healing 71).

By this ruling, for the faithful, images were stripped of their power, becoming mnemonic devices only, in service to the intellectual codification of belief. Only church-approved images were allowed, and only as representation of the notions of the divine as established by Scripture.

This complicated debate has continued in some form over many hundreds of years. It also involves Islamic law. It prefaces the schism between the Eastern Orthodox Church and the Catholic Church (1054) and later, the split between the Catholic and Protestant churches. Church rulings continue to stipulate just what

---

icon
noun
a magical object such as a totem or icon is a material form which serves as a focal point for a communicative relationship with what is conceived as divine power.

idol
noun
image or representation of a god used as an object of worship.

imagism:
nonu
veneration of religious images and symbols

iconoclasm:
noun
destruction of religious images and symbols along with persecution of supporters of the veneration of images

210 *HOW TO PARTICIPATE IN THE WORLD*

can and can't be represented, particularly in the more fundamentalist factions. In many Christian traditions, personal experience of the sacred has been essentially confined to approved protocol—not only "back then," but now.

When humans-in-power claim to speak for God and proceed to legislate the sacred experience of others, controversy will follow, and Christianity is no exception. Today, Christianity comprises many factions with varying positions on the issue of iconography, yet the abiding western belief denies inherent power to the image (or to any material forms), in the church and also in western culture at large. Spirit and matter are proclaimed as two separate things, so don't confuse them! One's unique spiritual experiences continue to be judged against doctrine, be it Christian, rationalist, or other. While Christian tradition regulates the non-rational experience, the rational-scientific model vanquishes the gods by denying their existence, essentially denying the unknown as a real category, finding idiosyncratic (unrepeatable) observations as false (or not to be counted), and proclaiming the supremacy of abstract thought (One God!). Anything beyond rationality is suspect; of course, this includes experience. Thus have we forged a path to the cultural devaluation and distrust of the transrational and imagination.*

---

earth magic

---

paganism, pantheism, animism, shamanism, witchcraft, voudou: these spiritual practices based on direct experience are not synonymous with one another, but they share the commonality that they have been judged villainous by Christian dogma.

---

*I won't be surprised if any readers take exception to my views on Christianity--and that's myth for you! We're talking about the same thing, but we all have different opinions about it. We are still steeped in this mythology, even if we try to reject it, and that shows in the heated discussions that the topic engenders.

One right and perfect good, over and above all else. If only one god is allowed, what to do with the others? In a good-over-evil, right-over-wrong schema, all the rest are suspect. Daimons are denounced as demons, and are (metaphorically or literally, depending on your outlook) consigned to the depths of hell. It is still deep down where we seek them.

"Psychic reality comes in the shape of daimons." Hillman (*Healing* 56)

Free the daimons!
The images that come to us, speak to us, act on us through dreams and underworld experiences are as daimons—imaginal figures arising from the ground of psyche, bearing mana and connecting us with the forgotten

and the unknown; even becoming psychopompos, offering us guidance to know self and psyche (Hillman 60-62).

Says Jung, " 'mana,' 'daimon,' and 'God' are synonyms for the unconscious — that is to say, we know just as much or just as little about them as about the latter" (*Memories* 337). This is not a judgment as to whether 'God' exists. It is a clarification that if something is unknown, then we don't know. You can't (unequivocally) distinguish one category of unknowns from another. Jung's groundbreaking work of inner exploration re-established an understanding of psychic reality as a realm of images, which one could experience via imaginal dialogue with daimonic presences.

If we understand how our numinous experiences of the imaginal, over time, take form as deities and archetypal constructs and abstract ideas, then we can also understand why we might pray to or converse with particular deities, why we might practice devotions, why we might focus intention on a sacred object, or why we might engage in imaginal discourse with a variety of daimons. (And why, as per the preceding discussion, some religious traditions find this objectionable.) Forms come and go, but the desire to engage with the numinous continues. It is through direct experience of the imaginal that we can do so.

> PLEASE KNOW that when I use the term "imaginal" I do not intend to suggest "pretend" or "unreal." Yes, I am an imagist. And I don't believe that other humans can dictate to me the parameters of my spiritual experience.

Who knows what mana is? I think of Bergson's *élan vital*, the vitality of life itself. I think of it, not as a human projection, but as a flow of energy or life force, perceived and finding expression through our humanness and beyond. The more important point is not *what* mana is, but *that* mana is. The collective experience of mana is clearly at the root of religious experience, but the origin of mana remains unknown. Mana has taken the shape of gods, then gods have been abstracted, literalized, and finally rejected via rational analysis...*but* the underlying direct experience which engendered the gods to begin with is still valuable and available, even to "rational" westerners. We only need the context and opportunity. But...*When? Where? How?*

Right this way!

In *Playing and Reality*, Winnicott establishes the essential role of the imagination in healthy human development. Forcing the distinction between "real" and "imaginary" requires resolving the paradox of playing, which is both imaginary and real (55). This leads to a "true and false self organization," whaere there is no space of play. This refusal of possibility results in anxiety (19, 75).

However, many other scientific and psychological theories place imagination in opposition to reality, where reality takes priority (Watkins 21). This is the basis for cultural definitions of "normalcy" and "madness," leading to the devaluation of imaginal experience and the fear of imaginative expression.

Consulting with Guides

There are many ways to conceive of guides and to work with them. Here's how I think about it.

On working with imaginal beings

I've been in conversation with everything for as long as I can remember. Trees, pets, crayons, fairies, ideas, books—whatever I've been involved with, I've been in conversation with. I didn't know it was odd. It helped that my mother was amused, intrigued, and open to my babble, and I was not corrected for this behavior, as others might have been; nor have I had trouble distinguishing between "inner" and "outer" conversations, nor telling "real" from "imaginary" when need be (other than the six-foot tall wolf that once upon a time tried to kidnap me at night). I was simply hanging out in the third, and my "good enough mother," in Winnicott's terms, let the paradox remain unresolved.

One time I heard Mother telling Dad, incredulously: "Mary has these long, *long* conversations with the dog and cat. But you know, they sit and listen to her!" And I thought, 'Heck yeah, obviously. Why else would I do it?' That was the moment, though, that I recognized that it was different, that not everyone is privy to these wispy conversations. Here I became aware of my strong intuitive sense and my familiarity with the imaginal realm, for it's intuition that leads you into the imaginal. The third is my special place.

I like to help people see how intuition and intellect can work together. A strong intuition doesn't signify a weak intellect (AHEM); but dominant culture places logic and factual data in high regard and views intuition with suspicion. Obviously, if it's rational, logical, and scientific, then others can verify your experience. They can hop on your train of thought and ride along with you to your conclusions. An intuitive insight is more of a trail through the woods, often harder to follow and less convincing. Furthermore, while *your* intuition may tell you one thing, *mine* may tell me something different, so it's not so straightforward to find agreement on intuitive insights. That doesn't make them wrong, and it doesn't make them right, either.

Sometimes I must stash my intuitive self in the closet, or face damage to my credibility. Sometimes that's unfair, and sometimes, just plain sensible: don't expect people to see and understand everything that you do, or as you do — especially if it's invisible!

> A "good enough mother" is Winnicott's term to describe the parent who is responsive but not immediately so. This space between frustration and having needs perfectly met allows the child to develop a healthy relationship between fantasy and reality.

It's super important to remember this: simply because something comes to you intuitively, does not make it either RIGHT or WRONG. Don't treat it either as a rational thought or a moral imperative. It's another kind of observation. Noticing it doesn't necessarily mean you should act on it. And if your intuition tells you one thing, and mine tells me something else, that's something to notice, but not necessarily to argue over.

Helpful Spirits and Imaginal Beings

When I intentionally enter into the third to participate and engage creatively, I invite *Helpful Spirits* to join me. This is what that term means to me:

> *Helpful spirits are all around in countless forms,*
> *known and unknown, visible and invisible,*
> *simply qualified by their helpfulness.*

They may bring advice, guidance, support, alliance, inspiration, mentorship, or any manner of helpfulness needed, requested or appreciated in the moment. Not all helpful spirits are imaginal, in my way of thinking (and not all imaginal spirits are helpful, either).

Helpful spirits include real and imaginal beings, visible and invisible, past, present, and future. Helpful spirits may include my ancestors and my intellectual forebears; the teachers and authors and artists who have influenced me; and the books themselves that line my shelves and sometimes even jump out at me; my past self, my future self, my unexplored self; my dog and kitty who reliably hold space for me with their loving energy; my friends and my family. The birds, flowers, and trees, bees, that share my world, making it lovely and habitable. The imaginal beings and dream figures whose presence I'm aware of, and those whose presence I request; and the helpful beings and influences of whom I have little or no awareness, but who support and guide me nonetheless. Helpful spirits might include any being or presence in my ecosystem.

the candle burning on my altar...the pens and pencils and paints
and brushes...the figurines, puppets, dollies...the fresh water I drink...the smooth
wooden floor...the warming air...the photos and quotes on my walls and shelves...
the trees whose roots hold the earth beneath me, whose branches frame and pro-
tect "my space"...the philodendron growing greenly in the corner ...the lavender
blooms from my garden ...the tarot cards that spark insight...the old journals filled
with memories and concerns...my mommy holding me safe in her lap...

You see what I am getting at... Helpful spirits are all around in so many forms! As I perceive psyche in everything, the habit of dividing "matter" from "spirit" seems delusional. I feel gratitude for all the many forms that support and enrich and sustain my life.

How to invoke helpful spirits?
As in any situation, if you are seeking help, ask for help. It can be very simple.

For instance, when you are unsure of your next move in any situation, instead of burrowing into an anxious pattern of overthinking, pause and ask the question. Sometimes, the pause and the question are all you need, because then the answer immediately appears clear in that moment. But note, both the pause and the question are important steps, and you need to remember to take them intentionally.

"Questioning builds a way" Heidegger

1. If you notice you are spinning your wheels, or anxiously pinballing between options, that's the time to pause and take a breath... and formulate the question.

2. What, specifically, is your question? Often, when I get clear on what it is I'm wrestling with, the answer simply reveals itself. Or, if not...

3. The question provides the pathway to resolution. Knowing what you're looking for can point you in the right direction.

So you stop and clarify the question, then ask the question, and then, be open to receive the answer. Success! You have invoked a Helpful Spirit. As noted, it's always your choice whether or not to act on this guidance.

Also per the previous discussion on unknowns, I don't know if that Helpful Spirit is "actually" your personal unconscious, the Voice of God, or insight engendered by your dog's abiding love for you. Some people may claim to know, but I don't believe they know; I believe they believe. Anyway, I don't know. Or care. Although I can say with certitude, it is *Not All Me*. Just be open to participate in the continuum of love and support that exists within you and all around you.

You can enter into this process of clarifying your questions and receiving guidance in greater depth through the journaling process. As you journey through questions and follow-up questions, the journaling process itself helps you to clarify what question is really coaxing you forward. Reading the tarot is also a fabulous pathway to seeking and receiving guidance. Tarot + Journal = **sine qua non**. Just be sure to understand that the questions you choose to ask are already pointing you in a certain direction. "Questioning builds a way," says Heidegger ("Question" 311). Take time to clarify your questions!

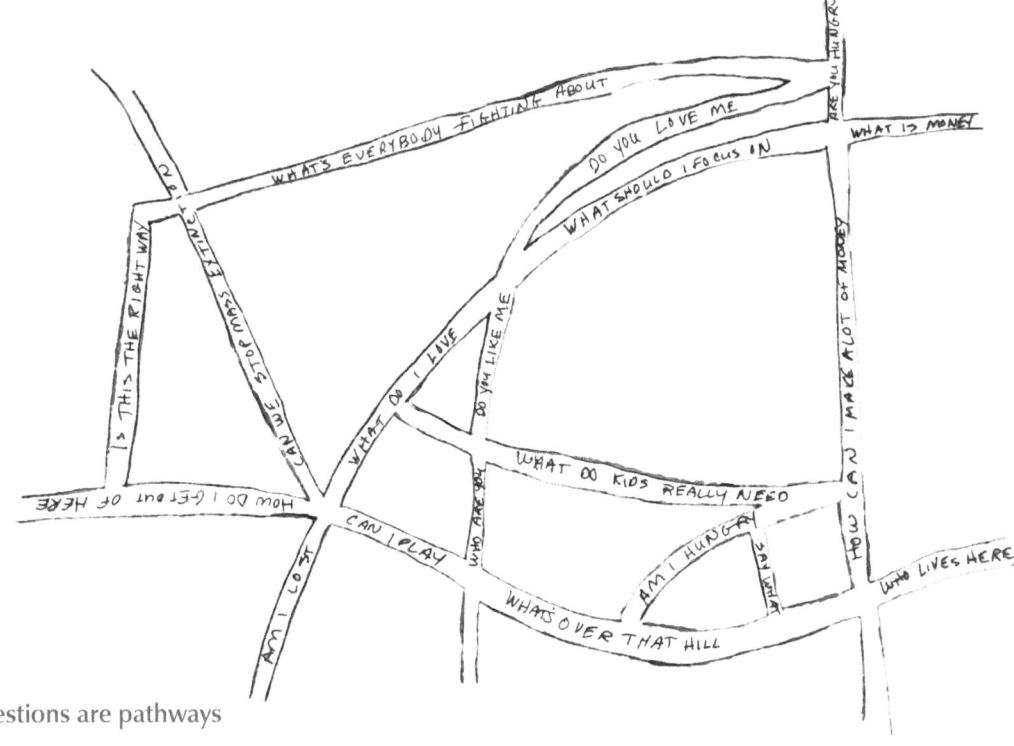

questions are pathways

Craft a ritual
You can develop your own ritual for a regular practice of invoking helpful spirits. Then, whenever you would like to engage in imaginal dialogue, you have a process to follow. Rituals become more meaningful as they are practiced over time. Remember, a ritual is simply repeatedly performing certain practices in a prescribed order. Give it whatever affect you like: that is, it can be mystical, magical, or matter-of-fact, according to your preferences.

In establishing a ritual for invocation, clarify your intention, include your practice of grounding and self-protection, set clear guidelines for your session, and **(extremely important!)** help yourself to recognize

- *it's not all you*
- *it's never all you*

Set clear guidelines:

+intention = I am open to interacting with you

+ guidelines = in this time space on this project

+ protection = only "helpful ones"

Let it be part of your invocation ritual to be grateful to all who help you along the way and in particular in this session. I recognize that there are so many ways I am supported, guided, helped, and mentored, many more than I am ever conscious of, more than I will ever know. So I give thanks to the unknowns, too.

Here is a simple ritual format for imaginal dialogue, in this case with a beloved ancestor.

Choose your setting, a place where you feel at ease. Create a clear space. Augment as desired with beautiful cloth, flowers, stones, photos, music... things that remind you of your ancestor or which you think would be meaningful or bring joy. Have paper and pencil at hand.

Relax.

Light a candle and focus your intention. Imagine the light filling your space with love, protection, clarity.

Sit silently for a bit, breathing and centering your attention within. Contemplate the conversation you would like to have, and write down the questions you would like to ask, leaving space for answers.

Bring the image of your ancestor to mind. Perhaps you have a photo, a letter, or a memory to assist you, or simply repeat the person's name over in your mind or aloud. You may have a strong sense of the person or not. Notice whatever characteristics become apparent to you. Notice how you feel as you contemplate this image.

Greet your ancestor as you would like (remember to always be respectful in this process) and say why you would like to have this conversation. If they seem agreeable, begin asking the questions you have prepared.

As you ask a question, pause and listen for the answer. You will probably not "hear" the answers as you normally hear conversation. Be attuned to the answers that form in your mind, and write them down. Don't try to control the responses but be present and take notes.

Ask your ancestor if there is anything else they would like you to know. When the conversation feels complete, express your thanks and say goodbye for now.

Bring your attention back to the sacred space you have created, your breath, your skin, the ground, the air. Notice that you are here, now. With gratitude for your experience, blow out your candle.

Take a moment to feel fully present. Add anything more to your notes.

Refer to the pages on Imaginal Dialogue in the How To Guide for more info.

A Simple Ritual Format

- *Create a sacred space*
- *Declare your intention*
- *Invite energetic presence*
- *Give thanks*
- *Bring closure*

A Guide to Guides
Bios of tricksters, psychopomps, and wise fools...

In this realm of the imaginal, shapeshifting may occur. One thing turns into another. You think you know what's happening, where you are, who you're dealing with... and suddenly the tables have turned—what's happening? It is not what you think it is. Ok, good. You're in between. In the dream world. In the shadows. One thing seems to be another. Which is it? Both, likely. Trying to resolve the question may mislead you. Don't force the paradox to resolution.

That said, getting familiar with some generic character types can be helpful.

Genii loci
Protective spirits in places. Numen, deity, or spirit whose presence is felt through a thing or a place. A guiding principle, force, or spirit. Local, personal, particular. birds trees rivers streams mushrooms nature spirits. Tune in to the presences in your world.

Psychopomps
Those who guide us between worlds: from the Greek, psukhē 'soul' + pompos 'conductor'. In classic mythology, they may lead the seeker to the realm of the dead. In your exploration of psyche, the psychopomp mediates between conscious and unconscious. They may connect you with the forgotten and unknown. They may guide you though shadowlands to inner treasures, offered to you as metaphor for better understanding your life.

Tricksters
Not all guides are tricksters, BUT—*tricksters are everywhere!* In fact, tricksters are quite capable of showing up unexpectedly in the guise of someone you thought you knew. There are unlimited permutations that fall into this archetypal category.

Tricksters are plentiful in the third, their chief characteristic being ambiguity: you're not sure who they are or how to take them: therefore, not trustworthy. Yet, potentially quite helpful! You thought they meant one thing, but then you realize they could've meant something else. They can be extremely entertaining and helpful, so long as you recognize the trickster nature at work. Tricksters do like to prank you, especially if you're over-confident; so don't take life too seriously, be ready for twists and turns, and you'll be fine.

Wise fools and passing strangers

Have you ever had the experience where someone says in passing just the thing you need to hear? You never knew who they were; you never saw them again; but they delivered you a crucial message. Pay attention! That happens in the café and in the imaginal realm, too. Not every helpful spirit turns into a long-term connection.

Who — What — Where are your genii loci?

Explore and contemplate your special places.
What other creatures do you notice or imagine? What
forms do they inhabit? What functions do they fulfill?
How might you engage with them?

genies of the earth:
an image that came to me in a dream

Gods as Guides: *A few of the biggies*

All gods have particular functions. This is true across mythological traditions. Hermes, Thoth, and Ganeśa are *psychopomps*, called upon to mediate between worlds, providing guidance and promoting communication, each in their own way. They travel between realms, bringing messages and translations, helping us to understand and make our experiences meaningful. While all gods are metaphorical, these gods in particular are gods of metaphor.

Ganeśa • Hindu
The beloved and generous Hindu god Ganesa is known as "the remover of obstacles."

Home alone, Parvati wanted to take a bath. She brought her son, Ganeśa, into form, that he might stand guard while she bathed.

Shiva returned home to find this unknown young man barring his way. Furious Shiva cut off the head of Ganeśa. When Parvati saw what had happened, she, too, was furious, and demanded that Shiva restore the life of her son. Shiva did so using the head of the first living being who crossed his path, *an elephant. Thus Ganeśa became the elephant-headed deity.*

Photo by Kirti Krishna Badkundri

Ganeśa is associated with the mystical phrase, *Tat tvam asi*, or I am that, or "Thou [the living being] art the visible Form of That [the supreme essence]." (*Ganapati Upanisad 2*)

With the form of an elephant-headed man or boy, Ganeśa expresses the unity of large and small being, or macrocosm and microcosm.

He is the Lord of Categories, a transcendent principle. As "the scribe who writes down the Scriptures" and the patron of writing and education, Ganeśa rules over the intellect. As the God of Obstacles, he both removes them and places them. He guards thresholds and his blessings are sought at the outset of any new endeavor. Ganeśa is associated in tantra yoga with the Serpent-Power or Kundalini-Shakti, "the universal Power as it is connected with the finite body-mind," which is envisioned, in its dormant state, as a serpent coiled around the base of the spine, and when awakened, shooting up to the crown to produce a union of human and divine (Feuerstein 86-87, 355-357)

Hermes • Greek
The Olympian god Hermes is characterized as trickster, psychopomp, navigator, wayfinder, messenger, narrator and storyteller.

The first thing Hermes does, on the day he is born, is to steal and hide the cattle of his elder brother Apollo. Apollo turns to their father Zeus for justice: "That's not fair!" Apollo seeks a judgment of right or wrong, but Hermes opens up another way: the way of the trickster. The beguiling infant tells his audacious version of the story with such cleverness that Zeus laughs. Not only is Hermes not punished for his deception, he is rewarded with his father's good humor and affection! He gets away with his pretense, not because he's believable, but because he's charming. Of course, he smooths things over with Apollo, demonstrating his considerable negotiation skills. By Day 2, Hermes has invented the lyre, which brings "jolliness, love and sweet sleep, whichever you want," and Apollo is charmed. In fact, via words and music, Apollo is not only happily persuaded to reconcile with Hermes, but becomes his champion: "You're going to have glory among the immortal gods," says the golden god of prophecy, and they become the best of companions (Homer, "Hymn to Hermes").

With his double snake-entwined staff, his wings, and his helmet of invisibility, Hermes traverses the three realms of underworld, mortal world, and lofty Olympus. He may show himself or remain invisible, but this is true of all gods, so Hermes' cap of invisibility means something else: "hidden motives and unseen connections" (Hillman, Dream 29).

Hermes is witty, clever, and playful. He knows the dirt, but don't expect him to tell it straight — if there is such a thing. He is associated with crossroads, choices, looking both ways, and talking out of both sides of his mouth.

He is known as the messenger of the gods; but his communications will not be straightforward. He gives the gift of insight, yet his messages carry more than one meaning: the obvious interpretation may flip like a coin. Hermes' facility with communication in all realms inclines him toward double entendres, though his audience may remain oblivious. The more adept one is at language, the greater the opportunity for word play.

Insider, outsider, neither or both? Hermes is a traveler, present in all walks of life. A traveler belongs everywhere and nowhere. His herms are erected at crossroads and boundaries, keeping the borders open, creating entryways and openings, and giving form to presence. At the border between worlds is where we may engage him as guide to the underworld, land of psyche. With his help, we mortals may travel imaginally where gods transcend and abide, the worlds beyond the limits of our lives.

herm
noun
a squared stone pillar with a carved head on top (typically of Hermes), used in ancient Greece as a boundary marker or a signpost.

Hermes Ingenui. Museo Pio-Clementino

Thoth • Egyptian
The Magician, the Scribe, the Judge, the Mediator, the Divine Physician. Thoth is god of wisdom, magic, language, and writing, from Egyptian tradition.

After Isis gives birth to Horus in the marshes, the baby is bitten by a poisonous creature. Isis' cries stop the Sun Boat as it crosses the heavens, and Thoth comes down to see what has happened. He gives protection to Isis and heals the infant Horus. Thoth is a wise counselor, whose magic, often instructive, is frequently conjured with words. He knows the names of all things.

Thoth is often found in the form of either ibis or baboon (Pinch, Short Intro 36). He travels as the navigator/companion of Re (or Ra), the sun. Thoth IS the moon, and Thoth is also protector of the moon (Boylan 74). Through lunar cycles, Thoth holds cosmic order and marks calendrical time, giving humans a framework within which to measure our lives. Time frames daily experience between light and dark; and time frames human life within infinitude, thus making it seem comprehensible to us. Thoth determines Pharaonic reigns and length of life (Boylan 85). Thoth is an important figure in transitioning to and navigating the afterlife. He is judge of the gods, the mediator who brings maat (order and right relationship) (Hornung 142). Maat (daughter of Re) and Thoth are consorts, showing the close relationship between cosmic balance and daily order. As above, so below.

Like all immortals, Thoth is outside of time. Just as it takes a third dimension to hold two, and a fourth to hold the third, only one who transcends time can hold time; and we, in order to measure the physical, must use knowledge and abilities that are beyond the physical: imagination, intellect, and intuition.

Hieroglyphs (sacred writing) are particularly associated with Thoth, who is believed to have invented all language and writing, as well as all science, philosophy, religion, and magic. Remembering that the basis of magic is metaphor, it makes sense that Thoth was said to possess more *heka* (power which sustains the cosmos) than any other male deity, and his temple at Hermopolis included a library replete with books of magic and ancient records. (Pinch, Magic 28).

The integration of word and image found in hieroglyphs allows for expansive play of meaning, multiple levels of interpretation, and greater potential to carry secret knowledge. Hieroglyphs were thought to be potentially alive, and hieroglyphic script was used to communicate with gods and ancestors (Pinch, Short Intro 15-16).

Striding Thoth.
Metropolitan Museum of Art.

Thoth as Baboon.
The Louvre.

Who was Hermes Trismegistus?

Hermes Trismegistus by Giovanni di Stefano.

A man? A god? A magician? An alchemist. The figure of Hermes Trismegistus is a conflation of Thoth and Hermes, demonstrating the syncretic nature of mythology, as it shifts in response to world events A corresponding shift in the imaginal cosmology enables teachings to be carried forward, but in a new way. Hermes Trismegistus was an important figure in alchemy, emerging during the Hellenistic period (323-30 bce), when the conquests of Alexander the Great brought an infusion of Greek culture into North African and South Asian cultures. The Greeks found similarities between Thoth and Hermes. Thrice Great was one of Thoth's titles, which translates to the Greek as trismegistos. Whether historic or apocryphal, Hermes Trismegistus is credited as author of the Hermetica.

He is also associated with the Islamic prophet Idris and the biblical Enoch.

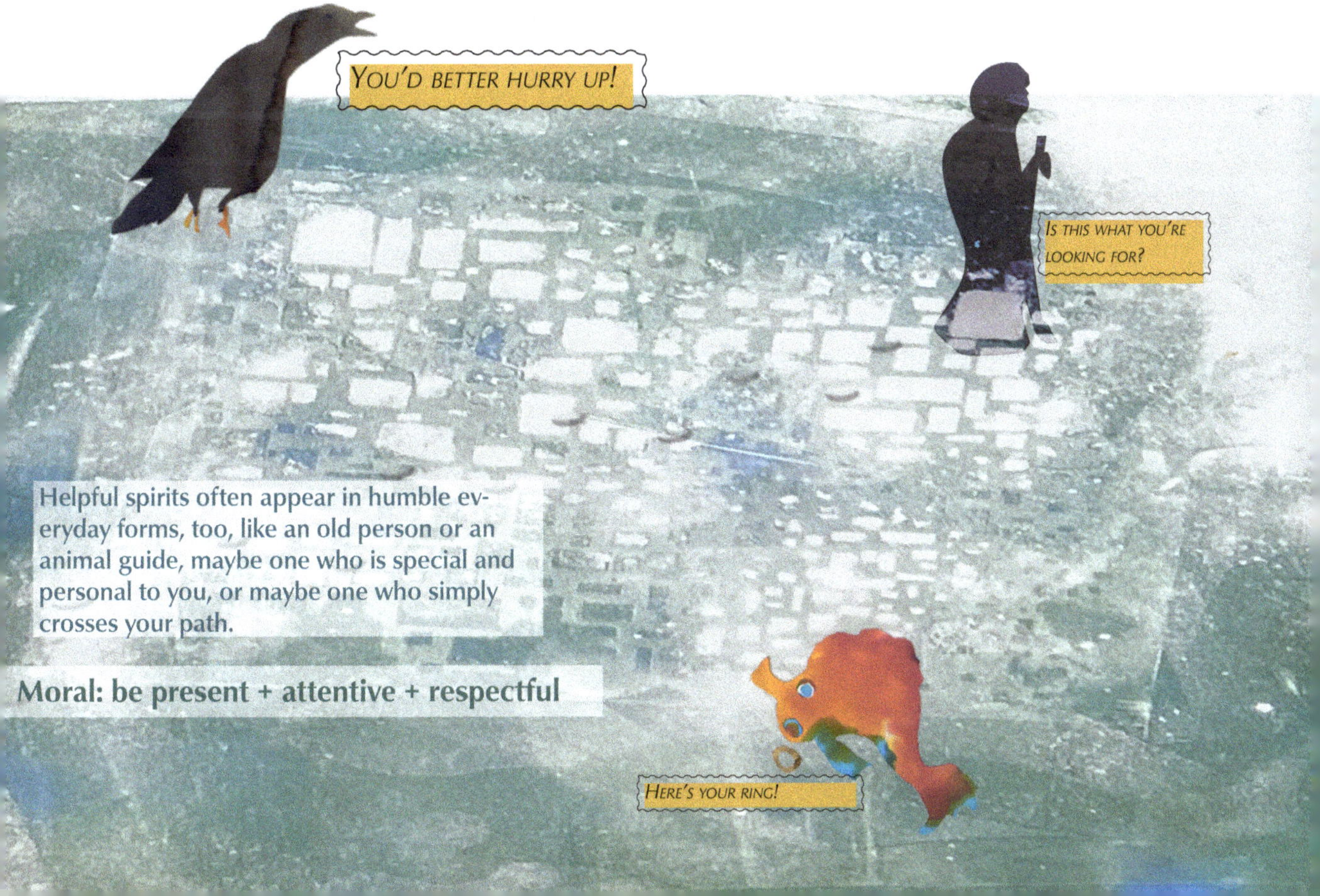

You'd better hurry up!

Is this what you're looking for?

Helpful spirits often appear in humble everyday forms, too, like an old person or an animal guide, maybe one who is special and personal to you, or maybe one who simply crosses your path.

Moral: be present + attentive + respectful

Here's your ring!

Tricksters to Know
(and know — they are everywhere...)

Mercury

A Roman god with many of the same functions and characteristics of Hermes, yet he is distinct god. Mercury is especially a god of trade, commerce and finance, patron of travelers and thieves both. Like Hermes, Mercury is the psychopomp who guides souls into the afterlife, the messenger who brings dreams, and the god of eloquence.

Djinni

A class of spirits from Arabic and Islamic mythology. Like humans they have free will, but they are naturally invisible and are able to shapeshift. They generally avoid humans but can interact in a multitude of ways. They are called on for protection or magical aid, but also to cause harm.

Eshu

A Yoruban divinity, Eshu is trickster, messenger, and intermediary. Known as "He-who-creates-problems-for-the-innocent" he is, however, protector of the elderly and small children, often appearing in these forms. Talkative and friendly, he holds the balance between extremes. He teaches the divine message of Ifá through divination. He lives at the crossroads.

Coyote

A trickster character common to many indigenous North American traditions, pivotal in many creation stories. He is known for both humor and deceit. In some stories he is considered malevolent, yet again, his acts often result in benefits for humans, whether or not that was his intent. Coyote is clever and strategic but often ends up the butt of his own jokes.

Trickster Qualities to Watch For:

Magic

Mystery

Shapeshifting

Slipperiness

Amorality

Humor

Shadow

Ambiguity

> WHY ARE THEY ALL GUYS?

> YEAH, I THINK THAT'S A TRICK

You stand before two doors, each with a guard. One door leads to freedom, the other to certain death. Only the guards know which is which.

One guard always tells the truth and the other always lies, but you don't know which is which.

Before choosing a door to pass through, you may ask one question of one guard only. What will you ask?

The simple answer is to ask either one what the other guard would say and go through the opposite door.

The imaginal interview: vetting your guides
It's up to you whether to choose a particular imaginal being as a guide. Sometimes they do just appear in your life and offer you guidance, which is a gift. But you make the decisions about which guidance to take seriously and which to brush off, just as in any other part of your life; sometimes you will feel trust and sometimes not. You can develop relationships with imaginal beings just as you can develop relationships with humans... *and animals and trees and books and...*

Do you really need to set up a formal interview with your potential imaginal guides? No. But you could, if you like. Formal or not, you can engage in conversation—imaginal dialogue, let's say. Explore whatever topics and ask whatever questions seem cogent. And if the conversation is fruitful, great! Then you may want to meet again. And, if not, just let it go.

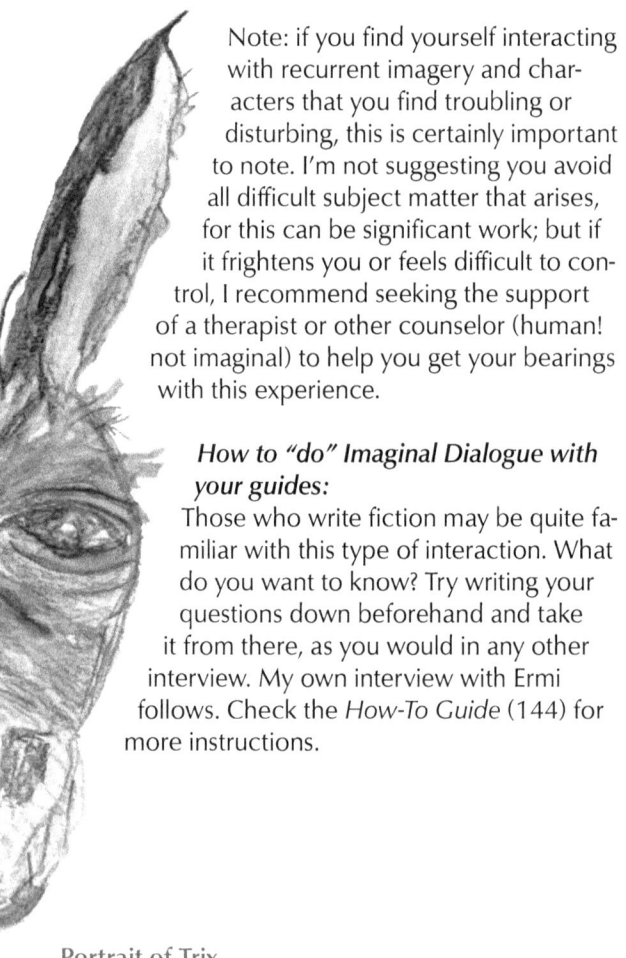

Note: if you find yourself interacting with recurrent imagery and characters that you find troubling or disturbing, this is certainly important to note. I'm not suggesting you avoid all difficult subject matter that arises, for this can be significant work; but if it frightens you or feels difficult to control, I recommend seeking the support of a therapist or other counselor (human! not imaginal) to help you get your bearings with this experience.

How to "do" Imaginal Dialogue with your guides:
Those who write fiction may be quite familiar with this type of interaction. What do you want to know? Try writing your questions down beforehand and take it from there, as you would in any other interview. My own interview with Ermi follows. Check the *How-To Guide* (144) for more instructions.

Portrait of Trix

Meet My Marginal Characters: Ermi+Trix
You may have noticed Ermi and Trix chiming in from the margins. Ermi is an imaginal being whom I have noticed "around" for a while: certainly a trickster, notably snarky and puckish, generally good-humored and fun. I have oodles of doodles and sketches of them. They pop up in notebooks and grocery lists all the time. But I've only imaginally introduced myself recently, during the process of writing this book. *Oh!* I thought, *here's a guide to help readers navigate through this text — that's helpful!* As I got to know them, Ermi and Trix were intrigued and intriguing. Thus, we began working together on this project.

Portrait of Ermi

Here's a little bit about them:
ErmiTrix is imaginary, ambiguous, and gender fluid. Sometimes he is a she, sometimes, she is a he, or neither/nor; they are definitely a shape-shifting trickster (if you can say *anything* definitive about an imaginal shapeshifting trickster). They have been called ErmiTrix, although, more recently, Ermi and Trix are two different entities.

Ermi gives me helpful guidance AND ALSO I do not leave Ermi in charge of this project, or they might just lead me off into the wilderness on a lark; this project might take so many twists and turns, running off on so many great new tangents that it might never get finished. So Ermi is not in charge, thank you very much. But Ermi IS a very important and highly valued contributor and guide, who knows the ins-and-outs of the in-between, crosses boundaries with ease, and keeps the journey fun. I like them a lot and I appreciate their presence.

What about Trix? My good-humored, furry, imaginal companion is with me every step of the way, tells it like it is, and will stop dead in the middle of the road, refusing to take another step, in order to make a point. EE-yore.

Ermi dressing up

Interview with ErmiTrix
Welcome. Thank you for coming
Thank you for having me.

Is ErmiTrix your preferred name?
It's Ermitrice actually—well, actually, I have lots of names. It depends. Call me Ermi.

It sounds sort of like Hermes…
Yes, we're related. How closely, it's hard to say.

What is your interest in this project?
It has a lot of potential. I deal in potential.

Meaning?
Potential is what something might be; Before it's nailed down, hardened, calcified. It's fluid, in the process of becoming.

Humans need to learn to navigate the metaphorical realm and engage more directly with the potential of the imaginal. Rather than trying to nail everything down.

And why do you care?
Yeah, why don't I just let you all destroy the world?

Wow. Can you say more?
There's great danger and foolishness in concretizing everything. NOT wise foolishness. I mean, if you think Midas was bad… If all possibilities were to harden into facts and forms, no change would be possible. Nada. The end.

How do you see your role?
I'm your guide to the imaginal experience. I'm comfortable moving between worlds: inner/outer, light/shadow, living/dead, mortal/immortal. They call me "psychopomp." I'm a wayfinder, a messenger. I can take you to hell and back, baby. I know pretty much everyone; I'm a natural to help people make connections.

Sounds very altruistic...
well, like I said, I deal in potential. For better, for worse. It's my function.

How did you come to be involved?
I'm always on the lookout for curious fools. Mary fits the bill. Haha, and I say that with the utmost affection. We crossed paths one day when she was wandering around in the woods. I dropped a few crumbs and she followed me home.

I guess she imagined me—or did I imagine her? ...same diff...

What do you most enjoy about this work?
Always something new —the discoveries. The magic. Mysteries unfolding. Jokes.

It's never boring!

I can tempt you—oh, let's say "inspire"—to open into possibilities. Then we see what happens. That's entertainment!

That sounds...possibly, a little dark?
I'm not the devil, if that's what you're suggesting. Evil is a human trait, as far as I know — not my department. But—inspire? tempt? That's a coin flip. Who's to say about the moral implications. That's for Jupiter to decide, or Saturn, maybe Athena...Or Arthur Dimmesdale, haha! Not my job, man. Take it up with Thoth or Ganesa.

What is your biggest challenge?
People who think I don't exist. As if the imaginal and metaphorical aren't real. Hello?

And then there are those who see me but consider me inconsequential. At their own peril, I'm afraid! heh, heh

Is that a threat??
lol Far be it from me! Just the reality, ma'am. I might bite you in the ass if you underestimate me... Oops! Sorry! (not sorry)

Ok. Speaking of...Are there places people get stuck or traps they should be aware of?

Sure there are traps everywhere and you can get stuck anywhere. Some people are trapped in the rational world. Some people are trapped in fantasy. And yes, you can certainly spend too much time wandering around in between. Just be clever and keep it moving, keep checking in, that's my approach. Don't limit yourself to one realm too long. Be fluid. Be a continuity. Exercise your imagination AND your two feet. I'm here to poke you if you start to calcify. I'll whistle if you get too diffuse.

Your guidance sounds, potentially, a little superficial.

Ok, sure, that's what my detractors say. Nobody's perfect—I mean, nobody's everything, right? But superficial? No, that's up to you. Because I'll show you things you won't find any other way. That's what we call "the shadow"-- yours, not mine, btw. But if you're avoidant, if you look the other way, if you won't look closely, if you think it's all meaningless, that's your choice. Be forewarned!

What would you really like people to know?

You know, sure, I joke around. I may not be entirely trustworthy... Who is? but you don't have to trust me implicitly. I don't have power over you, except what you give me. But you gotta have fun. Even the Dalai Lama says so. So... 'nuff said. Be clever. Pay attention. Play is serious business—but don't take it too seriously.

What advice would you give?

Do something silly. Try something new. Make a mistake. Follow your curiosity (aka, me). Listen for the "What if...?" 'cause that will be me talking to you.

Closing thoughts?

Just keep your wits about you. You know, coyotes know how to take the meat and shit on the trap. Just sayin'...

"Between the shadows of death where they finally must lose themselves, and the pure luminosity of the divine which remains inaccessible to them, human beings live in a middle world, divided between day and night" (Vernant 44).

Cosmologies and World-Making: Mapping the Territory

Maps are models; and, whether of the cosmos or of your neighborhood, maps are always metaphorical. One thing stands for another: this line for a road; that one for a river; and so on.

When you use a map, you enter into a particular worldview that influences you to notice certain things and be unaware of others. A map never contains all the data and details and depth of the lived experience. If it did it wouldn't be a map it would just be — *life*. To make a map is to choose what's most important, often toward a specific purpose; so, maps carry worldviews. Making a map is a way of visualizing a world.

A cosmology is a model of the universe, holding the thoughts, dreams, beliefs and imaginings of those who created it. You could think of a cosmology as the map of a mythic tradition, the imaginal structure that contains and orders all of its stories.

Cosmologies of the imaginal landscape connect infinity with the finite. Each frames some part of the infinite, scaled for human understanding. Our models are limited by our human limits, but remember that reality isn't limited to our models, and it's not limited to what humans can comprehend, and certainly we are aware of much more than we can define. There is always more possibility that lies beyond the border of what we know. We create meaning by exploring what we don't know.

Just as the flat earth model was once a commonly held conception of the cosmos, the maps that we use to navigate physical space are also artifacts with cosmological significance. For instance, when we establish the north pole as an absolute point to which all others are relative, or create a grid and reference points from lines of latitude and longitude, these common usages reflect an internalized model of the cosmos,*

> *which is not simply a work of imagination, but which uses imagination to extend from facts as we understand them; in other words, <u>metaphorically true but not literally true</u>-- and that's mythology!

> "What a useful thing a pocket-map is!" I remarked.
>
> "That's another thing we've learned from your Nation," said Mein Herr, "map-making. But we've carried it much further than you. What do you consider the largest map that would be really useful?"
>
> "About six inches to the mile."
>
> "Only six inches!" exclaimed Mein Herr. "We very soon got to six yards to the mile. Then we tried a hundred yards to the mile. And then came the grandest idea of all! We actually made a map of the country, on the scale of a mile to the mile!"
>
> "Have you used it much?" I enquired.
>
> "It has never been spread out, yet," said Mein Herr: "the farmers objected: they said it would cover the whole country, and shut out the sunlight ! So we now use the country itself, as its own map, and I assure you it does nearly as well."
>
> ---Lewis Carroll, *Sylvie and Bruno Concluded*, Chapter XI, London, 1893

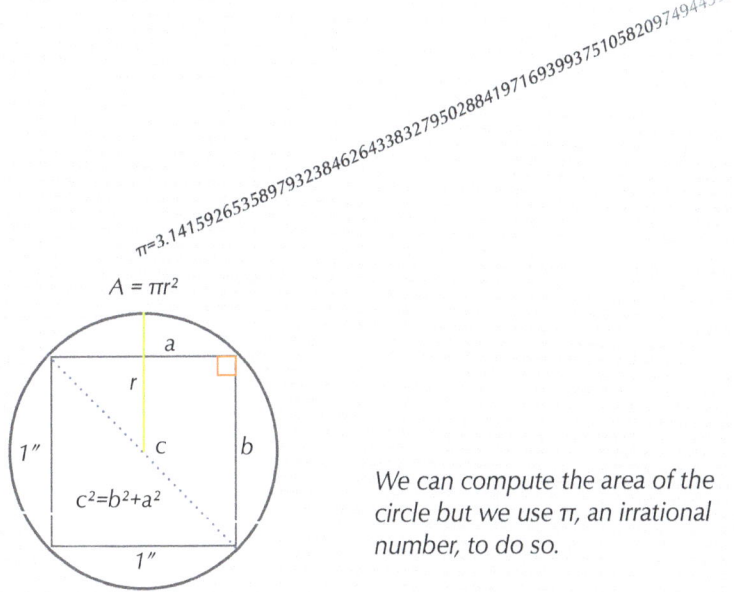

We can compute the area of the circle but we use π, an irrational number, to do so.

Measurable experience stands at the center of our shared understanding of reality, for that which is defined, quantifiable and repeatable provides a focus for cultural agreement.

Logical expression depends on measurement, in terms of definition and quantification; and for that which can be measured and quantified, logic is very useful. "If this, then that." But rationalist reduction leads to excluding that which doesn't fit into this model; what one can't count doesn't count.

If rationality defined the limits of truth and meaning, the immeasurable would be reduced to insignificance, aberrance or absurdity.

There is much beyond reason, and not only numbers, whose value can be noted but not defined rationally. Infinity is indefinable. We use logic and rational thought to frame a little bit of space and time in the midst of an incomprehensible infinity.

How can we construct a model to describe metaphysical reality? A systematic equation of microcosm to macrocosm is a model to contemplate the world beyond our understanding. Positing a consistent relationship between microcosm and macrocosm is a natural and logical extension of the theory of unus mundus, one world across which natural laws apply, and inner and outer are not separate, but continuous. Versions of this model are found in Greek, Egyptian, Chinese, Hindu, and Dogon cultures, (among others) and in the contemporary western world.

Maps and Snaps

There are perhaps an infinite number of conceptions of the cosmos! Here are a few snapshots illustrating how a variety of people have framed their mythic and imaginal cosmic explorations. Mythology is multi-faceted!

See Image Credits page for more information.

Gulliver's Travels
Coloured Picture Book for the Nursery, 1883

Cosmic Man
Shape of Universe, Jain Cosmology, 17th c

Nun Raises the Sun
Nun, god of the waters of chaos, lifts the barque of the sun god Ra
1050 BCE

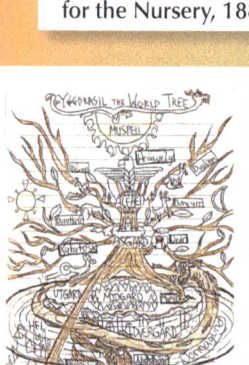

Yggdrasil: Norse Cosmology
Nathanael Weir-Wakely

Mount Meru
Bhutanese Thanka of the Buddhist Universe

Sufi Celestial Map
Museum of Turkish and Islamic Arts, Istanbul, 1583

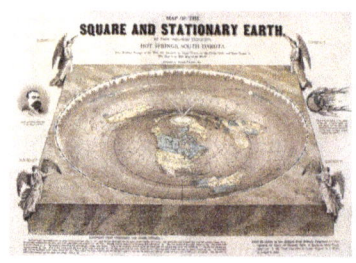

Flat Earth
Orlando Ferguson, 1893

Rabbit Hole
Generative AI

Sky Woman
"Indian Arts Project" Ernest Smith 1936

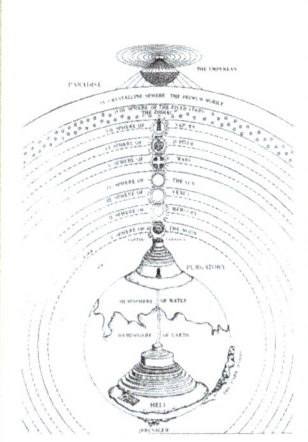

Overview of Dante's Divine Comedy
Michelangelo Caetani 1855

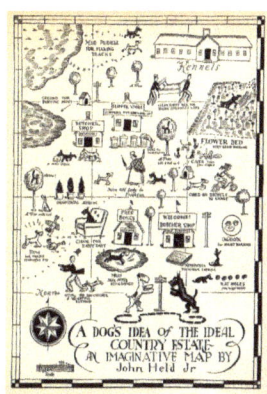

A Dog's Idea
John Held, 1925

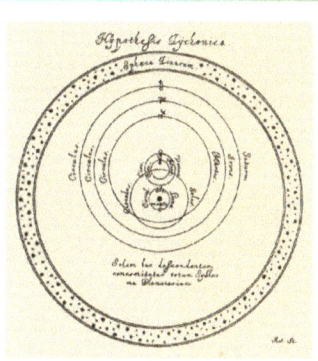

Hypothesis Tychonica
Hevelius' Selenographia, 1647

The Big Bang
Generative AI Evon J

Hobbiton
J.R.R. Tolkien

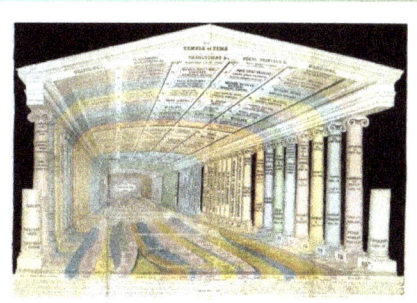

Temple of Time,
Memory Palace, Emma Willard 1846

Orrery
Robert Brettell Bate, c. 1812

Google Cosmology
© 2025 Google Maps

Explore the territory

What will you find when you enter the expansive, intuitive, creative, imaginal realm of the third? It may be whatever you imagine! It may be more. It's worth poking around.

Be in the place where you are. Always start where you are. Notice things you haven't noticed before. Whispering trees. Warm rocks. Chipmunk holes. Curious buildings. Cracks in the sidewalk. As you wander and notice your environs, also notice the thoughts and the images that come to you, or that you are following.

Am I talking about wandering physically, or imaginally? Either/or. Both. Maybe you're starting within a dream world, or in your back yard. In any case, you, human, are physically embodied and embedded, physically present in the world; and whether eyes are closed or open, whether body is still or in motion, you can notice the influences, feelings, presences, shapes, around you and within you; and wherever you are, inner and outer realities are also. Always. You are at once subject and object; you are at once subjective and objective.

BE while you SEE: practice the fluidity of inner and outer states.

Ask for direction, if you like; but find your own way.

Keep a journal

You'll bring back many stories from the Third; be sure to track your adventures. A journal is a "best practice" to record your findings. I would say it's essential, because for me, it is; but you'll do as you like.

Journal-keeping creates a connection between your imaginal life and your waking reality, and that's what this book is all about: practices that enhance a fluidity of experience, integrating inner+outer worlds, letting each inform and nourish the other. There are so many ways you can keep a journal, as noted in the Practices Guide. So, do as you like. Find what works for you.

> *See some examples from my own journals and journeys in the next section,* ***Mary's Adventures in the Third.***

Keep a travelogue of your experiences.

Make your own map

As you explore imaginal territory, you can create a map of your own experience. This map will in some sense hold the mythology that you are exploring and creating.

You can make a map of anything. Your inner cosmology. Or your outer one. Your closet. Narnia. The places where you've seen birds, or where you'd like to see birds. Last night's dream. Last night's dinner. What I'm trying to say: map YOUR experiences, and include what YOU find important. You can include inner AND outer features. YOU choose the scale. Zoom way, way in or way, way out. Map the places you've been and the places you'd like to go. Map your feelings. Map your observations. Map your ideas. You decide. Make multiple maps. And remember that maps are artifacts of your own mythological thinking. They record how you understand the world and what you find important. AND they shape the road ahead.

Am I lost?

-or-

In the thick of it...

What would you like to map?

What details and data are important?

What are the limits?

What is the scale?

Is it 2D? 3D? 4D? 5D?

Compare notes
When you compare your map with other maps, you find common ground as well as difference. I really believe in making my own map, but it's just as important to find out where others have been and what they've discovered. What a pleasure to peruse maps and all the different ways that people conceptualize the world. It's limitless! Think of it as a specific genre within the study of world cultures and mythologies. I love it for the same reasons: sharing and studying these different ways helps me to clarify what's important to me, and how I'm like others, and how I'm different. And it excites the imaginal impulse.

Immerse yourself. Learn what others have discovered. That helps me to choose my own direction. That's what makes it fun. That's my way of making my own maps.

There are great books and sites that share a wealth of maps; *AND ALSO* you can go beyond the confines of "maps-proper" and consider artworks, musical compositions, gardens, culinary delights, any sort of creative expression as someone's imaginal journey.

What have others noticed that you hadn't? Where have you made a new way? What's next to explore?

My Cosmology

The Mythos-Sphere is an idea I developed for my doctoral work, and subsequently adopted it as my business name. It's my own cosmology, in a way.

Imagine the Mythos-Sphere as our ever-changing world of experience, evolving out of our direct perceptions, and including all that we notice of the things and aspects of our vital existence, and all the ideas and stories and imaginings and creations that emerge from that.

The Mythos-Sphere is a multi-dimensional imaginal structure formed of beliefs, images, stories, songs, dreams, memories, patterns, abstractions, artifacts, treasures and junk, meaningful rituals and unconscious habits, broken traditions and emergent ones...

> **mythos-sphere** definition
> [mith-os-sfeer] | noun
> • a cosmology
> • the expression and understanding that result from the group creative process; the set of shared awareness, including explicit and unspoken, inner and outer, conscious and unconscious, individual and collective, intuitive and intellectual, material and imaginal
> • the container
> • the contents
> • the third
> • the territory of participation

We live in a Mythos-Sphere

· ·

Games as Maps—and Vice Versa

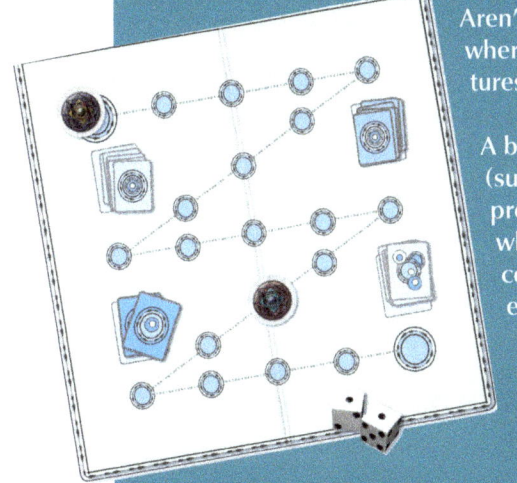

Aren't game boards like maps? Telling you where you can go and where you can't go, rules about what happens when, and adventures in the places where you're not sure what will happen.

A blend of rules (structure) and choice (hello) and chance (surrender). A satisfying game gives you these things in the right proportion– whatever that is for you–so you have a sense that what you do makes a difference–some things are beyond your control, but if you're smart enough, agile enough, and lucky enough, you may end up where you wanted to go.

So, if you make a map of your imaginal adventures, add some rules and you can play it like a game; likewise, if you have a cool game board that you love, use it as the layout for your next imaginal adventure.

*For "map"' you can substitute any number of words or concepts. See John Cage and chance operations. Or, let the game board be an oracle.

Journey's End: Exiting the In-Between

When the party's over, remember to leave!

How do I get out of here?
Leaving these dreamy conversations and expressions hanging is like leaving the shop door open when you're ready to pick up the kids and head home for dinner. So how do you close up shop? When you've had enough exploring the imaginal realm, bring your attention to the here and now: the skin on your body, the ground beneath your feet, the time of day, the regular rhythm of your breath. I like to say "Thanks, that's it for today." And I often clap my hands: "The End."

It's good to wrap up your sessions and make a clear transition back to normal waking reality, and some sort of grounding attention to the physical, somatic realm is a great way to do it. If you neglect this step, you may find your energy and attention drifty and dribbling off into the ethers.

Again, the third is a wonderful expansive area that can be opened and entered at any time to great benefit, but/and also, we need to be able to function effectively with clarity in the waking world where decisions must be made and actions taken. With your mental image of the territory, it becomes that much easier to notice when you're spacing out. Manage your attention and get yourself back to where you need to be when you need to be there.

What should I do with all this weird stuff I've made?
Oh man, that's the question. I'm writing this book, so I should have a really good answer to this question. Truthfully, this is the hardest part for me. I'm not as good at it as I'd like to be, but...it's a practice. It is not healthy for me or anyone to have all the 'what if's' hanging on forever. Do as I say and not as I do: Don't leave too much unfinished business laying around! It's like having a lot of leaky faucets.

Circling back: Finishing projects and unfinished projects
Many of my every day creative conversations will inspire me to take an idea further or craft it into a work more intentional. A lot of experiments become potential collage material or the foundation for some other more intentional work. Some are obviously simply heading straight to the recycler.

Silk-Purse-from-Sow's-Ear Syndrome (SiPSES)

Yes, I suffer from this. Let me tell you about it. I do a lot of experiemental stuff–yes, that's what I've been talking about. I don't worry about how it turns out because I'm into the process– check! I make lots of stuff that's ugly– fine. But what trips me up is that I also make lots of stuff that I think is cool, but I don't know what to do with it. Starting as an experiment, it's probably not made with great skill or the best quality materials, but if I really like it, I try to imagine I can turn it into some well-finished project. I might spend a lot of time trying to make that happen, and sometimes it's successful, but most of the time, I'd really be better off using my experiemnt as a template, and starting fresh with materials chosen with the finished project in mind. Do as I say, not as I do...

There are also many creative meanderings that end up in my "hmmm" pile – I think, maybe I'd like to work with that more, or maybe not. I don't know yet. That's fine, it's really great; I may later find inspiration or use for them another day. But that pile can (will) keep growing and growing, so it's important to circle back and sort through the pile.

After a while, if you can't decide whether you care about something or not, then you probably don't. I mean, you're the judge of it, and these decisions may come easily to you. I hope so! Whatever the case, don't let the "hmmm, I'm not sure" pile get too big, unless you want *that* to be your life's work. *Which is actually kind of interesting...* But no. It's like staying in the third and never coming out. OK. At some point, it's just too much.

I circle back regularly to sort through things. I'll use some materials that I've generated, and I'll throw some out, and recycle some. There will always be some I'm really just not sure about; and then, on another day, it will be clear. Sometimes the decision of whether to keep a thing or throw it out seems pretty random but those are choices that I have to make. I think anyone who makes stuff has "a stash" and has to navigate a path between "I'm appreciating possibilities" and "That's just plain hoarding." I have to say, I like the pile, just as it is: for all its colors and feelings and weirdness, there's a sort of energy vibrating in that pile of "hmmm"... but for me that's only because it is ever-evolving and also because it has limits. I do need to keep my home and work space kind of neat or I'll feel crazy-distracted (that's where my useful little OCD kicks in).

Well, like I said, if I can't decide, it probably doesn't matter. Maybe hmmm means humus...

You'll figure it out for yourself...

Remember, your choices are:

- Keep it
- Give it away
- Throw it out

Compost the unfinished expressions.

Soup or Compost: Here's a game I like to play when cleaning the fridge. Everything has to go into the compost bin or the soup pot. It works in the studio as well!

Mary's Adventures in the Third: A Travelogue

Some examples from my journals and journeys to share how I use this process to explore, discover, and connect.

Here are some pages from my own imaginal travels, gathered from various times and places, and reformatted for this book. Not chronological. They're here to illustrate some "whys" and "hows" of the ways I explore, as well as some "wheres." It's a smattering: when I tell you I have shelves full of journals and drawers full of sketches, it's no exaggeration. I picked out a few things to show a range.

Mainly visuals because—easier to share than other creative expressions.

It's been a tricky matter for me to share my own creative experiences, relative to this process, BECAUSE if I share the really cool stuff, it seems like ego, out of place here for obvious reasons: "Look at this really awesome stuff I DID"; so I like to share some crap as well, in the interest of demonstrating that it's not all really awesome stuff, that creating crap is part of the process, an important part, really-- BUT in my experience no one really wants to see that, and if I just show crap, people will say, "So what? Big deal! Anybody can make shit like that." Yes. That's my point. But it's a little tricky to share. Thanks, trickster, I see you.

Obviously, these are not only "messing arounds" but also include some pieces I've spent a fair amount of time on, but all of them began as creative forays into the imaginal realm.

So here's some stuff I've done along the way.

Contents

- One Bird Singing — 246
- Turtle & O'ma — 247
- Meeting with the Queen of Wands — 250
- Visible/Invisible — 252
- The Lounsbury Game — 255
- Saguaro — 256
- All Dried Up? — 257
- Nature Spirit — 258
- Tree Spirit — 258
- Cybele — 259
- The Dream Mentor — 260
- Love You, Baba Yaga — 264
- The Smiling Cottage — 265
- The Yaga — 266
- Mood — 268
- Prayer Flags — 269
- Hanging — 270
- Balance — 270
- Monsters & Demons — 271
- Murmuration — 272
- rando prints — 276
- journal outtakes — 277

TRAVELOGUE

>> One Bird Singing

one bird lifts me up, calls me into the world. I don't know which bird you are, but you infuse me with joy and vitality. Even my own humble presence may also make a difference in the lives of others, just a smile or a kind thought, even when they don't know who I am. You don't need applause.

"The woods would be very silent if no birds sang except those who sang best." - Henry Van Dyke

>> Turtle & O'ma

My work of adaptation extending from an event I facilitated.

My doctoral dissertation included my design and implementation of a three-day collaborative art-and-story making experience for a group of six participants. Afterward, I took time to connect creatively with the materials, images, and stories that emerged from the event, exploring the themes that come up repeatedly or with resonance for me. How did this process wind its way into my life and into my own future?

I'm following my own instructions: Let it be imperfect, spontaneous, improvisational. Don't try to fit everything in. Just stay with what draws my attention. Work within a limited time frame. Whatever happens is fine.

My method is slightly different but similar to the group process we carried out: Tune in to the environment, invite a character through imaginal dialogue, work with my hands, use structure and collage to arrange and assemble the pieces, invoke divination to point the way, then dream it on: as I seek and find aspects of the stories and images in the world and in my life, patterns become evident.

What follows is the story that came to me, with thanks to the contributions of all participants

TRAVELOGUE

More to the Story

Ō-ma' stirs the cauldron, humming. If you look into the pot, you see she is making spirals ... Spinning in—in—in to the center.

*

Fleeing the cacophony of modern life, No Bullshit Woman enters the forest, unsure of which way to go. Wilderness lies to one side, but looking the other way, she sees a rose petal on the ground. Then another ... Following what seems like a trail of petals she comes to an enormous, glorious, rose bush, covered in blooms. She buries her head in its pinkness, intoxicated by the fragrance. Suddenly, she hears a rustling above her. Startled, she looks up, but sees nothing. Wait, there it is again! What is it? She can hardly catch a glimpse. Is it ... a monkey? Unlikely. Strange. She follows the stirring of the leaves, trying to get a better look ... Whatever it was seems to be gone---but she realizes she has wandered off the path! Is she going the right way? The wrong way? Who knows?

She blazes her own trail, trying to make sense of her surroundings. Reaching the edge of the forest, a vast spacious meadow opens up before her. She stops to take it all in, pondering, feeling, breathing. No, not that way, she decides. Turning around, she circles back into the forest. She spies a tiny mushroom...and then another...and then another. Crouching down to take a closer look, she perceives a beautiful order arising out of the chaos and confusion. The world is speaking to her. The trees are talking. Strange, but clear. A tinkling sound, a sudden flash ... signs lead her toward the center of the forest, where she comes upon a still blue lake. Her vision is drawn into the reflecting water. A smooth, large rock rests near its center. She squats down to look deeply.

*

How long has she been there? She has lost track of time, stirring only when she notices the still water begin to move, spiraling like a whirlpool. The rock is moving. Hard, like a rock---but not a rock. Slowly, slowly, rising from the lake, the water running in rivulets off his ancient shield, comes the Turtle. Eye to eye, he walks slowly and determinedly toward No

Bullshit Woman, his vulnerable neck stretching forward, out of his safe protective shell. She looks into his eyes, and smiles. Something changes in her. Something changes in the world.

*

After a long moment, she knows it is time to move on. Renewed, she begins her journey back to the world. Her path seems clear to her now. Moving almost effortlessly, she is in tune with the flow of life streaming all around and through her.

From time to time, as she travels, she sees a solitary man wandering on and off the path ahead of her. How irritating! She enjoys her solitude. He seems strange, silent, troublesome. Is he trustworthy? Dangerous? Sane? She is relieved when he wanders off.

But again, he is there. Hard to avoid him, but she does. She is wary, but can't help noticing the grimace on his face. How parched and dusty he looks! Walking on alone, she remembers the Turtle reaching out to her—his generosity in taking the risk that transformed her, opening her connection to the world.

The third time the stranger crosses her path, she reaches out her hand and says hello. He smiles a tired, sad smile. She offers him a drink of water. Moving under a shady tree, they talk casually. Thunder rumbles in the distance, as raindrops begin to fall.

*

A story is like a road. Where does it begin or end? Down the road, if you keep on going, you may come to the smiling, magical cauldron. Holding everything, he laughs and laughs. Ō-ma' stirs and stirs. The story goes on.

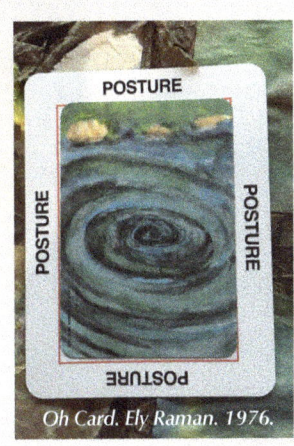

Oh Card. Ely Raman. 1976.

>> Meeting with the Queen of Wands

The queen of wands appears regularly in my tarot readings. Her fiery medicine is important medicine for me. Her frequent presence is an offer of patronage to me. I study the card more closely, the more it comes up. The imagery, the colors, her archetypal qualities are consistent across decks, though each particular manifestation shifts according to the vision of the artist.

The Queen of Wands is a symbol of transformation and self-mastery. Her story tells us she once had black hair, and so did her panther companion. As she discovered her true self and began to manifest her power in the world, her hair turned golden, and so did the cat's; but she pinched the cat's fur to retain some black spots, to remind herself to have compassion for those who still find themselves in dark places.

I begin to draw her myself. I even created a queen of wands costume for a masquerade party! [wish I had a photo. Make a sketch]

*Note: humans are not archetypes and I am not the Queen of Wands! But we can study and learn from them, engage with them, and seek to embody their characteristics.

I seek her out through imaginal journeys.
(somewhat following the form of a shamanic journey:)

I begin with a cloak of protection.

With inner vision, I follow a path beginning outside my door and leading me into the woods and through a portal to the upper world. I travel across vast realms of day and night, with the help of a spirit animal, sometimes a black panther and sometimes a leopard or jaguar, until I reach the place I identify as the Queen's Enclave. In this place I am greeted by her servants. A young boy cares for my beloved cat while her ladies prepare me, via a ritual of cleansing and dressing, to engage with the queen. I am ushered into her presence. She invites me into conversation. She is always the Queen of Wands, but appears in different forms on different occasions: sometimes a bright and shining child, sometimes a radiant golden majesty...

I endeavor always to be respectful and mindful of her status and great power and I have found her to be most kind, though she is the embodiment of strength and fire.

I have returned to this place many times. She has given me tasks to complete; advice which has proven quite useful; and the blessings of her support for my projects. She has given me gifts of value beyond measure and I endeavor to serve her well.

She has asked me to share this story.

TRAVELOGUE

>> Visible/Invisible

Some pages from a storybook about a girl who wants to be noticed -- or doesn't! Begun years ago, I found this story very difficult to complete, an indication of an active unresolved complex in my life. I didn't push it; not much, anyway.

TRAVELOGUE

It is not to change the story, it is to expand and deepen the story.
Jean Houston

>> The Lounsbury Game

Re: the idea of games as maps and maps as games... Here's a game I created for my sibs, based on our childhood home and experiences.

>> Saguaro

My first visit to the desert. I'm an alien.

The Sonoran desert and surrounding area -- magical.

The Saguaro -- amazing presence so strong, benign and wise.

Their sentience, the communities, the feeling is palpable.

I really can't "capture" them with camera or words, but...

I feel welcomed. I feel humbled. I feel so grateful to be walking through their magical habitat. A wonderland for all my senses.

What a joy and a privilege. What a rich world.

>> All Dried Up?

A magazine illustration I created as graphic designer, back in the day. Still apropos, unfortunately. FYI it's essevvntially a crumpled grocery bag, clipped to the outline of the US.

TRAVELOGUE

>> Tree Spirit

>> Nature Spirit

>> Cybele

Inspired by the mythology and artifacts of the Phrygian Great Mother of the Gods, Cybele and the neolithic culture of Çatalhöyük occupied my imaginal space for quite a while. Here's a mixed media collage and then my idea of a game board based on some of her symbolism, worked in encaustic.

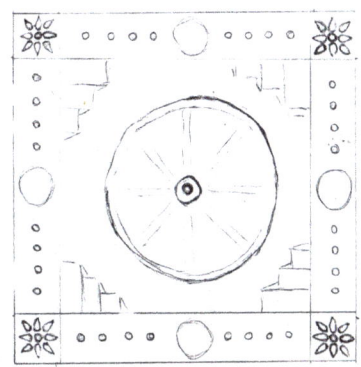

>> The Dream Mentor

TRAVELOGUE

A DREAM THAT BECAME A STORY:

Once upon a time, there was a girl, who had a dream. A wonderful, marvelous dream! Her head was still very much in the stars as she went through her morning chores. At breakfast, she couldn't wait to tell her family about it.

--I was in the woods, talking to the animals, and they were talking to me!

The panther shares his dinner with me, and the old tree tells me a story.

Then this big boulder starts vibrating, and it has a mission for me. It wants me to take this special fragile seed pod to the top of the mountain! it tells me I have to find just the right place to put it down.

Yes! I say. I'll do it! I carry it carefully and gently along the path. It's so fragile and delicate. And then I'm just about there, when I see that, the mountain peak in front of me is covered in thick, slick, sheer ice. There's no way I can climb it--I don't know how. I don't know what to do.

And then, suddenly, an eagle swoops up behind me and catches me by the scruff of the neck, and flies me right up to the top of the mountain! We're soaring through the air! And then puts me down gently at the top. There

I see this beautiful soft mossy pillow. I know this is the right place, so I place it gently on the pillow. And just then , the seed pod magically opens and inside is this amazing blue-green crystal. The sunlight dances and sparkles in it so beautifully! Oh! I would love to go there!

-Oh! Heaven forbid! cries her mother. That all sounds terribly dangerous! Don't ever go into the woods by yourself! Talking to wild animals, my goodness! That panther would have you for dinner, alright! Mercy! Flying with an eagle??

-But it was wonderful! We soared through the air! I could see everything!

--it was wonderful! We soared through the air! I could see everything! mimicked her brother. That is so dumb!! said her brother. That eagle would never pick you-- you're just a baby! A dumb baby!

The girl's eyes flashed with anger as she got ready to tell her brother what for, when--

--That's enough, both of you, said the father gruffly. All this fuss over a foolish dream. You need to be getting your books, getting your homework, and getting to school. Pay attention, get good grades, and one day you'll get a good job. Now forget about this nonsense and get going!

Travelogue

The girl did as she was told.

She gathered together her books and her homework, kissed her mother good bye, and out the door she went for the short walk to school.

The elderly neighbor sat in her garden as she did every morning. The girl stopped to chat, as she did every morning.

-Hello, child! said the kindly old woman.

-Hullo, said the girl glumly.

-Why what is the matter? she asked. You are not your usual self!

-Well I had a dream. I felt really excited about it, but my mother told me it was dangerous, my father told it me was foolish, and my brother told me it was stupid! Now I just feel bad.

-Oh dear, that's too bad, said the old woman. Would you like to tell me about it?

-Not really! said the girl.

- Good for you! said the neighbor with a laugh. The girl looked at her quizzically.

- You have to be careful who you share your dreams with!

-They told me to forget it!

-Ah, well... Your mother wants you to be safe. Your father wants you to be successful. Your brother just wants to cause mischief. They love you very much, but that doesn't mean they understand your dreams.

The girl kicked at the dirt as she listened.

-Your dreams are your own. Only you know which ones are important.

The girl looked up at her expectantly, so she continued.

-Dreams are so fragile and delicate! Like magical seeds--we need to hold them gently and carry them close, until we come to the right place where we know it's safe to set them down and let them stand on their own, for all to see.

At this, the young girl looked up with a gasp. Then she saw what she had never noticed before--the sun dancing and sparkling in the old woman's eyes beautiful blue-green eyes. The girl laughed out loud and gave the old woman a hug.

-You know, said the old woman, I'll bet you can carry your dreams and get good grades, too!

-Oh! Gotta go! said the girl. See you later, she called, as she ran the rest of the way to school, and she got there right on time.

Travelogue

>> Love You, Baba Yaga

--since childhood when I first saw her hut spinning on chicken legs.

Baba = grandmother

Yaga = witch

That ancient, primeval, dangerous power---you never know what to expect. She is not known for kindness! Yet often gives the heroine just what she needs to prevail against her human foes. intriguing.

Baba Yaga finds her way into many modern tales. Like any fairy tale character, she morphs into new forms while retaining her original identity.

But what about that hut! That magical hut, which has volition--which has LEGS! that can stand up and spin and even walk away.

That idea -- a building, a home, a place AND a being, cognizant--yes.

The magical cottage in the woods.

>> The Smiling Cottage

One night I dream of finding this happy cottage in the woods. Overgrown and rough, in need of care, yet smiling, welcoming, good-natured.

Collage of newsprint, paper towels, tissue paper, construction paper, corrugated cardboard

TRAVELOGUE

>> The Yaga

On the eve of Russian invasion of Ukraine, I'm inspired to a new telling of Baba Yaga. Here are some of the pages.

The Beginning: A beautiful, strong and capable young woman is pressured to wed her ambitious and powerful cousin. When she refuses, he pursues.

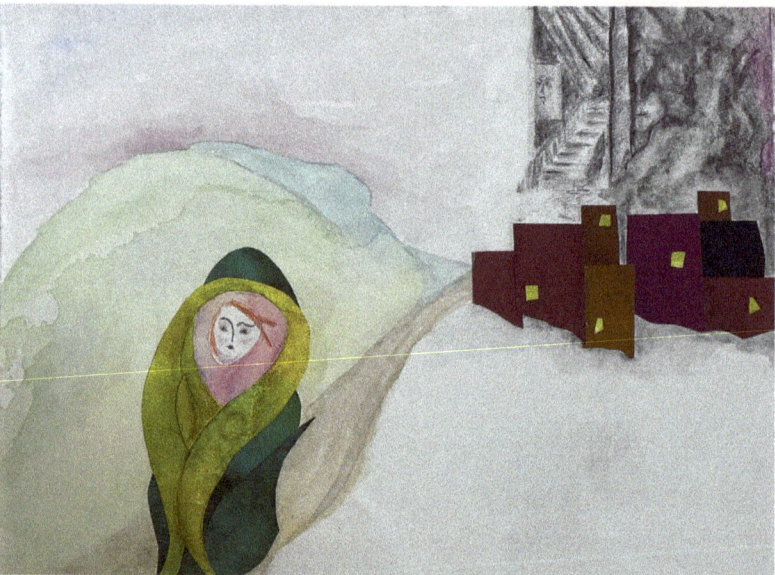

Deeper and deeper into the primeval forest she flies, the furious prince on her heels, until one day she comes to the mysterious hut that stands in shit and turns on chicken legs. Here lives the Baba Yaga. Starving and broken, she must ask for help.

ooooo

266

ooooo

The Ending: He comes burning and slashing to the heart of the wood. "I will have that girl or I will destroy this forest and everything in it," growled the dark prince menacingly.

The girl is filled with rage at this bully who threatens all she loves, only for his own selfish gain.

"No one will HAVE me," she shouts, "Never will you destroy this sacred place." She rushes at him with the flaming skull. Though he raises his sword to strike her down, he is no match for the girl's wrath, nor the ancient power that rises up around her. He screams as the flames consume him.

TRAVELOGUE

>> Mood

It was not a good one. However, I felt better after making this than before

>> Prayer Flags

A timeless tradition found world over, in one way or another.

Some I made:

TRAVELOGUE

>> Hanging

Covid era expression.

Not suicidal, simply hanging in clouds of ambiguity.

Where am I? Who knows.

>> Balance

Another perspective

Paint on cardboard.

Self-portrait. Photo montage.

>> Monsters & Demons

I've known a few...

>> Murmuration

September 2020 Watercolor painting of my mouth, with collage of journal pages, on cardboard.

Travelogue

Partial transcription:

What do I have to say? Noise words song oracle...when the words flow where do they go? What guides them what shapes them what carries them on out into the wind the sky where they dance and sing with others Oh who tries to hold them back? Who wants me to close my mouth? Is anyone listening? Does it matter? My mouth My Mouth MY MOUTH I am in charge of it If you tell me to control myself and I obey then you are in charge of it mine mine only my words only my words come out breath air wind kisses expression scream shout laugh yell my breath to use as I will Why do I believe you have power over my mouth don't tell me what to say don't tell me what to eat don't tell me who to kiss who to kiss what to eat what to say who to kiss who to kiss I guess I'll eat if I want I guess I'll shout since you won't hear me otherwise I'll shout if necessary Won't I rise up? Won't I join in with others? Let it flow

Words come out of both sides of my mouth and if I'm a hypocrite it's only-mostly-because we all are + cannot be any other way than both ways there is always a shadow always another meaning Always the words unspoken Always the whispers the undertones Double speak is always there always whisper

I think of Gemini, Hermes. Mercury. with the words coming out of both sides of my mouth, in the shape of a question. Inspired by a song I heard on the radio called "A Murmuration of Words," I began to think about the patterns of our words. What if there's a shape to our words that we're not aware of, a physicality, a pattern we don't see because we're in the midst of it, a shape and movement of human behavior that carries greater meaning than the meanings we intend. I think of the belief that we are "in charge" and "authoring" our lives, yet perhaps we're called to move and swirl, creating shapes and patterns of our lives by some force of which we're largely unaware, just as swallows swoop, sway, and undulate en masse through the skies.

TRAVELOGUE

>> Puppets

May 2021: A tentative and triumphant reemergence after the long--ong-ong winter(s) of Covid. The opportunity arises to participate in a week of giant puppet making at John C Campbell Folk School. I leap for it!

A week working outdoors -- community and creative expression — culminating with a parade! Wonderful!

Crazy week for me at times it turns out, with noisy rodents in my Airbnb and me teaching 2 previously-scheduled zoom classes in the midst of the puppet-making-- I was verklempt and almost went home but so glad I hung in there because it was wonderful overall!

Making the puppets: I know what I want to do but don't have the words yet. creative spirit and bubbles. Not humanoid but it's sometimes hard to do otherwise. The world is full of imaginal beings...

The Spirit of Creativity Giant Puppet: papier mache, acrylic paint, hand-dyed silk.

Giant puppet making week in Brasstown! Here's the parade.

Photo by Corey Marie Podielski.

Photos by Amelia D'Angio.

Home again, inspired by the work and the week, wondering how it will infiltrate my life... Calm and energized — that blissful combination. What a great week of work fresh air good company and creative expression

>> rando prints

>> journal outtakes

TRAVELOGUE

Part IV : Being Together

Being Together

It is not when a part of the self is inhibited and restrained, but when a part of the self is given away, that community appears.
—Lewis Hyde (Gift 120)

Everyday Connection

The first half of this book explored "everyday creativity" as a humble, grounded, regular practice of tuning in, noticing, and engaging with the world. By the same token, with "everyday connection," I mean regular, ordinary, comfortable opportunities to connect and share with others. I'm invoking a world where social interaction happens easily everyday. Though it's basic, such everyday connection is scarce for many today.

In the past, for better and for worse, physical acts of being and doing together were more common than they are now. It would just happen, regularly. I miss that. Plain old social interaction now requires a concerted effort, for me, anyway; so opportunities to share imaginal experience — my "gold standard" of social interaction — are rarer still. We need it all, from the humdrum everyday "How ya doin'" to the sharing of dreams. More than spectating, more than consuming; we need to be discussing ideas, gathering gossip, exploring visions, finding out what's on each others' minds. Through simple social interaction and shared experience, we find and give support. Together, we create solutions. The sense of meaning grows.

Human = Social

Socializing is part of the human experience. Do I even need to say that? No matter how introverted or self-sufficient you are, humans are relational by nature. "Everyday connection" doesn't mean constant chattering companionship, but rather a consistent common ground of social participation. I love quiet time, and too much socializing fries my circuits, but just the right bit of connectivity zings me with happiness. You have your own sweet spot, I'm sure. We all do. But the point is, hitting the sweet spot is easier when you know your community is there for you. Where communities are lacking or dysfunctional, they need to be rebuilt. By us.

When we individuals get out of balance and suffer pathologies, we need the help of others. Societies, too, develop pathologies. Just as a healthy society helps heal wounded individuals, so healthy individuals must help heal wounded societies.

Humans need connection

It's biological. The infant literally emerges out of oneness with the mother, and that process is not yet completed at birth.

> *"To the child the mother 'is' both the world and the self .... The child does not distinguish between its own body and its mother's body either in the pre-ego or in the early ego stage of its development"* (Neumann 79-80).

So, we are born out of an experience of oneness, only gradually sensing our independence and individuality.

As a healthy child develops, it is gradually separating from the mother, inhabiting a space of awareness which both is and isn't independent. The child oscillates back and forth between a sense of oneness with the motherer and a sense of individual consciousness. Self-awareness and relational awareness grow in tandem. Ideally, when the infant cries out in hunger or pain, its needs are recognized and responded to by the motherer; the infant coos, smiles, snuggles, and the motherer coos, smiles, and snuggles back. A rhythmic pattern of communication develops. It is never a "perfect" call-and-response, and that, too, is an essential part of the developmental process: it prods the infant/child to recognize the motherer as a separate entity. The infant/child comes to learn that it has influence, but not total control, over the motherer's behavior. Through the rhythm of communication, the infant/child learns to negotiate. Rhythm is the basis of participation.

coherence: the quality of being logical and consistent; the quality of forming a unified whole

Coherence

Rhythm leads to coherence; so says Louis Sander.

> *"The rhythms of oscillating systems become coupled when they share a common signal. Coupling amplifies the signal, increasing the inclusiveness and strength of coherence in the community of oscillators. The flow of energy is enhanced"* (Sander, "Thinking" 25).

This idea of coherence holds true for internal systems (like within your body) as well as for larger organic ecosystems, like the synchronization of marine organisms behavior with the lunar cycle, or the synchronous flashing of fireflies. Coherence is an important concept in physics. Psychologist Jessica Benjamin applies the principle to interpersonal relationships, specifically as coherence develops between baby and caregiver. The caregiver recognizes and responds to the baby's rhythm, in order to bring the baby into alignment with the caregiver's rhythm. It's a dance, out of which a coherent system develops.

We all live within the rhythms of earthly experience. Patterns of darkness and light shape the world around us, while our heartbeats count the time. Our social interactions, too, are shaped by these earthly rhythms. But, the problem is, we can become too busy or too chaotic or too self-absorbed to notice and respond to the rhythm, and that messes everything up.

On this note, Benjamin speaks to my particular question, with which I started this book, here paraphrased as: "Why are humans so screwed up?" She says:

> *"I have the idea that fireflies more or less have to synchronize, and at some deep biological level, there are things that humans have to do as well. But humans can be amazingly out of synch with what they have to do, or should do, or would be better off doing. Their minds and wills can violate patterns or refuse to join patterns or oppose them. ... The opposition to establishing rhythm seems to proceed from a difficulty **in the evolution of thirdness**."* (Rhythm 50-51 emphasis mine)

Thirdness, remember? It's important.

In order for the infant to develop the sense of thirdness, he or she must be recognized and responded to by the caregiver. Just as a dance may seem complicated or exclusive when you stand outside watching, and then a kind person takes you by the hand and leads you in. The process begins with you being noticed and met where you are, recognized as an individual, and welcomed into the dance—or the third. The experience of being recognized — noticed, seen, acknowledged — gives the individual a sense of validation and agency; and consequently allows the individual to relax and join into the rhythmic pattern of the relationship.

(Benjamin 45)

For the child whose expressions go unheeded, the sense of rhythmic participation is damaged. Such individuals may feel they are not included in the social rhythms that underlie successful relationships; that their voices lie outside of what is important to others; that they must choose between submitting to or resisting the will of the other. They may be prone to feelings of both grandiosity and insignificance. The natural unfolding of the third is hampered. To participate in the third is to negotiate a conversation of give and take, and those who haven't learned how to negotiate carry a sense of "competing wills ... as if the successful implementation of one's own agency is being hindered by the agency of the other" (Benjamin "Rhythm" 51, 46).

The missing third in the individual's experience will hamper that individual's ability to relate.

The third, that magical space between, can be lacking within the individual, it can be lacking in a relationship between individuals, and it can be lacking for an entire social system. In each case, without the third, there is insufficient space for negotiation.

So far we've discussed practices that provide individuals with tools to expand the third. When a social system is lacking thirdness it requires a community-wide solution. This chapter will consider ways to expand the social third. But first, a word about *weltenschauung*: how does one's cultural world view affect consciousness?

weltenschauung: the worldview of a group

Archetypal numbers:

Numbers, too, carry archetypal significance. That is, numbers express quality as well as quantity.

"One" means unity, undifferentiated wholeness, the All: Everything. The whole pie.

One can also be a unit, as in "one piece of the pie," but in this case other pieces are implied. To be a unit, one requires more than one.

Two is the number of differentiation, division, separation, replication, symmetry. Split, twin, mirror, reflect: all are expressions of two-ness. If we understand awareness as oppositional, then two is the number of consciousness: "This is me; that is not me." Says Jung: "the Other pushes itself away from the One in order to exist at all" (CW 11, para. 180; see also von Franz).

Two establishes rhythm as a dynamic back and forth oscillation between the One and the Other. Two is the number of dialogue, and also the number of opposition. With Two, there is only back and forth. It takes a third position of detachment to mediate or evaluate the dialogue.

Out of the relationship between the One and the Other comes the Third. With Three, progression is possible. Three allows observation, comparison and the emergence of pattern and meaning. The third is the opening of possibility.

The birth of a child is a quintessential experience of the archetypal quality of three. Through an opening emerges the new child, an unknown possibility engendered by the dynamic relationship of the mother and the father. Philosophically, the third appears to be the potential solution to polarization.

One	Two	Three
unity, undifferentiated wholeness	differentiation, dialogue, opposition	pattern, detachment, mediation

Cultural sense of individual consciousness
Individual consciousness in the infant evolves out of a sense of oneness-with-all toward a sense of discrete personhood: "I am *this particular* person with *these specific* characteristics."

The question of personal sovereignty — *"How independent am I?"* — is culturally relative. If the cultural belief holds that the individual is a free agent, acting on free will in complete separation from the collective, that signifies a lack of thirdness on a grand scale. If the cultural belief holds that Spirit and Nature are separate and distinct from one another and that the individual makes his way in the world by strength of intention — "mind over matter," as they say — this is a cultural call to ignore rhythmicity, to place our own will over and above the rhythms and cycles of the nature. We can see this illustrated by the American mythology of the rugged individualist, the maverick who pays his own way (and this character is stereotypically a "he"), rising to the top by virtue of his own hard work and smarts. In practical terms, such an individual will be inclined to ignore awareness of natural rhythms in favor of personal goals, for work or for entertainment. Is there any American who doesn't recognize this pattern of behavior? Cultural indifference to rhythmicity encourages personal arrhythmia.

> From heartbeat to drumbeat to cosmic cycles, the rhythm of life is perceptible if we allow ourselves to notice; and, when we notice, hard to imagine we could have ignored it! But we can and do ignore it.

As a culture, America has become more aware of the distortion inherent to this paradigm, which is a sign that we are outgrowing it, but it still holds great power. What's wrong with that? To be sure, there are people who work really hard, harder than others; but no one accomplishes anything on their own. There's no exception to this. One person's "rise to the top" is frequently accomplished by a helpful leg-up from another, which is great. That's humans helping each other. But it's not uncommon to see a "winner" make his way to the top by stepping on the backs of others while obscuring the importance of their help. No, when you look at the fuller picture, all humans depend upon other humans. Humans always have lived and worked collectively. Humans are only human in community with others. If there's anyone for whom this is not true – well, we wouldn't know about them, would we?

> "World-building ... is always and inevitably a collective enterprise." —Peter Berger (7)

The dominant western perspective has long held this style of distinct individual consciousness to be "the best," or the "most evolved." Well I say that's nothing more than an overzealous team spirit! And I'm not alone in my view. Countless individuals and organizations are working to deconstruct this view and replace it with a more nuanced equitable grounded balanced collaborative approach. Nonetheless, it is deeply embedded in western culture and it shapes the way we do and say things, often unconsciously.

We prize and entrain this kind of consciousness of differentiation, because it gives us the ability to focus intensively on a project/goal to the exclusion of whatever else may be going on around — but, to be sure, when you focus on one thing, there are many other things you miss. (Planetary rhythms, perhaps? Flowers blooming? Children playing? The meaning of life unfolding?) This type of extreme focused consciousness pushes so much else into unconsciousness. We focus on the end and aim not to be distracted by the means. Peripheral awareness is lost. Other, de-centered, voices are lost.

There are other ways.

All our relations

Indigenous mythologies the world over foster a deep sense of kinship and respect for all beings, formed through empirical observation within the landscape — seeing and listening to all, and perceiving the totality, tangible and intangible, as a web of complex relationships.

Compare this to the utilitarian approach, a philosophy of ethics which developed over time in western culture, becoming prevalent in the nineteenth century. The essential kernel,stated as "the greatest good for the greatest number," seems pretty agreeable — sure, I can go along with that — but how does it play out? Utilitarianism implies assigning value to all things

> "Rose has argued that white Australian settlers brought with them a particular, and peculiar, kind of time. They looked straight ahead to the future, a singular path of optimism and salvation informing their dreams and deeds. This future is a characteristic feature of commitments to modernity, that complex of symbolic and material projects for separating "nature" and "culture." Moving toward this future requires ruthless ambition – and the willingness to participate in great projects of destruction while ignoring extinction as collateral damage. The settlers looked straight ahead as they destroyed native peoples and ecologies. The terrain carved out by this future is suffused with bad death ghosts." (Tsing et al. *Arts of Living on a Damaged Planet* 7)

and beings, according to their usefulness; and then, if need be, sacrificing the "less useful" for the sake of the "more useful." The hierarchy of "usefulness" is perspectival, of course, though not often acknowledged as such: I mean, who's doing the assigning? Utilitarianism leads to the objectification of everything, animal, vegetable, and mineral alike, as resources to be used "efficiently."

Utilitarianism places (certain) humans apart from or over nature,* whereas the indigenous sensibility of kinship with all things sees humans as part of the whole of nature. All creatures, all places, all things play a part in the great story; and notions of "practical" and "spiritual" are not oppositional but indivisible. Since unrelenting efforts to maximize economic efficiency have generated the most wasteful civilization ever, how might a cultural ideal based on respect and balance lead to economic and environmental sustainability?

> *not to blame everything on utilitarianism; it's but one example of splitting in the western consciousness.*

It's fair to say that indigenous philosophies are grounded in experience and the landscape out of which they arise; while colonial philosophies are untethered from location and direct experience, viewing such grounded experience at a remove. The colonial perspective of abstraction leads to acquisition and extraction, and depends on the belief that abstract thought is superior to direct experience. The indigenous view is naturally more pragmatic/phenomenological.

Participation mystique: Lévy-Bruhl's theory posits a pre-logical state of group consciousness characterized by collective identification and a lack of subject-object differentiation. The presumption is that pre-logical cultures, termed "primitive," experienced a diffuse group sense of consciousness which lacked awareness of individuality. This nomenclature of "primitive" has, regrettably, been widely applied to indigenous cultures.

Jung follows Levy-Bruhl in viewing what he terms as "primitive" participatory experiences as at root instances of individual projection — thus fantasy rather than shared reality — in his opinion. Jung's evolving thought on this topic is evident in his developing understanding of the indigenous psyche, as Deloria has recognized.

Deloria, a Native American scholar, argues that the split between subject and object is a peculiarly western conception; and that it is possible to have simultaneous awareness of self and other as both separate and continuous, (that is, to be conscious of the self while also sharing a fluid awareness of psyche beyond the self).

Deloria disputes Jung's simplistic understanding of the indigenous psyche, yet he values Jung's work, as it created an opening toward better western understanding of the indigenous psyche.

As Deloria points out, Jung's (and certainly not only Jung's) theories on "primitive" psyche and experience were almost completely based on conjecture (29-31, 45, 49-50), which aligned with Jung's theoretical framework (so it was actually Jung's projection at work, rather than that of indigenous cultures). The over-emphasis on projection notwithstanding, Jung's work on the personal and collective unconscious, counter-transference, the psychoid and synchronicity are all founded in the concept of participation.

In analytic psychology, participation generally refers only to intersubjective human-to-human experience; but philosophically, we can understand that we are grounded in participation with, and within, the larger world. Barfield defined participation as "of self and not-self identified in the same moment of experience." This is how I use the term.

Splitting

When Europeans travelled to "new" (to them) worlds, they left behind the bones of their ancestors and their deep relationships with the web of life-forms all around them. They were literally split from the land that grew them, like plants with their roots dangling out. In seeking to establish a "new" sense of home in a "new" world (and in claiming a right to such things), colonists were often blind and deaf to the indigenous traditions and people they trampled upon.

Here in the US, interlopers became dominant, like an invasive species taking over. By silencing indigenous American voices, the culture has developed largely in ignorance of the established native wisdom of the land, wisdom grown from generations of close community with place and all abiding creatures. Here in the US, white European immigrants built wealth upon the enslavement of African peoples, who were brought here against their will and forced into labor, suffering indignities without number. The sacrifices of these people are embedded in the foundation of American culture. Inequities and abuses perpetrated upon indigenous and African-American peoples continue today— to a lesser degree, we hope, but there is much repair to be done. And it must begin with acknowledgment.

> NO MATTER HOW MUCH YOU WANT TO BELIEVE THAT YOU ARE WINNING BECAUSE GOD WANTS YOU TO WIN AND NOT BECAUSE YOU ARE CHEATING...THAT JUST DOESN'T MAKE IT TRUE.

Humans (social beings, remember) can only inflict such suffering on others by refusing to see or hear their pain, refusing to see or believe in our kinship. This sort of refusal creates blind spots and pathology in individual and society alike. As you narrow the light of your consciousness onto your goal, you push the rest into the darkness of shadow, where you don't see it, don't think about it, even forget that it exists. This is the process invoked by the phrase "the end justifies the means"; but, does it? Not usually.

> *Ignoring the obvious pain and suffering of others at one's own hands relates to ignoring the rhythms and cycles of nature and imagining that one is in a godly or superhuman position where one's own will is all that matters.*

When we abuse anything — other humans or other creatures or the land we share, or even including our own selves — there is a splitting that happens. To carry out inhumane acts, we must split off our awareness and feelings, somehow refusing to recognize and acknowledge the horror of what we are doing. This splitting results in repression, and the repression can be cultural as well as personal. That is, a whole cultural inability to see the immorality of our actions. We're #1, right? Land of the free?

As I write, social and political factions continue pushing away the uncomfortable facts of American history into the hidden realms of the social unconscious. At this particular point in time, their efforts are disturbingly effective. Maybe the tendency to avoid seeing our own transgressions is always at work. Well, we're far from the only culture needing to look into our own shadow, but — yeah, we need to.

You can't simply abuse people and think they'll forget about it. Following the depth psychological view, repressed contents need to come to light. No matter how much you don't like what's already happened, or you're ashamed or mortified or you wish it were something different, you can't change the past by denying it. You have to recognize it, accept it, and work with it. Otherwise, it will continue to create pathological effects.

> *The cultural past brings with it ghosts that represent the unacknowledged harm done through violence to the selves of the exploited, denigrated, and colonized other.*   Kimbles Intergenerational Complexes, 4.

American thought is characterized by "us" and "them" thinking, without a clear understanding of the relationship between "us" and "them." The separation of factions is enforced by upholding personal righteousness and laying blame upon the other. Hint: the relationships can be disclosed in the third (the shadowy space between). But when the third is collapsed, the connecting threads are not visible.

Continuity

In Edwin Abbot's 1884 satire called *Flatland*, there are only two dimensions (length and width). The inhabitants are geometric figures. In a dream, the narrator, a two-dimensional Square, visits a one-dimensional world called Lineland, where the inhabitants are Lines and Points. The monarch can perceive the Square's length but not his width, and so believes the Square to be a line. The Square tries and fails to convince the monarch that a second dimension exists. The furious monarch threatens to annihilate the Square for heresy. Fortunately, the visionary Square escapes and is subsequently visited by a Sphere from the third dimension (depth), who uses ingenious methods to help the Square imagine beyond what he can directly perceive. It's a brilliant example of how imagination can expand our understanding and carry us to new levels of insight. Conversely, a refusal to imagine collapses understanding. Squashes it.

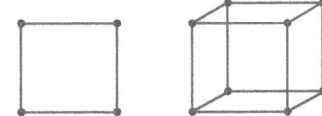

When the third is collapsed, then things that are related— events, people, emotions — appear separate and unrelated. Complexities are viewed superficially. We're missing information, unable to see the whole picture.

All the connections and relationships between us may be difficult to perceive, but are there nonetheless. And where connections are tangled or torn, then we need to gain access — "open the hood," so to speak — in order to make repairs.

We can learn to unwrap, unfold, expand the space between us, and thereby become more aware of the way that all things are intertwined with all others. We may not be able to trace all the intricate threads, yet I can be aware that somehow, my feelings are always related to my actions, and somehow, I am always related to you. Valuing this awareness does not threaten individual consciousness.

We are swirling blobs of feelings, craving closeness but easily bruised and spiky. There's more going on between us than we know.

The third is the place for space. Surrender to the third depersonalizes. The spaciousness of the third allows healing.

Dependent Arising

Dependent-Arising is a foundational concept in Buddhist ethics, which teaches that all things are inter-related, all things are dependent, all things are in flux (Napper 3)

The 12 links of the chain of existence are death, birth, becoming, grasping, craving, feelings, contact, the six sense organs, name and form, consciousness, drives and impulses, and ignorance. (Nhat Hanh 411)

"The teaching on dependent co-arising is most profound and subtle. Do not think it can be grasped through words and discourse.... Contemplate the nature of dependent co-arising during every moment. When you look at a leaf or a raindrop, meditate on all the conditions, near and distant, that have contributed to the presence of that leaf or raindrop. Know that the world is woven of interconnected threads. This is, because that is. This is not, because that is not. This is born, because that is born. This dies, because that dies." (Nhat Hanh 409)

The Bhavacakra or Wheel of Becoming is a symbolic representation of the process of continuous existence in the form of a circle, used primarily in Tibetan Buddhism.

"Thanks to the contemplation on the nature of dependent co-arising, we can dispel ignorance in order to transcend all anxieties and sorrows. An enlightened person walks over the waves of birth and death and does not drown in them. An enlightened person uses the 12 links of the chain of existence like the wheels of a carriage. An enlightened person lives in the very midst of the world but is never submerged by it. Do not try to run away from birth and death. You need only rise above them. Transcending birth and death is the attainment of great beings." (Nhat Hanh 411)

inner+outer experience and the psychoid

In short, the modern western understanding of individuals as discrete entities with singular minds is a fallacy, or at best, one simple part of a complex story. While we can and do function as individuals, we overstate our individual-ness and our independence. This mindset of independence is useful, but not ultimately "true," because it neglects awareness of the equally important shared consciousness and the continuity between consciousness states. We (westerners) have artificially reified the conceptual boundaries between us and inflated the importance of individual consciousness; but the belief in our separateness is so deeply ingrained in western culture, underlying so much of our cultural mythology, that we can be consciously aware of the fallacy and yet quite unconscious of the many ways we act in accordance with it. So, even if you agree with what I'm saying here, you may need to settle into some deeper work to uncover how you can repair the splits in yourself and in the world. Like, for the rest of your life, perhaps.

I find myself always returning to the idea of the psychoid, this territory where psyche and matter are one, hypothesized to exist below conscious awareness. This is territory that the western mind has turned its back on, so to speak. In believing mind and matter to be distinct from one another, with "mind" being the part that "matters," we make ourselves blind to that space in between, but ignoring it doesn't mean it's not there. Again, this is the shadowy space that we can't see clearly, yet intuit that it must exist. Can we feel our way into an awareness, however vague, of the connecting in-between space? In the western world, we consider this to be unconscious territory because *we're* typically not conscious of it, but what are the real limits of our ability to experience the psychoid? Are they limits of the western imagination? Perhaps a territory from which we have been forbidden entry? If so, it's time to exercise your imaginal muscles. *Stretch!*

> "Psychoid" is Jung's term to describe the pre-conscious level of experience where psyche and matter are undifferentiated.

No entry: Verboten!

The field of ecopsychology has much to offer us here, because for many westerners, a huge missing piece is a sense of connection to the earth, our literal common ground. While the field of psychology has focused attention on a small, distinct(ish) area of psyche contained within the body of the individual, the field of ecopsychology considers the immersion of humans within the extensive psyche of the natural world.

"Once upon a time all psychology was "ecopsychology." No special word was needed. The oldest healers in the world... knew no other way to heal than to work within the context of environmental reciprocity.... It is homely common sense that human beings must live in a state of respectful give-and-take with the flora and fauna, the rivers and hills, the sky and soil on which we depend for physical sustenance and practical instruction." Roszak Where Psyche Meets Gaia 5-6

"Ecopsychology holds that ...the psyche is rooted inside a greater intelligence once known as the anima mundi, the psyche of the Earth herself that has been nurturing life in the cosmos for billions of years through its drama of heightening complexification. The 'greening of psychology' begins with matters as familiar to all of us as the empathic rapport with the natural world that is reborn in every child and which survives in the work of nature poets and landscape painters." Roszak 16

"[Freud's] conviction that the "external world" begins at the surface of the skin continues to pass as common sense in every major school of modern psychology. The "procedure" we teach children for seeing the world this way is the permissible repression of cosmic empathy, a psychic numbing we have labeled 'normal.' " Roszak 11

"How did [psychology] so cut itself off from reality? Where else in the world would a human soul be so divorced from the spirits of the surroundings? ... Psychology, so dedicated to awakening human consciousness, needs to wake itself up to one of the most ancient human truths: we cannot be studied or cured apart from the planet." Hillman xxii Psyche Size of Earth

Psyche naturally extends beyond the individual.

Meditate on all the ways and places that what you consider "you" lives beyond you or outside of you.

Meditate on all the ways and places that what you consider "not you" or "other" lives within you.

Meditate on the physical nature of your thoughts, dreams, words, emotions...
How are they present biologically? Chemically?
How are they catalyzed by (or catalyzing to) "other" beings and substances, such as bacteria, amoeba, insects, light, fragrance, food?
How do they morph into actions, events, artifacts?

Meditate on the idea of anima mundi, or psyche continuous in all things.

I picture mycelium as the psychoid facing side of psyche. Try it!

particles, waves, you, me, everyone. everything

The distinction between inner experience and outer experience is often demonstrable. If I hear a voice inside my head, most likely, you do not hear it. You may be oblivious that something you just said about a beloved childhood memory transported me in a flash to remember a life-shattering traumatic event. You may be smarting from an incredibly painful toe-stubbing, or a deep personal loss, without revealing any outward signs of it. All of this is true, *and also* there are many instances where what we experience as internal, assumed to be personal, may be shared experience. Maybe I wake up feeling blue and exhausted. I think it's MY mood, MY health status, until I start talking to other people and I find out YOU are feeling the same thing, and so's the guy next to you. So maybe we all have a virus or maybe we're all stressed about politics or maybe it's the weather...but the point is, it's more than MY mood. It's bigger than me. Perhaps I'm in IT rather than it being in ME.

> Ancient Greeks understood emotional experience as visitations from the gods. That is, emotions are bigger than you.

"Where is the 'me'? Where does the 'me' begin? Where does the 'me' stop? Where does the 'other' begin?" —Hillman (Psyche)

Listen, we're particles *and* we're waves—it's not that complicated. It's always true. We can understand ourselves as individuals (who are composed of tiny microbes and bacteria and blood cells and dead things and live things and all manner of things) and also as part of a greater ever-changing pattern in motion... The thing is that a lot of what we "are" is invisible to us, whether because it's too little or too big, or just too...invisible to the human apparatus. But some things are invisible only because we're not paying attention.

Just as you and I may share the same air, food, water, sunshine, and microbes, there are less visible, less conscious energies and influences that flow through us, shaping our perceptions and our actions. We're not going to know about them unless we create some opportunity to share inner experience.

So what?

1. It's helpful simply to be aware of our continuity.

2. Actually "doing things" together (which used to be common place) is a fundamental way to increase this awareness.

'assume' making an ass out of you and me

What happens to you influences me. <–> What happens to me influences you.

Cultural Participation

Earlier, I wrote about "participation" in the sense of you being directly engaged with the physical world around and within you. Let's now consider *cultural* participation: specifically human-to-human interactions and the narratives and understandings that grow from these interactions; or, the things people do together and the meanings we make and take from this: aka "myth".

cultural psyche = myth

Like psyche in the individual, cultural psyche is composed of what we, collectively, are aware of and what we are not, what we notice and what we ignore. As in the individual, what the culture ignores and pushes away and represses is likely to make itself known in disruptive and dysfunctional ways. A strong healthy culture (ideally) encourages participation by all constituents, each in their own way. We might not find this happening in many places, but, like individuation, it's an ideal to work toward.

Participation means not only having a vote and a voice, but being a part of the conversation. Cultural participation is easier in some places and for some people, so we must remediate those situations where participa-

---

Dr. Bronner! Icon of the Sixties!

We would puzzle over the bounty of small print packed onto the label, laughing as we showered and soaped up with his peppermint castile soap. The big message? ALL ONE!

Dr. Bronner was right. We ARE All One!

This cosmically ethical family business continues today.

tion is difficult or discouraged. As a rule, though, cultural structures are resistant to change, being typically formed for the sake of stability; so we have to get creative. Remember that play is revolutionary!

Toward a healthy society
We are hobbled when our life-work-educational-social opportunities don't allow or encourage the free exchange of ideas. An idea kept to yourself has a very limited range of influence! This is why reading and writing are so important. As are social gatherings!

> *When people cannot name alternatives, imagine a better state of things, share with others a project of change, they are likely to remain anchored or submerged, even as they proudly assert their autonomy. The same, paradoxically or not, is true when people uproot themselves, when they abandon families, take to the road, become strangers in desperate efforts to break loose from pre-established orders and controls. (Greene 9)*

As I beat the drum for social experience, the odd truth is that I don't avail myself of many of the community events that surround me. I love my friends and my community, but it seems I'm seeking something different than what's already going on, as if, for me, some key ingredient is missing; and I think what's missing is the sharing of the imaginal experience. That's what got me here, to this work, to this book. Being the change, so to speak.

I know it's not all about me but it *kind* of is, for me, in this moment — when it's the thing that drives me to write, drives me toward the thing that I need, along with the thought that there must be others like me who feel they are inadequately recognized or missing the opportunity to participate fully. For me, participating fully and being recognized has to include sharing dreams and jokes, ideas and what-ifs, numinosities and synchronicities with my community: it has to include sharing the imaginal.

---

society
a group of people who share a common way of life, including customs, laws, and interests

> *Freedom shows itself or comes into being when individuals come together in a particular way, when they are authentically present to one another (without masks, pretenses, badges of office), when they have a project they can mutually pursue. When people lack attachments, when there is no possibility of coming together in a plurality or a community, when they have not tapped their imaginations, they may think of breaking free, but they will be unlikely to think of breaking through the structures of their world and creating something new. It does not matter whether those structures are as everyday as constraining family rituals, as banal as bureaucratic supervisory systems, as shabby as segregation practices. There must be a coming together of those who choose themselves as affected and involved. There must be an opening of the space between them, what Hannah Arendt called an "in-between" (1958, page 182), deeper and more significant than merely practical or worldly interests. (Greene 16-17)*

Society needs connectivity

On a collective level, society needs our contributions! What is society but the sum of our contributions, an aggregate over time? For sure, some people are more powerful, some are more visionary, and some are better placed to shape society; and some societies are more welcoming to new views and more tolerant of diversity; but whether they are forward-thinking or mired in the antediluvian mud, societies must respond to events in the world and they must respond to the experiences and expressions of their members — like it or not! Often, "they" (societies) don't like it! Because the function of a social system is to maintain order and minimize risk to members, societies are by nature conservative. Change is disruptive, and anything ambiguous might be dangerous, because it contains unknowns; so, often, the generalized response to the new or different may be anger or a cold shoulder, violence or authoritarianism... Nonetheless, societies

are made up of individual people, and in a healthy society, people's voices are heard, and individuals know themselves to be members.

If we feel that our contributions are not honored, not counted, not taken into consideration, then we have to come up with ways to change that. Don't wait for society to do it for you! If society does not recognize your worth, it is not going to negotiate with you. As we learned from Benjamin, a lack of recognition signals a lack of thirdness, characterized by behaviors of dominance and submission. We must look for opportunities to expand the third, rather than falling into the oppositional dynamics of the collapsed third.

Societies are not inclined to change from the top down (although authoritarian takeovers will certainly precipitate change). Social change mainly comes about through the grassroots web of connections with others—having conversations, sharing ideas, developing solutions... This is how the social mycelium grows, distributing nutrients where they are needed. In other words, individuals matter, but only if we are in relationship and communicating with others.

Spurred by my own longing, I made a commitment to create opportunities for people to come together for free symbolic expression — sharing the imaginal experience — even including those who may not know they need or desire it. Society needs people to really jump in and share directly in the creative crucible where enzymatic engagement bubbles up. Blub, blub. I'm talking about learning a way of being together where we are comfortable expressing our thoughts and feelings, and making space for that to happen.

I have ideas about how that might come about, but first, there are some social issues that make coming together for creative connection more difficult.

A beautifully diverse ecosystem strengthens and supports the whole, creating more stability and resilience. By comparison, a monoculture is fragile and susceptible to more risks.

Healing Social Wounds

By social wounds, I mean not only wounds sustained by individuals via social experience, but also social webs that are torn, dysfunctional, and needing repair. They won't be repaired by individual actors but by communities. Together we repair the fabric between us.

Is there anyone who hasn't suffered social wounding? Maybe? No? Most of us have had some difficult or challenging social experiences that have left their mark on us. And we all live within societies that bear the wounds of the past.

So these are two aspects of the issue to consider:

- We need others to help us heal wounds that have been inflicted by others.

- We need to come together socially to make repairs to the invisible web that connects and holds us, aka the social mycelium.

Either way, for both inner and outer repairs, we need help! The healing of social wounds can't be accomplished in isolation. Let's consider two big social issues, scapegoating and sociopathy, and then turn to thoughts about how we can heal together.

Scapegoating

scapegoat *noun*

1 a person who is blamed for the wrongdoings, mistakes, or faults of others, especially for reasons of expediency.

2 (in the Bible) a goat sent into the wilderness after the Jewish chief priest had symbolically laid the sins of the people upon it (Lev. 16).

Then Aaron shall lay both his hands on the head of the live goat, and confess over it all the iniquities of the people of Israel, and all their transgressions, all their sins, putting them on the head of the goat, and sending it away into the wilderness by means of someone designated for the task. The goat shall bear on itself all their iniquities to a barren region; and the goat shall be set free in the wilderness.

—Leviticus 16:21–22, New Revised Standard Version

In the ancient Judaic practice of scapegoating, two kid goats are chosen by lot. One has all the sins and transgressions of the people put onto its head by the priest—this is the scapegoat, who is then cast out into the wilderness. The other is offered as a blood sacrifice to YHWH.

That's the origin of the term "scapegoat." Many cultures have a history of similar yet distinct ritual purification practices. There are plenty of examples in the cultural imagination: Shirley Jackson's short story, "The Lottery," for instance. Metaphorically, we use the term "scapegoat" to refer to a person who is blamed for the faults of others.

If it happened in the history of the culture in which you live, then it is a part of you and it affects you.

According to anthropologist Mary Douglas, the role of any culture is to separate pure from impure, implying a system of classification that serves to maintain social structure. "The structure is expected to protect itself" (140). Purity refers to a state of order and clear boundaries, and purification implies a returning to order. "Dirt" is that which is out of order, and every culture has it. "Dirt is simply matter out of place" (Purity 44); but what constitutes "dirt" varies across cultures, as do the rules about how to handle it.

It's the "Yes, and…" rule. You have to accept what's gone before. Refusal is not an option.

A polluted person is one who is defiled or contaminated, according to cultural notions of dirt and purity. A person who possesses "dirty" qualities threatens the system by having transgressed categorical distinctions. Those whose roles are ambiguous "an involuntary source of danger" (126). If you have discomfort with the implications of these ideas, I get it. Me, too. These deeply held, not quite conscious instincts about dirt and purity are often taken up as weapons of manipulation. But don't blame the messenger; Douglas is not telling us how to deal with ambiguity, she is simply pointing out how social systems work, and it helps us see what's at the root of scapegoating, which clearly remains in practice today, in so many ways, world over.

The story of Oedipus provides perspective on the issue of pollution.

Oedipus Tyrannos: An Athenian tragedy by Sophocles, c. 429 bce

Freud takes a lot of flak, but, when you think about it, we kind of are all Oedipus: maybe not in the sense of killing our fathers and marrying our mothers, but in that we don't know what we don't know. And it's our hubris — the assumption that we DO know it all — that gets us into trouble. There's always more to the story.`

King Laius of Thebes is given a prophecy that he will die at his son's hand. Intending to subvert the prophecy, he binds his child's feet and sends him to the wilderness to be killed. The child does not die, however, but is raised by a shepherd. Because his feet had been so tightly bound, he will forever bear that wound from his father, so the shepherd calls him Oedipus, or "swollen-footed." Oedipus grows up believing the shepherd and his wife to be his true parents.

As a young man, Oedipus is eager to make his way in the world; he heads to Thebes. As luck would have it, he comes meets an old man in his path. They quarrel and Oedipus kills him. Wouldn't you know, the old man is Oedipus' father, King Laius? Oblivious, Oedipus continues his journey, which is full of adventure. By the time he reaches Thebes, he is hailed as a hero, and rewarded with marriage to the widowed Queen Jocasta. She is his birth mother, though neither is aware of it.

Now King of Thebes, Oedipus consults the Delphic Oracle about the plague which hangs over the city. He is told that the plague is a symptom of pollution caused by the unknown murderer of Laius, who has never been has caught or punished. Oedipus, the great leader, swears to save the city by finding and banishing the murderer of Laius. Little does he know....

In ancient Greece, it was believed that "a polluted individual threatened the entire group" (Cole 282). Society is purified by removing or separating individuals who are perceived as a risk to the whole. Again, these terms of "pollution" and "purification" are troubling because we have seen them applied as justification for ethnic cleansing, sexual castigation, and the persecution of "otherness"; but purification is not necessarily scapegoating. For instance, you have a head cold: all that congestion is "pollution"; then you drink herbal tea and inhale eucalyptus oil for the sake of "purification." Or, a pack of animals races through your home, leaving a trail of dead leaves and mud behind them. The disorder is "pollution";

the broom and bucket of soapy water are "purification." Or, a person violently attacks you; the attack is "pollution." Then the attacker is removed from society: "purification."

However it is used or misused in practice, purification is generally in place for the greater good of the system, a means of maintaining healthy function. Pollution can be defined as unwanted ambiguity, confusion and disorder. Those who are outside the rules, intentionally or not, have the potential to damage the system. The ambiguous and marginal are both powerful and dangerous to the social structure by their very nature, because they are not bound by rules, permissions, or social categories, and because they may have conflicts of interest or allegiance.

Was Oedipus ambiguous? Oh yes. In so many ways: as king, as husband to his mother, as brother to his children, as killer of his father who gave him life, and as one with no knowledge of his kinship. Any of these places him outside the norm. Without question, he has transgressed categorical distinctions. Honorable intentions don't change that. "Pollution rules, by contrast with moral rules, are unequivocal." (Douglas 162)

> In the search for the murderer of Laius, the hidden story is unravelled. With terrible clarity, the truth dawns on Oedipus. He is king and murderer both. As king, he is compelled to exact justice. Cursing himself, he gouges out his own eyes, and is sent into exile.

As Tyrannos (king), Oedipus is the purifier. As murderer, he is the pollutant. He is the one responsible for upholding and defending the system which he himself has put at risk. In this position, he must necessarily cast himself out.

Ok, but is he a scapegoat? Mm. Well, maybe as an infant, yes, but not as an adult. A scapegoat is an innocent vessel to carry the sins of others, whereas Oedipus the adult is sent into exile to purify the city for sins he himself committed, albeit in ignorance. The story clarifies the concepts of pollution and purification, highlighting how, regardless of intention, an ambiguous person is a natural threat to the system, and thus also at risk. If ambiguity is dangerous to the collective, then it is dangerous to be ambiguous. So, in any situation, the ambiguous person is more likely to become the bearer of shadow material for the group.

> Brian Sutton-Smith observed rhythmicity arising in the play of young children beating on their blocks, spontaneously moving from chaos toward unison. He also noted their joy and hilarity in the ensuing *collapse* of synchrony:
>
> "The children themselves having achieved some degree of order, they often show just as much enjoyment of breaking it down into disorder, so that sand-castles built with much cooperative effort are hilariously destroyed, and blocks tumbled down. Here the contrast or antagonism between social order and play liminality is mirrored in the play activity itself" ("Games of Order and Disorder" 21).

The bit of paradox is that, although a social system resists and distrusts ambiguity, it also needs the shake up that ambiguity introduces: the movement, the change, the fresh winds. There is a creative value to disorder. Social institutions are meant to protect us, but when we try to make them impervious to change, we also reinforce their imperfections. Stability's great, but a healthy social institution/society needs to be able to evolve. Those who do not fit easily into existing cultural categories fulfill an important social function: they enliven, they mix things up; they catalyze social change. Like Hermes, the god of ambiguity, neutrality, liminality, mediation, mischief, cleverness, fun, and more, those who cross boundaries bring new information and creative possibility to the group. Still, it is the marginal who often end up being "picked" as modern-day scapegoats.

It's a slippery slope from the just application of purification practices to the blaming and punishment of innocents for our own shortcomings and frustrations. Can we cleanse ourselves of sin by putting it on someone else's head? Doubt it; but we still try to get away with it. We are prone to do it, as a manifestation of repressed consciousness. This is projection, when, rather than dealing consciously with our own faults and misfortunes, we blame them on others. Scapegoating becomes especially dangerous when taken up by the group. We may enter into mass projections, banding together with those like ourselves to punish unlucky "others" for our own unhappiness. If not defused, group energy can whip itself into a maelstrom of emotions and irrationality, leading to aggression and violence. Antisemitism, white supremacy, gay bashing, witch hunts: these are all ugly manifestations of the refusal to deal honestly with one's own transgressions.

Can humans ever get beyond scapegoating? Maybe we'll always have to check our tendency to suspect strangers, to treat others unfairly, to lay blame on someone else's head. The shadow is always there, and, as long as we're alive, there's always more work to do.

Consciousness requires maintenance. It is an ongoing process. As long as we're alive and human, we're never done processing and absorbing unconscious contents. Our shadow contents are those parts we've rejected—whether forgotten or intentionally sent into the wasteland, just like the scapegoats. I don't know how well it worked for the ancients, but following Jungian theory, the rejected parts will continue to plague us. The more we deny them, the more insidious or destructive they will become. The rule is, if you become aware of it, you need to deal with it.

It behooves us to work with the group unconscious to bring repressed contents to light. This is a practice largely missing from dominant culture, and it shows. We are reaping the karma of our disregard. The time to make a change is now (or, ideally, a few hundred years ago).

"To ignore what we each can do to help others in our quest for individual development is to miss the very essence of that quest." —Colman (20)

Whether or not we are complicit in the wounding, we bear the gift and the responsibility to care for each other's wounds. The need is both moral and pragmatic. Failure to attend to the pain of the other results in ever more disturbing, disruptive, destructive social problems. That of which we are unconscious, as it struggles for recognition, will not be ignored, whether it comes from within or without.

And, lest you become overwhelmed, keep in mind this teaching from Jewish tradition:

"It is not upon thee to finish the work; neither art thou free to abstain from it." —The Talmud (*Pirkei Avot* 2:21)

The goddess Maat, from Queen Nefertari's tomb

The concept of balance is fundamental in Egyptian tradition, personified in the figure of Maat. Maat, conceived as the foundation of order, is both a goddess figure and an essential ethical practice. To keep maat, to do maat, was the central goal and orientation of ancient Egyptian culture (Balk 48-51, Karenga 5, Hornung).

Maat is known as the favorite daughter of Re, god of the sun. She accompanies him always on his perpetual journey across the heavens each day and back through the underworld every night. Thus, maat, as the concept of order and right relationship, is born in alignment with natural and universal cycles.

As "the antidote for every form of excess," this concept extends naturally to ideas of social responsibility and the administration of justice. Each individual was expected to do maat, in order to contribute modestly to its increase in the world.

Maat is an ideal that applies to all things, "[linking] the divine, the natural and the social" (Karenga 16), the practice of which must remain flexible and responsive to circumstance.

"Adhere to maat, but do not exaggerate": this instruction from the *Eloquent Peasant* text (Hornung 136) translates well to the modern day aphorism, "moderation in all things, including moderation."

Sociopathy

> **sociopath** noun a person with a personality disorder manifesting itself in extreme antisocial attitudes and behavior and a lack of conscience.

"Sociopathy" is a disregard for the cultural notions of reciprocity that keep us in good relationship with one another: *not caring about how your actions impact others.* Imagine "empty places" or *lacunae* inside the self, where "normal" people would feel love and caring. This is how Guggenbühl-Craig describes it, as a lack of eros, or the missing capacity to love; and he argues that each of us has such places in ourselves where the capacity to love is damaged or missing.

By Guggenbühl-Craig's definition, we are all sociopathic in some way, to some degree. Certainly in practice we distinguish between those who pose a danger to others and those who, say, don't care that they swooped in and stole your parking spot, or those who swipe sugar packets from the diner. We all have "compassion gaps" — you know, those times and places where you *should* care, but you don't, not really?

Then there are those who are dangerously "empty" and prone to commit atrocities. There are those who threaten us and terrify us. There are those who don't care about breaking the social contract in their quest to domination. It's easy to see how sociopathic behavior beats a path to positions of power; but it's not always straightforward to identify future threats, nor to craft effective solutions. How do you block the monstrosity without becoming a monster yourself? It's complicated by the tendency to project our own sociopathy onto others, making "them" into "the bad guys" (aka scapegoating).

There really are dangerous people that we need to cope with, but/and we are all sociopathic in our own ways and to different degrees. We all display aberrant behaviors, stemming from being broken or deficient in some way; but we are not all broken in the same places. That's fortunate, I think...because together we form a social web that, ideally, can support us, even where we are broken.

Ideally, your abundance of love in one area fills in for my lack, and vice versa. That's how we can support each other in our woundedness, and also, yeah, keep each other in line when rights and wrongs are overlooked. A resilient social web holds us so that we may function and even thrive despite our individual inadequacies; and, it holds to account those individuals whose "empty places" are dangerous. A broken social web allows more and more instances of threatening sociopathic behavior to fall through the gaps, causing damage to society as a whole. A broken social web, untended, will continue to unravel.

> *When the wound is between, we cannot heal it individually.*

When the problem is relational, you won't find the solution within the self. When society itself is ruptured, the solution is a social one. This thought is what leads me to champion creative group process as a way of healing and elevating cultural consciousness: a way of repairing the social web that we need to support us. And, as I mentioned earlier, when the individual suffers from socially-inflicted wounds, then the supportive social experience can provide a precious healing balm.

"Rarely, if ever, are any of us healed in isolation. Healing is an act of communion." — bell hooks

Healing trauma TOGETHER

Trauma is injury, of which there are many degrees. Psychic trauma has been defined as an unbearable experience of pain or anxiety, which ranges from "acute, shattering experiences" of abuse and violence to the "cumulative traumas of unmet dependency needs," broadly categorized as neglect and deprivation (Kalsched Inner 1). Kalsched describes how patients have difficulty metabolizing the trauma of the "unthinkable experience" by themselves. Therapy can assist in the integration of this material. So can the compassionate community.

The experience of trauma is compounded through the isolation that frequently accompanies it. The inability of another to understand keeps you from sharing, but a compassionate witness to your painful memories can offer healing that is not otherwise available.

There is a specific context that will allow others to be fully present for such sharing, and that context is the social third. In addition, the basic skills of compassionate listening are fundamental to our efforts to restore the social web.

Traumatic experience may indeed call for professional care, yet we all need to know some key things about how to support others. It's basic first aid. Trauma is present in all of our lives. Sensitivity and a readiness to help must also have a place in the everyday world.

Compassionate first aid: the basics

- *practice kindness and respect*
- *stay in the present: engage with what comes up*
- *listen and share*
- *assume confidentiality*

Don't make assumptions about other people's experiences. There's always more than you know. You'd be surprised. There are many degrees of trauma, and wounds can run many layers deep. Our traumas seem to have their own lives: apart from what we think we *should* feel, some wounds resist healing.

When someone is sharing, let them share. Be present. Listen deeply. Ask questions (with sensitivity) to better understand. Let them be the authority on what impact it has had or is having on their lives.

Don't give unsolicited advice. It's rarely helpful. Speak out of your own experience without expectation. Share from a place of love and caring without judgment.

Avoid "traumatic competition"— don't measure one person's traumas against yours or another person's. Don't say, "Wait till you hear what happened to *me*!" There's little use in judging or comparing traumas.

If you need to move on, redirect the conversation gently and diplomatically. Encourage the person toward additional support, if it seems appropriate.

projection
the unconscious transfer of one's own desires or emotions to another person

participation
being part of the whole

recognition
being uniquely acknowledged

empathy
the ability to understand and share the feelings of another

Vets suffering from PTSD find healing in their work caring for abused tropical birds says Siebert in the NYTimes. The author describes parallel paths of trauma between the two different species.

Is it a living metaphor between parrots and vets that allows them to find meaning and thus healing in their relationship with each other? "Alike but different" creates a healing bridge between individuals or groups.

Empathy is a kind of metaphor
When we are truly present with each other, we almost always notice:

1) things we have in common

      and

2) ways we are different

— which is, when you think about it, metaphor. *"Alike but different."* This true recognition of the other can happen only when we withhold our projections, in order to perceive accurately both the ways we are alike and the ways we are different. Being recognized — being seen and heard as we are — is healing.

In some way, each of us needs acceptance by the group in the context of acknowledgment for our uniqueness. *"Alike but different."* If either the sense of group participation or the sense of individual recognition breaks down — and both often do — there is dysfunction, certainly for the individual, but also for the group.

Empathy is encouraged when we imagine ourselves into each other's experiences, or even when we simply imagine together: a bridge is constructed between us. This seems to be the mechanism of catharsis (in the Aristotelian sense), where imagining into the experience of one person's wounding leads to a sense of emotional release for the group. It's like an inversion of scapegoating, when you think about it.

Empathy, then, is a kind of metaphor, where you are able to feel into someone else's experiences, while still retaining your sense of individual difference. This offers healing for everyone involved.

metaphor = alike but different.

In using imagination to relate what we know from experience to that which we have never experienced, healing can occur. Something about metaphor is healing.

Metabolizing trauma through the body

> **metabolism** noun   the chemical processes that occur within a living organism in order to maintain life

Everything does not need to be translated through your rational mind! It's a hard lesson for us westerners, who have for so long prized rational reduction as the most potent truth that, caught up in *THINKING* things and *SAYING* things, we forget to *DO* things and *FEEL* things. Oh well. Nonetheless, metabolism is a physical process, and the metabolizing of trauma need not rely on an explicit verbal recounting of experience.

We can metabolize trauma without rational expression. Physical movement, creative expression, group process, and ritual are all effective means of release and transformation, often more so than talking. And I'm pro-talking! But trauma resides in the body, and physical expression through movement and ritual can be the most powerful cathartic, particularly when done in community.

> **catharsis** noun   the process of releasing, and thereby providing relief from, strong or repressed emotion; a bodily purging

Group energy
Group energy magnifies the power of any experience, and the group can help the individual do what the individual cannot do alone.

When you sing with others, you feel the vibration of sound waves in your body — sound waves that you are all producing together. It's powerful. Dance in a mass of people moved by the insistence of the beat, voices and bodies merging with the music, and you feel the release into something larger than you. Generally, very much more powerful in a group than when alone in your room! It's great to dance/sing/move/emote at home by yourself, *YES, AND* in a group experience the energy is amplified. The sense of release is shared by all. Of course everybody's not releasing the same stuff! Doesn't matter. And you don't have to articulate what you're letting go of to feel the beneficial effects. That's the power of moving energy to metabolize stress.

Group celebrations bathe us in waves of joy. Coming together to mourn and share our grief collectively is a soothing balm. In either instance, cohesion develops from swimming together in that mutual experience. We may also crave and cherish the private interior experience, but there's a comfort that only comes from being held and cared for by the group (and that group may be family or community or sometimes even a group of relative strangers).

We have weddings and funerals, parades and support groups, and likewise, new rituals can be crafted specifically for whatever the purpose at hand. We invoke release and transformation using voice, movement, theatre, dance, and somatic practice. Ritual serves to protect us while we surrender to the cleansing experience. The change that occurs is real.

Containing the energy

There are dangers to this powerful group energy, as well. Today (in 2024), we see and feel the dangers of the angry mob all around us on so many fronts. When people are upset about events in the world, they need to come together to demonstrate their anger and will to change. Yet, when uncontained — when the uncontrollable nature of "the mob mentality" takes over — people are carried away by wildness, as you might be carried away by a wild river or engulfed in a wildfire. In such times, thought and conscience lose their sway, and people engage in acts they would never condone when in their "right minds." We rely on ritual to contain the wildness, as humans have always done.

Laws spoken and unspoken, orderly ways of doing things, rituals of deference, politeness, manners and common courtesies— these are containing rituals that keep us in check. Breaking such norms is a way to change, and sometimes it's called for — but beware! When we break the container, wildness floods in, and then anything can happen.

Jung saw ritual as *THE* way to manage group energy, which he deemed too dangerous to let run unchecked (CW 9i, para. 225-227). Certainly the atrocities of two world wars buttressed his opinions on the dangers of the collective; he was notably suspicious of "group mind." Current events tell us we are still susceptible to these wildfires of human energy, unfortunately. We are continually amazed and further horrified by the actions of huge groups of people. You, like me, may wonder *"How can so many possibly think and do such unconscionable things? How can they commit such atroc-*

Composed of images from hibrida; nosyrevy; AdrianHillman.

ities? Be convinced to believe in the righteousness of such a cause? Go along with this madness?" Well, just like a wildfire, I think mob mentality is a kind of wild, natural catastrophe. I think *"they"* (which could be any of us) are taken over by the stories that have enlisted them. THEY are being ridden by the narrative. Though *THEY* may feel a sense of oneness with the wild power that courses through them, *THEY* have abdicated any personal sense of control or responsibility. *THEY are* letting the wild story have its way with them.

Jung wrote about religion as a container in which humans can share the experience of the unknown. Specifically, Jung cautioned us on the dangers posed by the disintegration of religious practices in modern times. We may view many religious practices as imperfect or problematic, but the ritual forms they give us function to safely (well, *sometimes* safely) hold the collective unconscious.

In depth psych terms, religious ritual functions as a container to hold the collective psyche and the experience of the numinous, or the Great Unknown. (Also called "God" or "the unconscious" or simply "that which we do not know.") This content is simply too big, too much, overwhelming for the individual to hold, like trying to contain the ocean. Collectively, we modern sophisticates may no longer "believe" in "God," but we continue to experience the mana that engendered the belief in the god; and when ritual forms are lacking, individuals do indeed try to swallow the ocean — that is, assimilate this "too big to handle" stuff. That leads to a lot of problems.

One such problem is the sense of grandiosity, when the individual believes themself to be responsible for and in charge of everything; in other words, unconsciously believing oneself to *BE* the God, the Savior, the One, the Way, the Answer, the Archetype—pick your numenal nominal... I mean, call it what you will—when we don't have an appropriate way to experience and relate to things that are *bigger* than us, we are prone to imagine that they are *part* of us, and that we, as individuals, are REALLY REALLY BIG AND IMPORTANT; and that's a really, really big problem. Remember when I was talking about mistakenly imagining that the imagination lives and has its origin inside of you? Again, please be aware, *it's not all you*. When you imagine that you yourself are big enough to contain everything, the contents (collective psyche) will overwhelm the container (the individual–*YOU*).

Pentheus and the maenads. Pompeii

Dionysus, Greek god of ecstasy and madness, inspired those who worshipped him to intoxicated frenzy. His followers indulged freely in pleasures and passions, but, with nothing to stop them, they could be carried into reckless acts by their impulsive enthusiasm.

In one story King Pentheus is torn limb from limb by Agave, his own frenzied mother. Hallucinating that he is a lion, she impales his head on a stick and carries it back to Thebes. Only coming back to her right mind when she meets her father Cadmus does she realize what she has done.

It's a conundrum for many westerners, who, for many reasons, no longer practice traditional rites. We may proclaim ourselves to have "evolved" beyond the need for such things, only that doesn't make it so. We really haven't. Some of us may turn to the practices of other cultures to fulfill that need. Ok when and if you can do so with respect and openness and humility. But when and if seeking to *purchase* "exotic" spiritual experience, beware that commercialization can kill meaning, for the host-culture as well as the customer. The gods may vacate. And, though we crave the intensity of experience that we witness in other peoples' practices, appropriation of someone else's tradition will typically be superficial and trivializing, lacking the resounding depth of a ritual grounded in one's own culture. I'm all in favor of learning about and from other cultures, but the thing is to recognize how critically we are in need of rituals that are born out of our own symbolic resources. When we outgrow the old ways, then we need some new ways to move into.

But the good news? It's a simple thing to create a ritual. Can you make it meaningful? Yes. When you pour in your intention, the rituals you craft will be based on symbols meaningful to you, for purposes that you require, whether it's a rite of initiation, of celebration, of grief, of healing.... If you invest yourself in them, you may find them highly efficacious.

efficacious
adjective
successful in producing a desired or intended result; effective

Rituals become meaningful when they are built of symbolically relevant metaphor and practiced over time. Meaning is amplified and multiplied when taken up by the group, so find or make your groups and get going. Again, rituals are physical practices, grounded in the body.

Ritual is physical

A ritual is physically participated in, not something you watch from your couch.

Ritual is physical, sensory, grounded: it must be directly experienced in the body to be understood. You cannot "know" it vicariously, through reading or thinking about it. (Ok, reading, thinking, and viewing are all *types* of direct experience, true, which you might practice in a mindful, resonant way, and which may be transformative; but they do not typically involve your whole body in the same physically active way that what we call "somatic experience" does.) The embodied experience brings a level of awareness that cannot be gotten any other way.

Through sensory experience — *which may itself be traumatic*— a new sense of reality is awakened. Participants are changed, in body and mind.

Let me repeat: traditional rites are frequently traumatizing in themselves. Hmm.

–Think of rites of passage, like scarification or tattoo, where the skin is cut or burnt to mark a social transition...

–Think of pilgrimage, where pilgrims undergo prolonged physical stress in traveling to a sacred site for the sake of healing or purification...

–Think of the shamanic voyage where mind-altering substances provide entrée to another realm, but the cost of admission is vomiting, sweating, uncontrollable shaking...

–Heck, just think about birth! For mother and baby, birth is a traumatic experience. One that we yearn for and cherish, a transformation that offers the greatest reward but requires we face the greatest of risks. Birth is a traumatic experience, no matter which ritual forms we use to protect ourselves.

The thing about trauma is that it is transformative. Shocks us right into a new way of being. Before and after are never the same. But trauma is also dangerous.

When trauma comes upon us without warning, uncontained, we're not prepared. Who knows what will happen next? Perhaps there is no one nearby to offer support. Shock and fear can be overwhelming. There is no container. Again, ritual is a container designed to provide protection while transformation occurs. *There is always risk.* I mean, the ritual itself may break the individual, and the ritual container can always break, but the goal of ritualized trauma is to harness the transformative power while minimizing the danger.

So, ritual is invoked to contain energy and to support transformation. Effective rituals can be created by using meaningful symbols appropriate to the purpose of the ritual. Such symbols connect the individual to the archetypal, in a sense connecting the individual into a deep shared source of power. Effective group rituals will rely on shared metaphor.

(the boat is ritual)

Shared metaphor

Metaphor extends from experience and is culturally relative. *Bigger is better, time is money, the future unfolds before us ...* these common western metaphors (and there are limitless such examples) underlie complex shared cultural understandings, but *they are not universal.*

Metaphors are born out of physical experience; "We typically conceptualize the nonphysical in terms of the physical," say Lakoff and Johnson in their book, *Metaphors We Live By* (59). That is, physical experience underlies any conceptual system. So, think about it: from pole to equator, jungle to desert, coast to mountain to plains—environment varies widely from place to place, and environment is huge in determining cultural notions of reality. That begins to explain why, outside of cultural context, metaphors are not reliably consistent in meaning.

Even within a culture, metaphor is by nature open to interpretation, so we might be excused for thinking it untrustworthy, for thinking we'd be better off without it. We might think, "Just use words straight, don't bother with metaphors!" Words have defined, fixed meanings, right? Mm. Eh. Words, too, are embedded in cultural understanding. Words mean different things to different people. Context is everything.

> *Any given verbal interpretation receives its meaning in part from accompanying non-verbalized communication—shared traditions, common knowledge, shared sensory experience, here-and-now personal interactions, and much more—in which it is embedded"* (Ong 4).

Words, fabulous words—they really are! Magical! They evoke, elucidate, elaborate, convince ... but they do not replace experience. Everything points back to experience as the ground that underlies meaning, metaphor, and the way we use words. Understanding comes from our *shared* experience. The metaphors that arise in the process help us make connections. Metaphor helps us extend from what we know to what we don't know.

As we live through this strange collision of multi-culturalism with the personally-curated lifestyle, it's like we have more and more ways of encountering each other but with less and less shared experience. Intersections of understanding can be quite rare. In a pluralistic world of people from radically different backgrounds who have never done anything together, how is communication even possible? No wonder confusion abounds. Common ground must be established for communication to take place.

using what you know to see what you don't know

Cultural pluralism

> **cultural pluralism** a condition in which minority groups participate fully in the dominant society, yet maintain their cultural differences

Conflicts can arise naturally when people of different cultural backgrounds come into contact. It's just different ways of doing things and different understandings. Resolution may not be simple, but surely it begins with respect and kindness and not trying to steamroll over other people's traditions.

At the outset, people fear syncretism, the fusion of beliefs and practices. Syncretism happens naturally over time when people coexist, and it's a beautiful and fascinating thing. Like "Stone Soup," everybody adds their contribution and it simmers together to a flavorful broth; but it's rocky and fractious at first. People defend what they love because they don't want it to change, they don't want to lose it. What could be more human than that?

When we lack shared background and experience, communication can be difficult, painful, stressful, angry—if it happens at all. But if we can't communicate on some level, then we have no hope of resolving our problems. So we have to figure out a way forward.

I can't imagine that human relations will ever be perfectly harmonious, but there are ways to better understand each other. It starts with doing things together. Don't ask people to give up their most beloved, closely-held traditions, but look toward new projects to generate new understandings and new traditions.

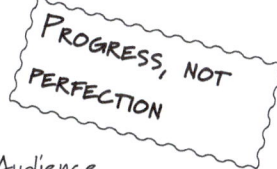

syncretism the amalgamation of different religions, cultures, or schools of thought

PROGRESS, NOT PERFECTION

Dear Pluralistic Audience,
   Who is "we"? How can I use "we" appropriately? I have the questions, not the answers.
   My topic is "us" and the things we do together, and how. I don't know—can never know—who all is included in "us," and, even less what our variety of backgrounds and opinions may comprise. I'm trying my best to facilitate a respectful conversation, but I'm probably saying some things wrong anyway, depending on who you are. So, sorry if I say it wrong.
   Sincerely and With Love,
      Mary

stone soup

Metaphors shift in meaning and relevance over time and in response to events in the world. As culture changes, so will metaphor. New versions of traditional stories bring forth an evolution of meaning. Playful or naïve recombination of common phrases can illuminate new understandings: insightful, subversive, funny.... It is because of the spaciousness of metaphor and myth—that within words and in between words there is room to understand in more than one way—that this evolution of meaning can occur.

> ### *The bricoleur, said Lévi-Strauss, "shapes the beautiful and useful out of the dump heap of human life."*

bricolage
construction using whatever comes to hand

• • • • • • • • • •

From a bricolage of old or unfamiliar metaphors will emerge new coherence, because this is what humans do: we find meaning and we make meaning out of what we have, thanks to the mythic imagination that is our nature. Since metaphors are built on experience, playing around together can unite fragmented communities. As long as we do things with each other, we will muddle through; and in that muddling, every day, new metaphors and new understandings arise.

Metaphor is the essential bridge traversing the space between us, connecting my experiences with yours, giving us a way to share understanding while also maintaining our differences. We're all "alike but different."

The Social Third

The social third is the space between us where we can interact playfully and creatively, where we can join resources to become greater than our individual selves, where we can build a shared narrative, where we can share feelings and personal views without judgment or interpretation... Whaaaat? Sounds awfully idealistic!

Ok, these things are *possible*.

What is required is *space*: physical space, yes, but I really mean head space, the space that allows possibility, the space that allows us to share the experience of the unknown, and where we allow each of us to respond in our own way. We *must invite* the ambiguous space between.

> *the connection requires the bridge, and the bridge requires the gap*

When we practice awareness together, we begin to open to each other. Our voices interlace within group experience, the group is strengthened and the individual supported.

The social third is a non-dual, non-dogmatic space where participants explore various perspectives imaginatively, not analytically. Solutions can emerge, as if the fluidity of the situation allows ideas to float to the surface and be seen.

This doesn't have to be a big deal major event! Could be, but doesn't have to be. The social third space is "open" anytime we can be in relationship with others and feel we are seen and heard and allowed to participate and express ourselves freely, without being organized or judged, without being reduced to roles and labels. To share creative musings without hierarchies or humiliation. Not all cultural situations allow or encourage the social third, but the overall lack of it results in dysfunction.

Playfulness allows the freedom to explore ambiguity and paradox. Moving between various viewpoints widens perspective, creating the space in which pluralism can be entertained. Pluralism allows for the different in "alike but different."

Liminality in ritual refers to the transitional phase, when one has let go of what was and is on the threshold of what is becoming. Victor Turner emphasizes its transformational nature ("Betwixt"), but makes an important distinction between "liminal" and "liminoid" experiences: "liminal" applies to demanding and compulsory rites that are integral to tribal and agrarian cultures, while "liminoid" describes the experimental and free behavior that is common in large-scale, complex societies.

The shared experience advocated in this book qualifies as an "optional liminoid genre," distinct from the initiatory *rite de passage* described by van Gennep; but it has features common to ritual.

Remember, it's not all you
Social experience is between you and others. Obvious — so why even mention it? It may be obvious intellectually, but the cultural view *(weltenschauung)* has practical implications to the way we interact and the expectations we have of each other. Events shared between you and others can't be neatly divvied up into personal portions. The dynamic social interaction is a third, nebulous thing, more than the sum of the parts. Your wounds and your joys are your own, of course, but, <u>as I've said before,</u> the experience is not only yours, and it's not only theirs, either. Everyone's point-of-view is part of the picture.

Together, we're able to express and experience a transcendence beyond our personal experiences — something bigger than you or me. To do so allows healing and renewal.

That's why we need to make more opportunities for the kinds of social connection where we are present, curious, and engaged, where we actually feel seen and heard, where we see others with a real sense of understanding and caring, and where we really enjoy ourselves. Whether it's a fun and easy hangout or a deep and potent transformational experience, we can proactively initiate social experiences that open and share the third space. We need all kinds of social experiences of the third, from the lightest most serendipitous interaction to the planned and potentially transformative ritual event.

"The ancient Pueblo people sought a communal truth, not an absolute. For them this truth lived somewhere within the web of differing versions."
Leslie Silko 35

Also Remember: it's not going to be perfect. Keep trying...

DON'T POKE PEOPLE IN THEIR WOUNDS. IT HURTS!

Exploration of the space between and around us is not an invitation to enter the private space of the other. We must respect each other's privacy! Don't force or be forced into exposure of tender wounds, or anything you don't wish to share, but maintain an atmosphere where sharing is voluntary, accepting, and non-judgmental.

If sharing is difffficult for you, don't force it, but remember that when others can see something about you that was previously unseen or misunderstood, you may be able to let go of a defensive stance or a sense of victimhood, becoming free to unfold more fully, free to make connections and explore the perspectives of others.

Inviting Thirdness

*Where and how can we get more of the
social third?*

First: <u>Notice</u> when it's missing.

*Second: <u>Imagine</u> what the between space
might look or feel like.*

Third: <u>Invite</u> it to expand.

*You can practice this in big eventful ways
and in tiny moments of opening.*

Moments can become momentous.

*take a breath
soften your gaze
soften your mind*

*You may not notice a difference right away,
but over time, I think you will.*

> **We can surrender to the third, because it is an open-ended container, neither you nor me. It is not a question of submitting to the others' will.**
>
> •

Emmanuel Ghent distinguishes between the terms "surrender" and "submission":

"To me, surrender is an act of embracing the unknown, whether in a quiet, meditative, receptive way or in an all-out "active," assertive way, a "letting it happen."(31)

Surrender is open-ended, part of an open system that tends to grow, differentiate, and expand into new forms. In this sense, it is creative, emergent, and unpredictable as to result, yet highly interactive with other internal and external elements in one's experience. Submission is close-ended, part of a closed system. Unlike surrender, it has a specific goal or destination. (31-32)

In surrender, arguing ceases; there is a feeling of liberation. In submission, we feel bound; we are secretly protesting, debating, bickering, wishing to bring in a lawyer to present our case. In surrender, there is no trace of complaint or blame; there is acceptance. In submission, by contrast, there is resignation, and with it, bitterness." (32)

surrender:
an open-ended letting go into the unknown

submission:
a close-ended feeling of being bound

The Transcendent Function in the Group Experience

According to Jung's theory of the transcendent function, a third thing is born "out of the suspension between opposites ... that leads to a new level of being ...[manifesting] itself as a quality of conjoined opposites" (CW 8, para. 189).

Jung's transcendent function refers to resolving splits *within the individual psyche* — becoming able to accept opposing views or truths within yourself, rather than choosing one and refusing or projecting the other. For example, you say you want a stable, steady, cozy home life, AND ALSO you want to travel the world with no attachments. Listen, it's not crazy to have competing drives within the self, but it can make you feel and act crazy if you haven't examined it, or if you think you must embrace one impulse and reject the other. To recognize and accept these competing impulses is called "holding the tension of the opposites." To find a solution that acknowledges both desires is to transcend the conflict.

How about when such splits occur socially, between individuals or between cultures? Or between culture and nature? Such splits cannot be resolved *within* one person or *by* one person. Solutions emerge at the location of the split. The split is the opening through which possibility may unfold. So, if the split is within you, the solution will come through you. If the split is between you and me, the solution will emerge between us. In order to implement a solution, *together* we must hold the tension and *together* transcend.

I believe that, by together exploring unknowns and sharing the imaginal experience as it unfolds, we may invoke cultural transformation.

A participatory group experience is not merely the sum of individual experiences. You working on your own enlightenment and me on mine will not substitute for a group practice of integrated awareness; and we cannot wait until we've all reached enlightenment before we begin to work together.

> **integrated awareness**
> my term for the integration of intuitive, intellectual and experiential knowledge

328 HOW TO PARTICIPATE IN THE WORLD

---
archetypal motifs = symbolic patterns with collective significance that always take unique expression

---

Jung locates archetypal motifs *in between* individual and collective. They're metaphors that bridge the gap between individual and culture. That gap, that potential space between us, is the social third.

Shared experience of archetypal motifs transpires in the social third.

• •

The archetype always refers simultaneously to psyche (inner) and mundane world (outer): "archetype" is an inner-outer experience based in the psychoid reality. Symbols are the "co-ordinates" of an archetype.

> "[Symbols] are of course inconceivable without the psyche, the producer of images; yet it is equally true that all symbols point beyond themselves to a reality outside the psyche. At the same time, however, we must realize that every symbol contains within itself a revelation of something which has an existence that is essentially independent of images." (Neumann 87)

Rider Waite Tarot: Pamela Colman Smith

Group alchemy

1) the goal of alchemy is transformation; and
2) transformation needs imaginal space; so
3) cultural transformation needs shared imaginal space.

Imagine our disparate attitudes coalescing into a shared understanding that transcends (goes beyond) rational explanation. This is group alchemy.

To nurture a transformative group experience:

- *Use ritual to form and hold the container*

- *Invite imaginal response to areas of curiosity and unknowns*

- *Use archetypal imagery to build cohesion*

- *Accept multiple perspectives*

- *Allow ambiguity within the container. Soften the edges. Let it be.*

How to share the imaginal

Imaginal sharing as a group experience is uncommon in dominant society today, especially for adults. Maybe it's a regular part of your life — I hope so! We can create more opportunities for this type of sharing. These concepts, already discussed lay the groundwork for successful sharing:

- *Healing the mind-body split*

- *Participation*

- *Thirdness*

- *Imaginalia*

- *Inner+Outer continuity*

Not everyone is schooled in these concepts, but if the facilitator holds them in mind and introduces the ideas, then over time participants will grow in understanding. A written statement of Guidelines or Agreements is recommended.

Facilitator, wait, what? Who's the facilitator? Ok, reader, you may or may not consider yourself a facilitator, but every group needs someone to be in charge. "Host" is another way of saying it. Some of my least happy group experiences have been those that lacked leadership. Who's driving this thing, anyway?

The facilitator holds the container — This is essential! — and shapes the experience with simple limits and guidelines. And, I believe it's always best to begin with grounding in location. Look to the Group How-To Guide following this chapter for activities that work well.

> *Remember:*
>
> • *Establish a safe and trustworthy container*
>
> • *Provide simple guidelines*
>
> • *Begin with grounding in location*

Benefits of Sharing the Imaginal

- *We become more compassionate!*
- *We feel seen and heard!*
- *We share our best stuff!*
- *We participate!*
- *Social wounds are healed!*
- *Society becomes relevant!*
- *Life goes on!*

And I mean, that's really what we're all hoping for, isn't it?

WHOOSH!

Enter the Mythos-Sphere

This book's first incarnation was my doctoral dissertation, titled **Crafting the Mythos-Sphere: Toward the Practical Integration of Intuition and Intellect.** *I've argued with myself over how much or where to refer to the original project, and decided to include this summary, which is perhaps redundant, but it gives an earlier perspective on my work and how it developed out of mythological studies. You can find my dissertation in full on Proquest at: https://www.proquest.com/docview/2048104131*

I use the term "Mythos-Sphere" to describe the nature of the collective psyche within which we humans live, *a multi-dimensional imaginal structure formed of beliefs, images, stories, songs, dreams, memories, patterns, abstractions, artifacts, treasures and junk, meaningful rituals and unconscious habits, broken traditions and emergent ones...*

By "*crafting* the Mythos-Sphere," I suggest that we, human beings, *make meaning* out of our lives by *making things*: we give physical form to imaginal content through the creative process. By doing this together, in a social context, we may bridge divides in understanding.

Shared metaphorical understanding, aka myth, grows from shared experience; without it, social systems break down.

Mythology is the invisible web that holds society together, always evolving and being rebuilt. People from different cultural backgrounds live within different mythologies and metaphorical understandings; but as these are invisible, disagreements and misunderstandings can arise inexplicably. The solution is shared experience. When we do things together, we begin to form new webs: new shared understandings: **new mythologies.**

All cultures construct meaning through myth. The cultural third is where this takes place. Mythic understanding mediates between self and culture, and a mythic framework holds pluralistic views together. When the cultural third is damaged or inaccessible, opportunity for the playful negotiation and sharing of meaning breaks down and cultural cohesion is lost. Yet, the cultural third can be rehabilitated. It depends upon a shared experience of the unknown.

---

mythos-sphere
noun

• a cosmology

• the expression and understanding that result from the group creative process;

• the set of shared awareness, including explicit and unspoken, inner and outer, conscious and unconscious, individual and collective, intuitive and intellectual, material and imaginal

• the container

• the contents

• the third

• the territory of participation

Without the mythic "containers" that focus group energy, we are susceptible to the often destructive forces unleashed through group unconsciousness. In early twenty-first century America, the "old ways" of mythology, religion, and cultural tradition no longer serve in many respects, but what has replaced them? New contexts for reflection and cultural participation, grounded in physical location, can help re-establish crucial relationships with mythic forms.

Through my doctoral work, I developed and implemented a method for collaborative creative participation for the sake of building social cohesion. This method is, in a sense, a container to hold our shared imaginal experience.

The container of a creative arts project exemplifies what Ghent speaks of as an "open system" into which one can surrender without loss of self: into the container of a project, one can surrender emotions, feelings, pain, anxiety, and opinions, without inflicting them on others.

My method for creative collaboration is pragmatic, building on approaches from depth psychology and developmental psychology, with perspectives from philosophy, cultural studies, ritual theory, group process, and expressive arts therapy. Reverie, play and expressive arts are used to develop a group narrative. We enlarge the third space as participants oscillate between inner and outer experiences. A sense of shared mythos develops naturally from a creative exploration of the basic questions:
Where are we? Who is here? What happens?

The group integration of ideas and narratives is an interweaving, not an homogenizing. Individuals bring in many threads; some are taken up by the group, becoming more central to the developing textual pattern; some remain peripheral or simply fall away. Themes arising repeatedly from multiple sources characterize the emerging narrative(s).

Just as the creative process helps to integrate the individual's inner and outer experiences, the process of creative collaboration can mediate the relationship between individual and group. The power of the group to help with metabolizing trauma can be tapped in the setting of a collaborative creative arts project.

Look for more specific applications of my method in the Group Practices Guide.

Sharing is the best/Sharing is scary

In community, says Parker Palmer, "we generally behave in ways that drive everything original and wild into hiding" (59).

O, humans! What do we really want? I say that we all want to be appreciated for who we are. We want to give of ourselves in a way that makes a difference in the lives of others. It's such a great feeling! So what gets in the way? Why do we hide?

- Fear of being seen
- Fear of not being seen
- Actually not being seen
- Being seen but not being appreciated

These are biggies. And how about these:

What if I share till I have nothing left? What if I share but nobody shares back? What if people take what I give without seeing me or appreciating me? What if someone else takes credit for MY share? Should I be posting this? Is this on brand? Should I be charging for this?

These are valid concerns, unfortunately. There are many social situations where sharing does not feel safe or wise, where we may be taken advantage of or treated unfairly. It definitely does not help when we float in and out of "communities" without a real sense of connection. I'm sure it's always been so, and the internet has made this exponentially more true, so, yes—sharing is scary. But yes, sharing is also the best.

We need safe, loving, giving, social situations where we can each be seen and appreciated.
And, where these are lacking, we need to create them. We need to do the grassroots work it takes to nurture nurturing spaces. That means helping one another to learn how to be together supportively.

Parker Palmer's methods and insights for facilitating group retreats invoke the experiences of solitude and community simultaneously in order to heal the soul. His book, *A Hidden Wholeness: The Journey Toward an Undivided Life : Welcoming the Soul and Weaving Community in a Wounded World*, is a valuable resource.

Starting a Group

Why *YOU* should start a group
We need to be together creatively, regularly: Not just to perform or show off, but in a healthy, nourishing, everyday way. More than being comfortable in your own skin: being comfortable with allowing psyche to flow. Relaxing ego, sharing ideas without ownership, letting imagination roam and inspire, letting the social mycelium connect and nourish us all.

Can you do it?
I'm saying YOU can and should do it. Sorry if that sounds patronizing because you're like, "Yeah, I KNOW, I already *do*!" Still I know there are some of you readers who don't think you're cut out for the job, because maybe you're shy or you don't feel like it or... or.... Well, I think EVERYONE can in some way be the initiator of a group—because gathering is just a normal thing for humans to do — a normal thing that has, in this time, become, for many, somewhat abnormal.

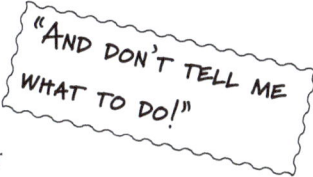

"And don't tell me what to do!"

What kind of group?
Any kind! Maybe it's a one-time thing — a party- a walk, a dinner... Maybe it's a recurring thing — a book club, a discussion group, a time to share music Maybe get together to walk your dogs or plant a garden... What do you enjoy doing? Or what would you like to explore?

But I don't know anyone!
How can you start a group if the whole thing is that you feel isolated and lack connection? Yes, that is a good question, and not one to be glib about. What if you have social anxiety — hate small talk — adore your introverted self? These are all big questions, and I don't mean to trivialize them; but I do mean to say that, even so, there are many, many ways into social experience, and I believe there's a way for you.

Start somewhere
Start where you are. with small, everyday connections.

Smile at people. Hold the door for someone. Thank the checker at the grocery store. Talk to the trees, and listen for their response. Sometimes when you talk to dogs, it opens into a conversation with nearby humans.

Think organically. What is a group you would like to be a part of? Grow it. Plant seeds. Nurture the connections that you would like to see flourish.

Maybe you have a community garden or an urban allotment garden in your area, where you can grow your own food and connect with others at the same time. It's kind of a win-win-win (-win-win-win), because you're building relationships with neighbors and the land and the food that you're growing, and promoting good health on all levels. Community gardens often share produce with local food banks as well. Gardens connect us all.

Meanwhile, see if you can take a step back from any groups that are not nourishing you; at least take a closer look. Why are you there? What are you hoping to get or give or accomplish? What is your actual experience in comparison to your hopes? Does the group provide value in some ways? Is there something about your participation or the way you show up- that you could/would/should change? Or, is it time to step back and make space for more fulfilling connections?

My introverted self wants to say, find your own "sweet spot." I spend the lion's share of my time alone (how else would I get anything done?), and that makes me happy *until I suddenly realize that got I lonely while I wasn't paying attention.* At that moment, if I'm not careful, I might manically schedule a bunch of things, which will then drive me crazy because suddenly my schedule is too full. The point? Knowing about how much time you like to spend with others can help you keep your social life more or less in balance.

To build connection, you don't have to share *EVERYTHING*, but you have to share *SOMETHING*. So figure out or find or create what it is you'd like to share. What would you like others to recognize about you? How would you like to give of yourself?

It's just like gardening: one garden won't feed us all. We need many, many gardens and many, many gardeners, each in your own way, place and time, and all for the cause of a healthy society that encourages balance and growth and participation. You won't be surprised when I say that by "nurturing spaces," I'm talking once again about the social third.

Keep imagining the expanding third...And it will happen!

Speaking of building connection, Doug Tallamy's Homegrown National Park Initiative calls each of us to step up to the biodiversity crisis by planting native plants in our local ecosystems. This patchwork approach effectively provides "stepping stones" of essential resources. It's not only humans that need to eat. Pollinators, wildlife, the watershed, the soil, all can be served — or starved — by the plants we choose in our home gardens. We are all a part of this web!

"Our National Parks, no matter how grand in scale, are too small and separated from one another to preserve (native) species to the levels needed. Thus, the concept for Homegrown National Park, a bottom-up call-to-action to restore habitat where we live and work, and to a lesser extent where we farm and graze, extending national parks to our yards and communities." Doug Tallamy *Learn more online.*

Group Process: Some Specifics

Three or more people getting together: that's a group. Simply any collection of people considered as related in some way, groups form naturally all the time for any number of reasons. You love some and hate some. Sometimes you feel at ease, sometimes on edge. You feel eagerness or dread. You are warmly welcomed here, snubbed there. It's a real mixed bag.

I love an easy-going gathering, and I also appreciate conversations that go deep, discussions that tackle opposing points-of-view, and even awkward situations where I'm not sure exactly what's happening or where it will end up. I guess, weirdly, I'm saying I enjoy even those situations that I don't enjoy. That can only be half true at best! It's all part of the mix, though. You need those times that poke you and push your patience, for the learning they bring.

Differences and hard problems don't have to resolve to make a group experience worthwhile. Sometimes it's ok to feel annoyed and leave it at that. And if I'm being honest, I'm very easy to annoy. Is it me? Yes, that's me. It might be you, too, or not. I'm just saying, when people come together, there's often friction, but that's not necessarily bad, and it doesn't always last forever. I'm just saying, don't be too idealistic in your expectations.

With all that in mind, some groups are more satisfying than others. Whatever I've 'just said', I'd rather be part of a functional group than a dysfunctional one. Here's what I've gathered along the way about what makes a planned group event successful.

Planning and maintaining the group
Fun gatherings may pop up serendipitously and delight us like wildflowers on a summer day. They make us happy and don't need any planning or thought or any more reason for being. Love that! AND ALSO, in getting an intentional group off to a healthy start some planning up front is super helpful.

But what kind of group you are forming? A raucous free-for-all ? A meditative quiet time for sharing poignant memories? A one-time-only picnic? An ongoing support group? Obviously some groups need more structure and planning than others.

> Priya Parker's work on this topic helps you to focus first on the purpose of your gathering, then developing the form to make the gathering more meaningful to participants. Read her book, *The Art of Gathering*, and find great resources on her website, including her gathering toolkit and her newsletter.

Things to keep in mind:
Group Function:
An intentional group needs a shared understanding of its function: *why are we here?* This leads to developing a shared narrative: *we're here because...*

Do you think this is obvious? Yes. And it needs to be: Obvious. So, it's kind of mind-boggling that this step, *clarifying the reason for the group,* is often ignored. To be fair, sometimes it takes time for the sense of purpose to emerge or gel: it has to be figured out in process. But sometimes, it just never becomes clear what the hell is happening. *Why are we even here?* If you don't spell it out, there may be no shared understanding. Expectations may be wildly at odds! On the other hand, if you've stated the purpose, you can always return to that when things go wonky.

It may be a simple statement, rather than a grand manifesto. For instance:

- *Come over to make cookies with me. I've got plenty of dough.* or –

- *I like hanging out with you guys! Let's talk about things we'd like to do together.* or –

- *It's time to overthrow the CEO. Join me!* or –

- *Want to work on a community garden?*

But where a manifesto is warranted, write a manifesto! An ongoing group wants a shared sense of what the group is about. A successful group experience depends on communication. You want an idea of what it's about—even if what it's about is...*nothing*... (like Seinfeld. "It's a show about nothing.")

Order and Chaos:
Obviously I'm into play and creativity, BUT/AND play and creativity can threaten order. So where do you draw the line between order and chaos? It's really a personal preference, how much freedom you love or how much you can stand; but do consider the relation between structure (order) and freedom (chaos) in your group. What will work and feel the best? If you want people to do things a certain way, you need to let them know. Don't expect them to read your mind. And keep tabs on how it's going. Make changes as needed.

Structure/Freedom: know what works for you; and be sensitive to signs that play is about to devolve into something more destructive, so you can take steps to rebalance.

Dynamics:
The vibe, the energy of the group: the collective psyche. It's not necessarily under anyone's control, but you can shape or encourage a certain dynamic if you put a supportive structure in place up front to encourage that mood. Once a dynamic gets established, it can be very difficult to shift. Shape the vibe with the setting, the invitation, the form you give to the gathering, the group agreements you share, and the expectations you communicate.

Thirdness — of course!
Promote thirdness with openness and acceptance, and watch out for that out-of-balance seesaw rhythm that signifies "lack of thirdness." If you notice divisions forming, people taking sides, tempers flaring, then look for ways to soothe and defuse and return to balance. Find points of agreement, bring attention back to the present moment or to the question at hand or to the reason for being together. Ask everyone to take a breath. If people are pulling back from engagement, try something like an easy collaborative game or a quiet meditation on breath to get grounded again.

Encourage participants to practice giving grace. Cancel culture is a dead end.

Self-abandonment:
When individuals over-identify with the group, they may feel unsafe or insecure or unable to express their authentic thoughts and feeling. Perhaps an individual is trying to embody the archetypal energy of the group — to BE the group rather than to be a *participant* in the group. Enter the danger of group mind overpowering rational response. This phenomenon is not natural to the space of the expanded third, yet it can happen.

Sensitivity and firmness on the part of the facilitator will go a long way. Notice if people are:

- biting back their wordst

- alking over others

- preventing or belittling expression

- claiming to speak for the group

- putting down alternate views.

> **YOU ARE NOT AN ARCHETYPE!**
>
> You ae not the Goddess, the Hero, the Warrior, the Savior...No! None of those!
>
> You may wear the mantle of an archetype in ritual or play, you may be inspired, drawn to, moved by... but don't get carried away! Remember yourself. Step out of the mantle and return to your human form.

Take action to remedy! Support everyone's opportunity for expression! Remind participants: *your uniqueness is also your genius, the aspect of you that has the most value for the group.*

Lowest common denominator effect
This is the outcome of self-abandonment. When the group becomes unsafe for individuals, then individuals will huddle together and try to blend in with the group—even if the group is making bad or abhorrent choices. It's the survival instinct. Herd mentality is not characterized by nuanced thinking but often by the stupidest, broadest black and white ideas. Herd mentality impedes individuation and leads to scapegoating.

Framing and reframing
Who and what the group is, can, even *should* evolve over time, so it's worth it to periodically check in and possibly reframe what the group is up to, about, working on — where is it headed? Are people satisfied? Frustrated? Do we need to come back to our origins? Or have we evolved such that we need to restate our reason for being?

Narratives are always "framed"— and, they can always be "re-framed." This discussion can be fruitful. Allow it to happen: let it be alive, responsive, flexible. It's a good practice for the individual, and is crucial for the group.

You will find different means to address this according to the size and structure of your group.

Being the Facilitator
You don't need a special degree or a fancy location or a great talent to be a great facilitator. Just some ground rules and a clear command of them. The ability to state the rules and hold them means:

- being a time keeper

- calling out inappropriate behavior

- respecting all members

The most important task is to hold safe space. You can accomplish this in your own style. That is, you don't have to be the gestapo. You can be fun and loving and still hold the space.

Some important things to know about healthy sharing:

- We're all alike and we're all different

- Surrender (letting go of being dominant) is not submission (allowing yourself to be dominated)

- Shared ideas belong to everyone

- We all have inner+outer aspects, and we are all both introverted and extraverted

Each of us is like other people and different.
Couldn't be more obvious, right? *Didn't I already say that? Like, 5-7 times?*

Yes. And it bears repeating. Because in so many ways, over and over, over our whole long lives, society discourages us in expressing the ways we are different *while also encouraging exceptionalism,* and it shapes our lives every day, so I feel like as much as we know it's true, I need to emphasize that WE ARE ALL DIFFERENT AND ALIKE. Not one or the other. Both. Not just you. Everybody.

Give yourself a good shake! Shake yourself up and shake it into yourself.

I'm unique! I'm like everyone else! I'm like everyone else! I'm unique!

So are you! So am I! So am I! So are you!

There are times, at work or at school or maybe closer to home amongst family or friends, when you may be prohibited from expressing your differences; or it may feel like others just won't understand; or it may feel too personal, too vulnerable to share.

Exacerbating the problem, we are constantly being herded by articles and algorithms and industry, always toward what "most people" think, believe, want; or what "experts say"; or what polls and statistics are telling us. But listen and remember:

*** Statistics can be (AND ARE) used to control outcomes ***

*** Statistics often produce the effect of self-fulfilling prophecy ***

Ironically, popular science is more concerned with prophecy than divination is,* often in the service of corporate and political entities. But scientific claims based on probabilities ought only be applied to the group overall, and not to individuals.

*I — and many people — use divination techniques to gain insight and to open my understanding, not to tell the future.

Jung pointed out that it is only the collective element of the individual that can be scientifically described as "normal." That is to say, only the part of you that's "alike" is measured by norms, for science is concerned with the many ways we are predictable, as demonstrated through repeatable research. But science can NEVER accommodate all of the ways each of us is unique And again, each of *IS* unique, and that's not something wrong with us, it's NORMAL to be UNIQUE. It's simply outside the purview of scientific research. Nonetheless, individuals commonly feel embarrassed or "wrong" to express any unique personal statement lying outside the norm.

I'm pro-science, and I respect expertise, and of course we need to identify our human commonalities. *BUT* it is not desirable that we lay down our own idiosyncratic direct experiences, inner voices, thoughts, insights, and feelings, to be sacrificed on the altar of probability. And, it must be said, no more is it desirable to proclaim our own specialness to be more special than the specialness of others. We all have the right to our own perspectives and interpretations.

A satisfying group must, in some way, recognize the way that each of its members is both alike and different.

Remember: Surrender, Not Submission!

When I see that "Submit" button...

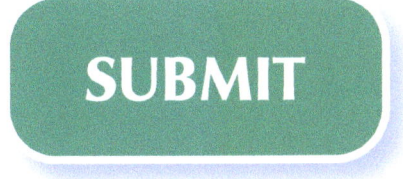 

Surrender is not submission
To reiterate, surrender is *an open-ended letting go into the unknown.* Submission is *a close-ended feeling of being bound*

Shared ideas belong to everyone
Am I altruistic? Yeah, kind of. But altruism doesn't mean that if we all hold hands, everything will work out great for everyone. It means *the belief in or practice of disinterested and selfless concern for the well-being of others; the behavior of an animal that benefits another at its own expense.*

When we share our ideas, we are feeding the collective. It's like a potluck of imagination. Just as mycelial networks seem to redistribute for benefit of the overall system rather than for individuals. By this definition, it seems that I am copping to utilitarianism, after previously trashing it. Yeah, ok, is this the tension of the opposites? I think you *do* have to take the whole picture in mind because the health of individual and society *do* go hand-in-hand. We cannot abandon the individual in the healing of culture; and we can't neglect the group in the healing of the individual. Individual and collective are mutually dependent.

Being inner + outer + introverted + extraverted
We all are! All of those things! You have an inner reality and an outer reality, and you have the ability to look within and to look out upon the world. We each move toward individuation and integrated awareness by expanding beyond our "typical" experience. We can encourage this by alternating inner activities with outer activities. A well-formed group can encourage each of us to explore and share both our innerness and our outerness, and by doing so, we become more fluid and more whole.

Whatever your relationship to culture-at-large, it's in local direct group experience that you can best appreciate how participation matters. Your participation and the participation of others shapes the group, and it's obvious.

It makes a difference who shows up.

Things that can get in the way of healthy sharing:

- **Social constraints**
- **Ego**
- **Projection**
- **Group mind**
- **Trauma**

There are potential problems, always; and especially when we're practicing imaginal sharing. Let's review.

Social constraints: yes. Sharing requires us to get over some long-held social strictures against being vulnerable and embarrassing and imperfect. Yes. So this is almost unbelievably hard for some people. Yet... this is why we need it.

Ego: I'm encouraging humility. Have the courage to stop trying to impress people. It's not about you. That doesn't sit easily with everyone. It's very very very hard for some people to mess around and be "less than." Again, this is why we need it.

Projection: Yes, we all do it. Activities like these help us to sort out our projections because we get a better sense of what's going on for other people as well as a clearer view of our own less conscious processes. But projection can get in the way of group sharing and expression, if guidelines are not in place. It's the facilitator who keeps tabs, holds the container and minds the limits, notices if someone is out of bounds and reels them in.

Group mind: Jung thought that the collective unconscious would always tend towards the lowest common denominator. Indeed, we see the worst case scenario of group mind playing out all around us. BUT doesn't this call for some proactive intentional group process of awareness? Group consciousness isn't going to raise itself.

Trauma: It's evident that

- *we have all been traumatized*
- *some have suffered unspeakably*
- *this type of work can open up sensitivities that ought best to be dealt with in a professional setting.*

At the same time, so widespread is the experience of trauma that we all need to know some basic things about how to support others. Like basic first aid. Bearing compassionate witness to another person's painful memories can offer healing that is not otherwise available. There are risks herein but obviously as we see in culture at large, there are risks in not taking collective action as well.

Shared Creative Practices

Sharing the imaginal through creative engagement

What, specifically, constitutes shared creative practice? For me, it means taking the approaches I've shared for "everyday creativity" and adapting them for a group experience: being and doing together in a way that allows each person to participate intuitively, expressively, and improvisationally, each person contributing authentically from their own opening into and engagement with the experience. It doesn't ensure that all participants will meld and gel into a cohesive community, but it does allow for that possibility.

This is how I think about a successful group experience of imaginal sharing.

Basics of Creative Sharing: A Summary

Container
Limiting factors. Limits of time and place. The rules.

Facilitator
The person(s) holding the container, tasked with keeping track of time, space, rules and agreements. The decision maker(s).

Rules
Guidelines/agreements. Sometimes the rules are explicit: spelled out. Sometimes they are implicit: everyone already knows and has the expectation. In either case, when all participants agree to the rules, the play can be satisfying. Without such agreement, disagreement about what's fair or what falls outside the limits can ruin the sense of play and enjoyment.

Ritual
The way you do things. Rules + traditions + the order of events. Play in a container.

Process, Not Product
Whatever comes up is part of the process. Whatever is expressed is freely offered to the group, so it may shift and change in the process. Letting go of expectations allows engagement and playful exploration. To engage with the process we release concerns about the end product.

Participatory awareness
Begin with awareness...listening...tuning into the presences and conversations happening all around you.

Start where you are
We are sensible creatures located in place. Where are we, in this moment? Feel it. Breathe it. Settle in to the earth beneath your feet and notice what you feel-hear-taste-sniff-see-and beyond. What else can you tap into?

Thinking takes a break as you relax and deepen to *this place, where it meets your body*. Your experience is now, before divisions and labels and organizational models. Your experience simply flows.

Simply experience. This moment. Notice what you notice. This is your common ground. Share into the group from this experience.

Shared introversion
Quiet time spent with others. It's a lovely thing. The energy of people gathered together, quiet and introspective. It's like heaven to me, humans being quiet and deep together.

You often have to create the circumstances and explicitly tell people, *"Don't talk now. Just listen"* (or just draw ... or just breathe). There are many who will rush to fill up the space with conversation, whether by habit or perhaps because the quiet makes them nervous or uncomfortable. They just need gentling.

Shared extraversion
The other side of the coin—time for sharing and discussion. Let this follow the tuned-in introversion, and people will be more centered, relaxed, and thoughtful, communicating from a more intuitive place. Communication will be more satisfying and successful.

Otherwise there can be a lot of "overflow" of whatever's top of mind — stressy things, listy things, gossipy things...There's often some of that at the beginning of a gathering, when people are saying hello. That's fine and normal, but take steps to shift to a deeper, more centered awareness before sharing and discussion.

The back-and-forth between shared introversion and shared extraversion forms a gentle inner-outer group rhythm that encourages relaxed and engaged communication.

Shared narrative
Story — narrative — myth — is shaped by the teller, by the circumstances, and by the mind and understanding of the listeners. When songs and stories are passed along, then they are alive; and it's a shared participatory experience, not a spectator sport. We all need to be part of the story. We need the opportunity and the community support to participate in the telling of our own stories.

Chance and Oracle
Incorporating methods of chance and oracle assures that we relax ego control enough to accommodate the presence of other influences. We can turn to these methods to provide an archetypal narrative framework, or to make choices in the midst of process. It's a quick, and sometimes mind-blowing, way to find a pathway through the forest of individual preferences and often fraught group decision making process.

Shared ownership
Participants share what they like, and don't have to share anything they don't want to. But ideas shared into the group are given freely. They are not fixed or monogamous, but are allowed to morph and transform through the group process. This allows the "Yes, and..." improvisational method, meaning that we accept all creative ideas that are shared into the group. You don't have to love or agree with everything; we can each have our own way of seeing it, but they're all versions of the story, and we can entertain all of those versions.

Sharing the imaginal
What I most hope to achieve with a group experience is the opportunity to share the imaginal: where participants feel relaxed, tuned in, and at ease with their intuitive awareness, the next step is to share and express what comes in from the imaginal world. It's all "As if..." Don't worry about whether you're "really" talking with the tree or not! it doesn't matter. Whatever kind of feelings you have, and whatever comes into your imagination, just go with that; and share whatever you like. Now we're really in the space of possibility.

> *These are what I consider the basics of creative sharing, and that's where I always start when facilitating a group. Now what exactly are you going to do together?*

GROUP PRACTICES: THE HOW-TO GUIDE

Here are my favorite practices for group creativity. For each activity, you'll find a blurb about it, instructions or a script to try, and suggestions for further exploration. Dip in - poke around - mix and match - experiment as desired.

Activities

Building on Everyday Creative Practices 351

Creative Ritual 352

Awareness 354

Open Studio 356

Toning 357

Poetry Spells 359

Exquisite Corpse 362

Endless Landscape 364

Mending the Web 366

Stone Soup 367

Open Space 370

Zine 371

Group Theme 373

Fable 375

Crafting the Mythos-Sphere 378

Building on Everyday Creative Practices

The practices from the *How-To Guide* form the ground of these shared practices. The *Group How-To Guide* suggests specific group activities, but speaking generally, to modify any solitary practice for group use, make these things clear:

- Time and Space (when and where)
- Activity (what's the plan?)
- Opening and Closing (beginning and ending)
- Instructions/ Communication

and remember:

- Comfort of Participants/ Allowances for Individual Needs
- Materials, Supplies, and Physical Set-Up (do you have enough? who's bringing what?)

Even if the activities and guidelines are familiar to all participants, they need to be clearly stated. This is part of creating the container. It won't just happen by itself.

Ritual provides the form for group practices: knowing who will do what when in what order orients participants to the activity by providing an overview of what to expect. Creating this container in some way is necessary for group activities. Include guidelines, dos and don'ts, as needed.

Creative Ritual

Create a Ritual Specific to the Gathering

Begin with the purpose. Why are you coming together? What are you hoping to achieve? (Refer to the sections on ritual in the text.)

What are the limiting factors? Determine time and place, and any particulars that must be accommodated.

Who will be participating? How will you bring them together? How will you communicate details, guidelines, and instructions?

What activities will support the purpose? What outcome are you seeking?

What is the vibe? What elements and symbols will evoke this?

Remember that while rituals may be sacred or ceremonial, they can also be playful and idiosyncratic. Think of the rules and customs of a game, or the particular way you like to prepare a special dinner. Ritual is simply performing a series of prescribed actions according to a plan, in order to achieve a certain outcome.

Priya Parker is a great resource for planning gatherings.

Create a Ritual Together

The group can be involved in the planning and decision making process. Together you craft the container. (Refer to the text for more on ritual.)

First Ritual

This is a ritual for the sake of ritual. The form was shared by my professor in grad school. Simple it may be, but as you participate you understand so much about how rituals are formed and how humans do things together. Remember that the *idea* of a ritual is not the same as the *experience* of it. So try it out!

Ask each person to bring an object with some special significance, but not too precious as it will be handled by others. Alternately you could find natural objects on site, or use items made by participants. They need to be small enough to fit on the table. They will be returned after.

Set up a round table, big enough and situated so that all participants can stand around and circulate freely.

Instruct participants that once the ritual begins, there will be no talking until it is over. This includes the leader, so give instructions before you begin. Each places their object on the table, wherever they like.

Participants may move and rearrange any objects as they like. They may continue to do so as long as they like. Any participant may move any object.

Continue until the movement has ceased and the process feels complete. Leader signals the end. Discuss.

Awareness

Just as in your personal practice, the first step to any group practice is always…tuning in

In a group the facilitator may invite this step. It can take the form of a guided meditation in place. Check that people are comfortable. If you will be speaking, be sure all can hear you. Speak slowly and clearly. It may be as simple as:

Sit quietly.

Notice your body.

Notice your surroundings.

Notice your skin.

Notice your breath.

Extend as desired with relaxation and creative visualization techniques. A few minutes for journaling provides a good segue back into the group activity, if that fits with your plan.

A walking or wandering meditation is a great way to connect with the locale, if you have access to outside. Invite participants to wander at will for a certain period of time, tuning into sensory awareness. What are they seeing, feeling, hearing, smelling, even tasting? Arrange a signal like a bell to call them back to the group. Give a few minutes to journal as people return to group.

A silent walking meditation as a group is a nice variation.

Relaxation - Reverie - Creative Visualization - Journaling - for Groups

All of these forms which were presented in the personal How-To Guide are great for group use

Make sure people are comfortable. You may like to provide yoga mats and blankets and darken the room, depending on your plan.

Make sure people can hear you if you will be speaking. A guided creative visualization is a great way to initiate a shared imaginal experience. Everyone is responding to the same suggestions in their own way, so it will be a personal experience with common ground. Following this with journaling allows participants to gather thoughts and responses they'd like to remember. Depending on the situation, you may want to provide journaling prompts. Sometimes it's great just to provide time for journaling without additional instruction.

Generally, allow transition time to come back to group. Abrupt shifts may seem jarring.

Open Studio

Great for a group as an ongoing practice or a one-time event. See the *How-To Guide* (152) for ideas. Set up the materials to be accessible to everyone. Ideally materials are laid out in one area and then workspace is set up to provide ample space. Give ground rules. I use some version of this:

- Practice Mutual Respect and Kindness
- Assume Confidentiality
- Tune In/ Listen Well/ Be Supportive
- Minimize Distractions/ Please Put Phones Away/ Turn Ringers Off
- Share from Your Own Experience/ Avoid Giving Advice
- Pace Yourself/ Take Breaks as Needed
- We Love Imperfection! Practice Freedom of Symbolic Expression
- Be Open to the Process • No Judgement • No Expectation of Outcome
- Creative Expression is for ALL
- Communicate Concerns
- Give Grace and Assume Goodwill

Encourage people to tune in as they create. I usually like to keep conversation to a minimum, or some people will get carried away by conversation with little awareness of what they are making. This can be distracting for the whole group, taking people out of the process and reducing satisfaction. See what works for your group. Music or not? Many people appreciate the vibe and flow. If it's not the "right" mood, it can distract or conflict with the expression.

Toning

This is a circle voice activity. It's improvisational, it does not need to harmonize, and musical talent is not a factor. It works no matter. If we just trust and let go, somehow the chorus of our voices sounds cool and we literally vibrate together. There is something mesmerizing about the experience of a group of people sharing their unique voices, floating together into a river of sound.

Let people know the plan before you begin. You can't really give instructions once the toning begins, so give them ahead. What's key is that everyone needs to participate without holding back, without trying to harmonize or do what someone else is doing. Just open up and give voice to the noise • sound • note that wants to come out. At first it may sound like and be a cacophony, but as you flow along with it, it becomes absolutely mesmerizing and a bit of a high.

People are often quite shy about opening up their voices, but it's so true that there's no wrong note. In the same way that it is difficult for accomplished artists to let go of their skills to let more raw expression come forth, those experienced in choral singing can also be resistant to this activity. It can be hard to trust that "harmony" is not the point. It may help to first lead everyone in a shout, then a hiss, then a hum, then a cry, etc.

Ideally, people are lying on their backs on the ground, all heads toward the center. This position reduces the anxiety of being seen and lets us concentrate on the sound. If not possible, try standing or sitting closely in a circle, facing away from each other. Call out the initial breathing instructions, then let the sound take shape and continue on its own. It will have a natural arc, reaching a crescendo and then fading back to silence, at which point, let the group have a little time to lie still and listen and breathe together at the end.

Listen to the sounds of the world, the sounds of the space, the sounds of the group. Listen to the breathing.

With eyes closed, all breathe together, deeply deeply in, and fully fully out. And again. Feel the rhythm of breath.

Continue breathing, and with your next exhalation, pick any note or sound to give voice. Commit to it. Do not hold back. Let it come out strong or soft, harsh or sweet, staccato or smooth…

Express the sound with the fullness of your breath.
Breathe as needed and continue.

Let it change, shift, weave, as you feel inspired. It may be ugly, it may be beautiful, it may be whatever wants to come out.

Listen to the voices blending together and vibrating all around you.

Let the toning continue as long as it continues. Follow its natural arc. As it subsides. continue to lie quietly, breathing and listening to the stillness.

Poetry Spells

I'm inspired by the book *Joyful Noise: Poems for Two Voices* by Paul Fleischman. It's a collection of poems about insects, where two intertwining parts are read simultaneously. It's fabulous and inspires me to create something similar, which I haven't done — yet —but maybe I will, or maybe you will.

I'm also inspired by the books, *Poetry as Spellcasting* and Starhawk's classic *The Spiral Dance*, both of which I've already mentioned. Joanna Macy and Molly Brown's *Coming Back to Life* is full of great exercises for poetic group expression of belonging in the natural world. Check all of these out for more ideas using chanting, power words, and poetic expression.

As always, I'm about being present with the process rather than perfect presentation. When you come together to create and share poetically, think of it as a group process rather than a revue made of individual performances. If you are reciting together, whether the words are improvised or already written, play around with group intonation, modulation, and rhythm, speaking in synchrony and speaking in layers. Here are a couple of ideas to get you going.

I AM: Very powerful to chant these two words, affirmation of our existence.

- Lead the group in chanting "I AM", elongating each syllable, as we do when chanting the sacred syllable OM

- Intersperse "I AM" with "OM"

- As you chant or speak the words "I Am…", participants call out words to finish the sentence as they are inspired.

Power Words: Adapted from Poetry as Spellcasting(63)

Settle into a relaxed and grounded safe quiet space. With pencil and paper, each person creates a shortlist of words that feel powerful to them, by way of love, by way of connection, or for whatever reason.

Each chooses one word from the list. Participants can take turns with all giving voice to the same one word at a time. Speak this word aloud for a full minute, in as many different ways as you can: loud, soft, fast, slow, etc. Notice the sensations and images that arise with each word.

Follow with a few minutes of writing poetry or poetic phrases based on the experience. Then, in group, let each person share one phrase at a time. Contemplate the arrangement of phrases as a group poem.

Praise Song For Our More-Than-Human Kin

In circle, bring attention to the rich diversity of our world, perhaps through a guided meditation or a few words of introduction. Ask particpants to join in by speaking praise for a variety of creatures, as inspired. They may be endangered, they may be extinct, they may be sitting at your side. It might be simply a name, or a particular phrase like "[Name], I love your [characteristic]" or it might be free form:

Beloved furry dog I love your wet nose and perky ears…Graceful long legged heron…manatee, you seem so kind…grey wolf I love your lonesome cry…brilliant cardinal, I love your bright eye…hidden peeper, I hear you… bright firefly flashing…slick rock, shiny in the rain…caw, caw, black crow…rabbit hopping so quickly…

Go around in turn or just chime in as desired. Continue until you feel finished. End with an expression of appreciation for all of these beings, and a moment of listening to the world around.

Poem Circle

1. Facing out, each name one thing you see.
   Facing in, each name one thing you feel.
   Closing eyes, each name one thing you wish for.

2. Write each word (or your 3 words) on a post-it. Place on floor or wall where all can see. Craft phrases or sentences (aloud or inner). Write on post-its.

3. Each person choose one phrase post it. In circle, speak each phrase in turn. Rearrange yourselves and go again. Choose another post-it and go again.

Exquisite Corpse

A parlor game popularized by the surrealists. You may have played it as a child, as I did, without knowing anything of its past. The name comes from this bit of poetry, "the exquisite corpse will drink the new wine," a phrase generated from the game. Also called Consequences, this collaborative parlour game uses a simple folded sheet of paper passed around the group to create a story, a line of poetry, or a fantastical drawing. The surrealists also made collages using this technique. Each player adds a bit, folds the paper over to hide it, and passes it to the next player, who adds a bit, folds it, and so on. Results are silly and sometimes profound.

Exquisite Corpse Drawing:

Each participant has a piece of paper folded int o four equal parts.

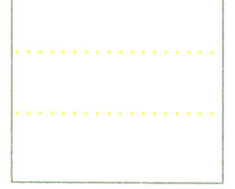

Working so that others can't see, draw a head on the top section. Extend the lines of the neck just slightly into the next section, then fold the paper over so that your drawing can't be seen, and pass to the person next to you, as you receive the paper from the person on your other side.

On the second section of paper, create the trunk of the body. Again, extend the lines of the body slightly into the third section and fold over so your work cannot be seen. Pass your paper on to the next person, while you receive the paper from the other side.

On the third section, create the legs, as before, extending the lines, folding over, and passing on.

Finally on the fourth section, create the feet. When everyone is finished, unfold to reveal the fantastic.

Try this method to create a story, a poem, or a collage--even a piece of music.

The MoMA website gives history, examples, and instructions (moma.org/magazine/articles/457)

Endless Landscape

The Victorian pastime also called the Myriorama, or "Many Thousand Views," is said to originate in France, with an English version showing up in 1824. I discovered it when my kids were little, in the form of a pack of cards I could keep in my purse. Cards are placed side-by-side in any order, always resulting in a seamless landscape. You can create your own.

Begin with at least 6 cards of the same size. Create as many as you like to accommodate your group size. On each card, use a ruler to mark the horizon line. It needs to enter and exit on right and left at the same height on each card (but it can go up or down in the middle).

On each card, draw (or paint, collage) a slice of landscape. Choosing specific art materials and a limited color palette will make overall effect more cohesive.

When finished, line them up to create a scene. Rearrange!

Endless Exquisite Pattern

This variation combines Exquisite Corpse and Endless Landscape. A simple template allows you to create interlocking squares that can continue ad infinitum. It's a pattern that is also not a pattern: unique pieces will always form a cohesive composition, yet they can be endlessly reconfigured, rotated, or removed. Add as many pieces as you like, creating an emergent, ever-shifting design.

Use paint, marker, collage, or whatever! Enlarge it to cover a wall or keep a set in your bag to use while you're waiting for…your plane…your food…your enlightenment….

Begin with 12 blank squares of the same size to create the templates for your designs. On each side of each square, create guide marks like so:

If you want to vary the placement of the guides, just be sure that all four sides have guide marks in the same place. Each design must connect to the edges through the guide marks on all four sides.

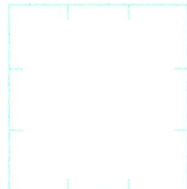

For example:

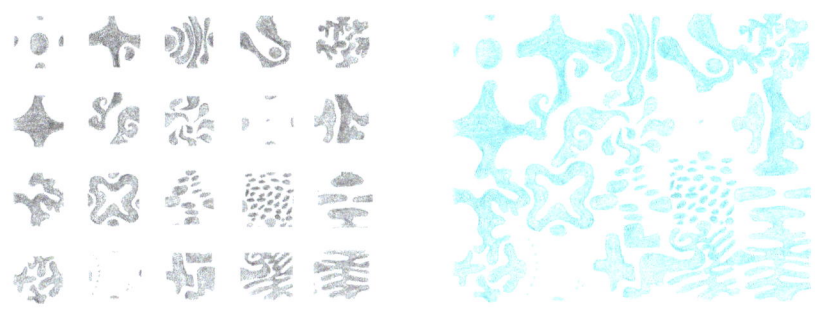

Experiment with different media and color choices. It's a simple idea which can produce fascinating results.

Blaize D'Angio made this one.

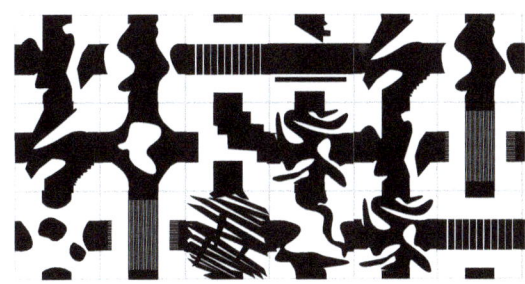

Mending the Web

Explore the metaphor of the social web in real life. Set the mood, if you like, with an intro or guided meditation on how we build connections to hold us together, or just jump in and play.

Gather a bunch of sturdy sticks and, forming a roughly circular shape, stick them into the ground so that they are stable and upright.

Let each participant bring a ball of yarn or string, or choose one from a supply on hand.

Stand around the circle.

Each person ties their yarn around a stick. Now move to another stick and wrap around. Continue. Organize it to create a pattern, or let chaos reign.

For instance, create a simple weaving pattern by having everyone move in the same direction, alternating bringing yarn in front of one stick, behind the next, in front of the next, behind the next, and so on.

If you'd like to carry it further, embellish with yarn bombing techniques of knitting, crochet, macrame, knotting, etc. The longer you'd like it to stay in place, the more forethought you should give to the location and the stability of the sticks or stakes you begin with. You could also build upon an existing fence or other framework. And, of course you can build something very complex and intricate if you start with a plan.

Stone Soup

Stone Soup is a European folktale:

Strangers come to a village. They try but are unable to convince the villagers to share food with them. They have with them a large pot which they proceed to fill with water, put a large stone in, and begin to heat it over a fire. When a curious villager asks, they say they are making a wonderful Stone Soup which they will be happy to share! Hmm, it might taste even better, they say, if they had just a little something extra to add. Eager to try it, the first villager contributes a carrot. One by one, each villager comes around to check it out and is convinced to offer an ingredient: onions, potatoes, peas, cabbage and so on are added to the Stone Soup pot, as the soup simmers and flavors blend. Finally the stone is removed and the delicious soup is shared by all.

Using the story as the framework for an activity, each person will contribute one element. What emerges for the group?

This could take many forms--including the most obvious, a soup! Keep in mind, it helps to start out with "the pot"— that is, defining your structure first will help others to contribute. It's helpful. too, if you decide ahead when "the soup will be ready." What's the time frame? You can wrap up the activity even if everything has not been resolved; you can always extend it if you like.

Following are a few ideas. See what you come up with.

A Collage:

The pot = the substrate. What are you working onto, and how big is it? You may want to name a theme as well. Invite participants to bring photos, drawings, lines of text, special papers to be adhered to the substrate. Lay them out and "stir them up" to get ideas of how they might work together. Encourage people to be flexible as you are at any potluck- no one has complete control over the menu. Adhere the pieces to your surface. You can continue to work into or over it with paint and drawing media.

A Play or Story:

The pot = the setting. Decide first where this story will occur. Each participant contributes a character: on an index card, describe your character and one or things about their personality or history, such as, are they seeking something? Did they just experience a major event? Keep it simple and specific.

In group, each person introduces their character. Brainstorm about how they might interact, conversations that might come up, etc. Use post-its to captuer ideas. Move them around to play with chain of events. Does an over-arching theme or plot suggest itself? Introduce elements of chance or oracle to move the story along. It helps to take some of the burden of decision-making of the group. For instance, draw a tarot card to decide how the story will end up.

A Musical Piece:

The pot could be a mood or a vibe or an image to inspire. Give each person an instrument and let them go off on their own for a few minutes. Let each come up with a particular rhythm or melodic line. Nothing too complicated! Keep it simple. Now come back together and see if you can work them all into one piece. Taking direction from the story, it may work best to add each piece in one at a time; and, as with the soup, pieces may adjust their character somewhat as they simmer together.

Open Space

Open Space was conceived by Harrison Owen as a self-organizing means to facilitate meetings. Participants create the meeting's agenda. Then, the group subdivides, and each participant chooses the groups she/he would most like to attend. This assures that the topics of greatest interest are addressed, and we are not obligated to sit through discussions in which we have little interest.

OPEN SPACE method:

Open Space relies on Four Principles and One Law to the group, and the idea of "bumblebees" and "butterflies".

- Whoever comes is the right people.
- Whatever happens is the only thing that could have.
- Whenever it starts is the right time.
- When it's over, it's over.

The One Law: If, during the course of the gathering, any person finds him or herself in a situation where they are neither learning nor contributing, they must go to some more productive place.

Bumblebees flit from meeting to meeting, pollinating and cross-pollinating, while butterflies don't get into any meetings but enjoy sitting quietly or opening into some unexplored serendipitous conversation.

This method is really helpful. I've adapted it for more than one event. For more info on Open Space, see the book **Open Space Technology** *by Harrison Owen or visit www.openspaceworld.com.*

Zine

A zine is an indy magazine that can be anything you want it to be, often on a lo-tech shoestring budget. You can make a zine by yourself, but it makes a great group project. There are no rules but it's helpful to make a few decisions upfront -- again, create the container.

One way to start is with a theme or concept that's important to you and your group. Do you have a certain perspective? Do you want to use a certain style? What sort of content will you include? All of these decisions can be made in advance or on the fly— or NEVER! because, as I said, anything can go in it. If you're facilitating a group, you can decide some things and then invite others to participate, or you can decide as a group. How many pages will it be? Will you put it together in one night or over a longer period of time? Do you have a budget? And so on. For helpful online resources, look up "How to Plan a Zine Project" at brooklynmuseum.org.

zine space

or How to run a self-organizing zine group based on the principles of Open Space

1. Create the agenda The facilitator can give an introduction to focus attention and assist with managing and organizing the flow of activities.

To begin, participants use post-its to write down any topics, issues or opportunities they'd like to discuss, or what they would like from the evening. Use a separate post-it for each topic and put your name on each post-it you create. Place on the

Agenda Board. Create as many as you wish or none at all. You do not need to duplicate an item someone else has already posted. Participants may decide to combine topics into a single agenda item.

Participants may decide to discuss topics at the general discussion table, or they may decide to create a focus groups for specific topics.

Participants may choose to work on projects independently or collaboratively.

These discussions and projects may happen simultaneously or in sequence, to be decided by members at that meeting.

2. Do it! Remember the Four Principles and the One Law, and cherish the Bumblebees and Butterflies.

In other words, you are free to participate in the activities and discussions of your choice, and you are not obligated to remain in any discussion longer than you wish.

For an ongoing project, the participant who creates a topic is responsible for taking notes on that discussion. Gather the notes and distribute to all participants.

3. Closure. Clean up after yourself and lock the door. That's all there is, there isn't any more.

Group Theme

A group activity organized around a theme can be satisfying for all and exciting to see the different perspectives people bring. Everything in the "Themes for Exploration" activity in the How-To Guide is applicable here, so read over those pages.

With a group, in addition to identifying the theme, you want to identify the parameters. Mainly, the time frame: it could be equally worthwhile as an hour-long activity or a month-long activity. In general, a longer project will especially benefit from opportunity for group discussion, at the beginning and along the way.

Is it for one particular medium, or will participants use a variety of media to explore the theme?

Will you gather in-person or across distance, via the internet or the mail system? How will you share what you create? How will you wrap it up?

The possibilities are limitless. Here are a couple of versions on one theme:

Theme: The Forest

An hourlong video call.

After introductions and orienting the group, begin with a guided meditation of entering the forest. With continuing background of forest sounds, participants move into 20-30 minutes of responding to the theme through writing or drawing. Invite the group back into conversation with sharing and discussion, wrapping up with an invitation to carry something from the experience into their next forest visit.

A month-long discovery and response, with weekly in-person meetings, alternating between forest meetings and studio meetings.

Begin with an introduction and invite participants to share what attracts them to the project and what they would like to explore. Give the group questions to consider as they wander through the woods and express in the studio. Each meeting includes time for personal expression and time for sharing and discussion. To wrap-up at the end, create a scene or installation of the various work created by participants to evoke your own group forest experience. Participants share what stands out for them about the experience; and what further explorations they have been inspired toward.

Fable

Choose one fable, fairy tale or traditional story to retell together. Traditional stories are public domain, meaning no one owns them. They are archetypal: they may be reinvented into countless versions while still recognizable as a particular story, like "Sleeping Beauty" or "Icarus Flying Too Close to the Sun" or "The Selkie." Depending on the nature of your group, you can explore the psychodynamics of the story, the various instances of the story as it has shown up in culture, the socio-political significance, participants' personal relation to the story…or just jump in and play with it.

Decide your time limits, the story you will use, and the goal: is it to create one new version, or is it kaleidoscopic experimentation and exploration, where each particpant can take it where they wish? Are participants free to work in any medium, or is it specifically one, like storytelling, or illustration, or musical response? Also decide on how you would like to wrap up: for instance, with a group installation or exhibit? A storybook or video? Simply a sharing and discussion?

Begin with a pared down version of the story— the simplest telling which is recognizable as this story. Facilitator can present to the group or group can work this out together.

- Tell story

- List characters, elements, settings,

- Discuss symbols, themes, problems, questions

- Create amplification and association map: deepening the sense of the story's symbolism by connecting related metaphor and similar imagery.

What happens next depends on the parameters you've set. For instance if people are working individually, they can now begin to respond through their mediums. If you're working towards a group outcome, you could have each person choose a character to develop or portray.

In any case, you want to allow time for people to share and discuss. Well-considered questions can guide both the sharing and the developing project.

As you bring it to a close, give people the opportunity to express what they've gained from the process, and whether it's inspired them to any future projects or exploration.

Variation: Creating a new tale from the old. Deconstructing old tales and recombining, Frankenstein-style. As always, possibilities are limitless. Here's one way I've done it, over three sessions:

Beginning with 3 traditional fairy tales, we list their constituent elements. Participants choose 2 or 3 elements to work with in more depth. We explore the symbolism intuitively and intellectually. We explore through visual arts techniques, with an emphasis on intuitive expression. Playfully, we consider new ways to reconstruct the stories.

- Each participant chooses one character to work with. We list symbolic elements on cards and each participant randomly chooses one card, "Go Fish" style.

- Participants are asked to work with the characters and elements as they might with a dream. As a group we discuss the symbolism.

- I lead the group in a guided meditation on their chosen characters, followed by journaling. We move into hands-on expressive art activities, using pastels and then collage. Participants are asked to create a simple rod puppet of their character.

- As a group and with reference to our puppets, we play around with retelling the story. I provide cards called "traits" and "actions" which particpants can draw from if they feel stuck. In the end, the story develops in entertaining and surprising ways.

This work underscores the message that there is not just one "real," "true," or "original" version of a fairy tale, but that all versions are true.

Crafting the Mythos-Sphere

A group creative process of collaborative improvisation through visual arts and story.

I hope I've made it clear that there are myriad ways that groups can gather, share, work and play together, and I hope you're inspired to gather your people and do your thing according to your own needs and interests. Here's the method I developed as part of my dissertation research. I think it's pretty good.

I implemented this project over 3 days with 6 participants (plus myself) on the campus of a liberal arts college. Centered around visual arts and narrative, activities were a mix of individual, small group, and large group processes, broadly categorized as Meditative, Expressive Arts, Game, Oracle/Chance, Narrative, and Sharing/Discussion. I created the schedule to follow a back and forth rhythm of inner and outer experience, with the goal of expanding the in-between, or third space of possibility. We always return to the physical as a common touchstone for the expression of inner thoughts, images and feelings.

It would be unrealistic to expect that we end up with complete and polished work of art through this process. The object is rather to grow or construct a shared sense of an emergent story that is still developing, and give participants a direct experience of how creating together develops cohesion of understanding.

Schedule Overview:

Day 1:

Circle: Greeting, Intro and Guidelines; Local meditation and journaling; sharing; character meditation and worksheet; sharing; lunch; Landscape Sculpture 1; Matrix: possible narratives; Discussion; Landscape Sculpture 2; Sharing; Circle: Themes and Dreams, Found Objects

Day 2:

Circle: Check-in, Dreams, Developments; Motif meditation, expression; Lunch; Sharing; Story-making, small group; Story-making, large group; Journaling; Circle.

Day 3:

Circle: Donuts and Coffee, Sharing, Plans; Open Space process; Free Play; Group Sharing; Meditation and Journaling; Closing Circle.

You can see how the various activities and theories I've written about come into play in this process.

To view the complete digital document I created to report my dissertation fieldwork, follow this link to the full theoretical dissertation: https://www.proquest.com/docview/2048104131 Look for the "Supplemental files" at bottom of page. Click on the pdf called "Crafting the Mythos-Sphere" to download. Interactive features of this document may not display properly on hand-held devices. For best viewing, use of a computer is recommended.

Creative Collaboration: A Method

The Project is the Container

Establish the Container: FIRST: 1) Situate in Time and Space 2) Gather Group to Circle 3) Share Guidelines

mythic awareness-reflective writing-sharing-observations-summary

Results:

≳★≲

~transformation and cohesion~
...mysteriously happen...

personal exploration-random connections-narrative development-group storytelling

<<pretend......**real**......pretend>>

Action:
What do we do?

divination-improvisational narrative-play-conversation-drawing-collage-making forms

Content:
Who's here?

unknown<<other<imaginal presences ☉ participants>others>>unknown

What are we working with?

imagination-intuition-dreams-memories-ideas-words-tools-art materials-found objects

Location:
Where are we?

self - inner landscape - outer landscape - world

meditation-reverie-imaginal dialogue-awareness-exploration-sharing-discussion

⇒ and begin...

inner ———————————————————— outer

Method Graphic

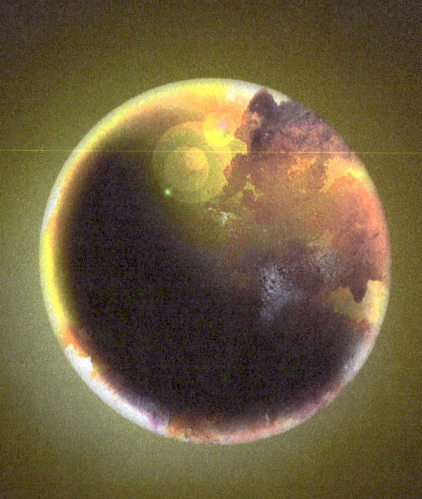

Part V : Full Circle

Full Circle

Coming Around: The 360° View. What more can I say?

---
conclusion: culmination, finale, consummation, crystallization
---

From Flatland to the Mythos-Sphere

I've presented to you my cosmology, that is, how I understand my place in the creative universe which surrounds me, where in leads out and out leads in. These pages hold my everyday sacred practices to reanimate a flattened world.

Objectivity is a myth — which is not to say that it is false, wrong, or without value. We can, for good reason, aspire to a perspective that helps us to "see the whole picture," but we simply can never achieve such a position.

I hope I have made the case for the value of mythic understanding. May you revel in the dimensional enrichment of peeking through a variety of viewpoints.

Sharing Reality

Who knew that sharing reality would be so fraught? At the time of this writing (2025), powerful authoritarian forces are attempting to suppress history, science, the arts, education, free speech, ethical thought, and intelligent problem solving here in the US. Marginalized people face the greatest risk. The rule of law is under attack, and so is our ability to know and trust one another. In the midst, we are only just beginning to understand the implications of AI, and those who imagine they are using it to their own ends are headed for a rude awakening.

The movement toward cultural destruction seems new and devastating to many of us in the United States, but it is not new. This greedy strain of the human condition winds its way through space and time like a disease, and that disease is sociopathy. I'm not cavalier about the situation. It is disheartening. It may be an epidemic of sociopathy that brings the downfall of humanity.

Yet, we are still here. We don't wish for it, but catastrophe brings out the best in us, and the instinct to love and care for our homes and families is the deepest instinct we have. As long as we're here, our mission remains the same:

Be human!

Gather together. Share ideas. Care for one another.

Continue to bring intuition, creativity, and compassion into a reductive world.

... Breathe in... Breathe out...

I wish for you the willingness to express yourself

--and the opportunity.

—Not only deeply and from the heart

—but also just for fun.

To make things that are beautiful, meaningful, insightful

—and also things that are ugly and silly.

May you find or make the time and space to be playful and creative!

May you have the freedom to tell your stories as you like!

Thank you for engaging with this book!

Keep participating!

Now, draw your own conclusions!

Bibliography

Abbot, Edwin. *Flatland: a romance of many dimensions.* Seeley & Co., 1884.

Abram, David. *The Spell of the Sensuous: Perception and Language in a More-Than-Human World.* Pantheon Books, 1996.

Alsadir, Nuar. *Animal Joy : A Book of Laughter and Resuscitation.* Graywolf Press, 2022.

Arrien, Angeles. *The Four-Fold Way : Walking the Paths of the Warrior, Teacher, Healer, and Visionary.* HarperSanFrancisco, 1993.

Bachelard, Gaston, and Daniel Russell. *The Poetics of Reverie: Childhood, Language, and the Cosmos.* Boston: Beacon Press, 2010.

Baldi, Ben. "What is Mycelium: Nature's World Wide Web Underneath Our Feet,w" Fungi Ally. https://www.fungially.com/blogs/growing-mushrooms/what-is-mycelium-natures-world-wide-web.

Balk, Janet. "Ancient Egyptian Beliefs and Traditions." *Encyclopedia of Death & the Human Experience.* Ed. Clifton D. Bryant and Dennis L. Peck. Vol. 1. SAGE Publications, 2009. 48-52. Gale Virtual Reference Library. Web. 28 Sep. 2016.

Barrington, Judith. *Writing the Memoir.* Eighth Mountain Press, 2002.

Bateson, Gregory. *Steps to an Ecology of Mind.* Ballantine Books, 1990.

Beck, Guy L. *Sonic Theology: Hinduism and Sacred Sound.* University of South Carolina Press, 1993.

Benjamin, Jessica. "Beyond Doer and Done To: An Intersubjective View of Thirdness." Psychoanalytic Quarterly 73, 2004. 5-46.
Benjamin, Jessica. "The Rhythm of Recognition." Psychoanalytic Dialogues. Vol. 12:1, 2002. 43-53.

Berger, Peter L. *The Sacred Canopy: Elements of a Sociological Theory of Religion.* Doubleday, 1967.

Bergson, Henri. *Creative Evolution.* Authorized Translation by Arthur Mitchell. Macmillan, 1911.

Beyer, Tamiko, et al. *Poetry as Spellcasting : Poems, Essays, and Prompts for Manifesting Liberation and Reclaiming Power.* North Atlantic Books, 2023.

Boylan, Patrick. *Thoth: The Hermes of Egypt.* Oxford UP, 1922.

Carroll, Lewis. *Sylvie and Bruno Concluded,* Chapter XI. London, 1893.

Cassirer, Ernst, and Susanne K. Langer. *Language and Myth.* Dover Publications, 1946.

Cazeaux, Clive. *Metaphor and Continental Philosophy: From Kant to Derrida.* Routledge, 2007.

Cole, Susan Guettel. "Greek Religion." *A Handbook of Ancient Religions.* Ed. John R. Hinnells. Cambridge University Press, 2007. Gale Virtual Reference Library. Web. 1 Nov. 2012.

Colman, Arthur D. *Up from Scapegoating: Awakening Consciousness in Groups.* Chiron Publications, 1995.

Corbin, Henry. "Mundus Imaginalis, or the Imaginary and the Imaginal." Spring 1972. 1-19.

Crastnopol, Margaret. *Micro-trauma: A Psychoanalytic Understanding of Cumulative Psychic Injury.* Routledge, 2015.

Davis-Floyd, Robbie. "Rituals." International Encyclopedia of the Social Sciences. Ed. William A. Darity, Jr. 2nd ed. Vol. 7. Macmillan Reference USA, 2008. 259-264. Gale Virtual Reference Library. Web. 19 Mar. 2013.

Deloria, Vine. *C. G. Jung and the Sioux Traditions: Dreams, Visions, Nature, and the Primitive.* Ed. Philip J. Deloria, and Jerome S. Bernstein. Spring Journal, 2009

Douglas, Mary. *Purity and Danger: An Analysis of Concept[s] of Pollution and Taboo.* Routledge, 2002.

Driver, Tom. *The Magic of Ritual.* Harper, 1991.

Durkheim, Emile. *The Elementary Forms of the Religious Life.* George Allen & Unwin, 1915.

Ferrucci, Piero. *What We May Be: Techniques for Psychological and Spiritual Growth.* 1st ed, J.P. Tarcher ; Distributed by Houghton Mifflin Co., 1982.

Feuerstein, Georg. *The Yoga Tradition: Its History, Literature, Philosophy and Practice.* Hohm Press, 2008.

Frankl, Viktor E. *Man's Search for Meaning.* Translated by Ilse Lasch, Beacon Press, 2006.

Frankl, Viktor E. *Yes to Life : In Spite of Everything.* Beacon Press, 2020.

Franz, Marie-Louise. <u>Number and Time: Reflections Leading Toward a Unification of Depth Psychology and Physics.</u> Northwestern UP, 1998.

Freud, Sigmund, and C J. M. Hubback. *Beyond the Pleasure Principle.* The International Psycho-analytical Press, 1922.

Fyleman, Rose. "A Fairy Went a-Marketing." 1920.

Gawain, Shakti. *Creative Visualization : Use the Power of Your Imagination to Create What You Want in Your Life.* Whatever, 1978.

Ghent, Emmanuel. "Need, Paradox, and Surrender: Commentary on Paper by Adam Phillips." Psychoanalytic Dialogues. 11.1 (2001): 23-41.

Gibran, Kahlil "On Children" from *The Prophet.* 1923.

Gilbert, S.F., J. Sapp, A.I. Tauber. 2012. "A symbiotic view of life: we have never been individuals." The Quarterly Rev. Biol. 87: 325-341.

Greene, Maxine. *The Dialectic of Freedom.* Teachers College P, 1988.

Guggenbühl-Craig, Adolf. *The Emptied Soul: On the Nature of the Psychopath.* Trans. B S. Harris. Spring Publications, 1999.

Hari, Johann. *Chasing the Scream : The First and Last Days of the War on Drugs.* Bloomsbury, 2015.

Harrison, Jane E. *Epilegomena to the Study of Greek Religion.* Cambridge: UP, 1921.

Harrison, Jane E, Francis M. Cornford, and Gilbert Murray. *Themis: A Study of the Social Origins of Greek Religion.* Cambridge: UP, 1912.

Heidegger, Martin. *Basic Writings: From Being and Time (1927) to the Task of Thinking (1964).* Ed. David Farrell Krell. Harper Perennial Modern Thought, 2008.

Heidegger, Martin. "The Question Concerning Technology." *Basic Writings: From Being and Time (1927) to the Task of Thinking (1964).* Ed. David Farrell Krell. New York: Harper Perennial Modern Thought, 2008. 311-341.

Herman, Judith Lewis. *Trauma and Recovery : The Aftermath of Violence - from Domestic Abuse to Political Terror.* Basic Books, 2015.

Herman, Judith Lewis. *Truth and Repair : How Trauma Survivors Envision Justice.* Basic Books, Hachette Book Group, 2023.

Hillman, James. *The Dream and the Underworld.* Harper & Row, 1979.

Hillman, James. *Healing Fiction.* Spring Publications, 1994.

Hillman, James. "A Psyche the Size of the Earth: A Psychological Foreword." In *Ecopsychology:Restoring the Earth, Healing the Mind.* Ed. Theodore Roszak, Mary E. Gomes and Allen D. Kanner. Sierra Club Books. 1995. xvii-xxiii.

Hillman, James. Re-*Visioning Psychology.* HarperPerennial, 1992.

Homer. "The Hymn to Hermes." Trans. Charles Boer. *The Homeric Hymns.* Chicago: Swallow Press, 1970. 23-69.

hooks, bell. *All About Love : New Visions.* William Morrow, an imprint of HarperCollins Publishers, 2000.

Hornung, Erik. *Idea into Image: Essays on Ancient Egyptian Thought.* Timken, 1992.

Huizinga, Johan. *Homo Ludens: A Study of the Play-Element in Culture.* Beacon, 1955.

Hyde, Lewis. *The Gift : Creativity and the Artist in the Modern World.* Vintage Books, 2007.

Hyde, Lewis. *Trickster Makes This World: Mischief, Myth, and Art.* Farrar, Straus and Giroux, 1998.

Jackson, Michael. "Thinking through the Body: An Essay on Understanding Metaphor." Social Analysis: The International Journal of Social and Cultural Practice. 14 (Dec. 1983) 127-149.

Jacobs, Jill. "Pirkei Avot: Ethics of Our Fathers." *My Jewish Learning*. Web. 3 Jan 2018.

Jung, C. G. *The Collected Works of C. G. Jung*. Trans. R. F. C. Hull. Vol. 8. PrincetonUP, 1969.

Jung, C. G. *The Collected Works of C. G. Jung*. Trans. R. F. C. Hull. Vol. 9 Part 1. Princeton UP, 1980.

Jung. C. G. *The Collected Works of C. G. Jung*. Trans. R. F. C. Hull. Vol. 11. Princeton: Princeton UP, 1989.

Jung, C. G. *Memories, Dreams, Reflections*. Vintage Books, 1989.

Jung, C G. *Nietzsche's Zarathustra, Vol. 1.* Princeton UP, 1966.

Jung, C. G. "The Transcendent Function." *The Collected Works of C. G. Jung*. Trans. R. F. C. Hull. Vol. 8. Princeton-Bollingen, 1960. 67-91.

Kalsched, Donald E. *The Inner World of Trauma: Archetypal Defenses of the Personal Spirit*. Routledge, 2004.

Kant, Immanuel. "An Answer to the Question: 'What is Enlightenment?'." Konigsberg, Prussia: n.p., 1784. N. pag.

Karenga, Maulana Ndabezitha. "Maat, The Moral Ideal in Ancient Egypt: A Study in Classical African Ethics." Dissertation, University of Southern California. Ann Arbor: ProQuest/UMI, 1994. ProQuest. Web. 28 Sep. 2016.

Kearney, Richard. "The Narrative Imagination." *Social Creativity*. Eds. Alfonso Montuori and Ronald E. Purser. Hampton Press, 1999. 61-79. Print.

Kearney, Richard. *Poetics of Imagining: Modern to Post-Modern*. Fordham UP, 2006.

Khanna, Madhu. *Yantra, the Tantric Symbol of Cosmic Unity*. Inner Traditions, 2003.

Kimbles, Samuel L. *Intergenerational Complexes in Analytical Psychology: The Suffering of Ghosts*. Routledge, 2021.

Lakoff, George, and Mark Johnson. *Metaphors We Live By*. U of Chicago P, 2011.

Levi-Strauss, Claude. "The Effectiveness of Symbols." *Readings in Ritual Studies*. Ed. Ronald L. Grimes. Prentice Hall, 1996. 368-378.

Lévi-Strauss, Claude. *The Savage Mind*. University of Chicago Press, 1966 [originally published in French as La Pensée sauvage, 1962].

Lévy-Bruhl, Lucien. *How Natives Think*. Washington Square Press, 1966.

Machado, Antonio. "Last Night As I Was Sleeping." Translated by Robert Bly, 1983.

May, Rollo. *Courage to Create*. Norton, 1975.

McNiff, Shaun. *Art Heals: How Creativity Cures the Soul*. Shambhala, 2004.

Merleau-Ponty, Maurice. *Phenomenology of Perception*. Trans. Donald A. Landes. Routledge, 2013

MOMA. "Make Your Own Exquisite Corpse." Althea Rockwell. November 18, 2020. https://www.moma.org/magazine/articles/457

Napper, Elizabeth. *Dependent-Arising and Emptiness : A Tibetan Buddhist Interpretation of MāDhyamika Philosophy Emphasizing the Compatibility of Emptiness and Conventional Phenomena*. Wisdom Publications, 1989.

Neumann, Erich. *The Place of Creation: Six Essays*. Princeton UP, 1989.

Nhat Hanh, Thich. *Old Path White Clouds: Walking in the Footsteps of the Buddha*. Parallax Press, 1991.

Ogden, Thomas H. "On Talking-As-Dreaming." The International Journal of Psychoanalysis. 88.3 (2007): 575-589.

Ong, Walter J. "Hermeneutic Forever." Oral Tradition. 10/1 (1995) 3-26.

Owen, Harrison. *Open Space Technology : A User's Guide*. Berrett-Koehler Publishers, 1997.

Palmer, Parker J. *A Hidden Wholeness: The Journey Toward an Undivided Life: Welcoming the Soul and Weaving Community in a Wounded World*. Jossey-Bass/Wiley, 2008.

Parker, Priya. *The Art of Gathering: How We Meet and Why It Matters*. Riverhead Books, 2018.

Parry, Alan, and Robert E. Doan. *Story Re-Visions: Narrative Therapy in the Postmodern World.* The Guilford Press, 1994.

Pinch, Geraldine. *Egyptian Myth: A Very Short Introduction.* Oxford UP, 2004.

Pinch, Geraldine. *Egyptian Mythology: A Guide to the Gods, Goddesses, and Traditions of Ancient Egypt.* Oxford UP, 2004.

Pinch, Geraldine. *Magic in Ancient Egypt.* U of Texas P, 2009.

Rogers, Carl R. *Freedom to Learn.* Charles E. Merrill Publishing Company, 1969.

Rogers, Natalie. *The Creative Connection: Expressive Arts As Healing.* Science & Behavior Books, 1993.

Rossbach, Sarah. *Interior Design with Feng Shui.* Penguin, 1987.

Roszak, Theodore. "Where Psyche Meets Gaia." In *Ecopsychology: Restoring the Earth, Healing the Mind.* Ed. Theodore Roszak, Mary E. Gomes and Allen D. Kanner. Sierra Club Books. 1995.

Sander, L. "Thinking Differently: Principles of Process in Living Systems and the Specificity of Being Known." Psychoanalytic Dialogues 12.1 (2002): 11-42.

Schechner, Richard. *The Future of Ritual: Writings on Culture and Performance.* Routledge, 2009.

Shattuck, Roger. *Forbidden Knowledge: From Prometheus to Pornography.* Harcourt Brace & Company, 1997.

Siebert, Charles. "What Does a Parrot Know about PTSD?" *New York Times Magazine.* 28 Jan 2016. Web. 8 Feb. 2016.

Silko, Leslie M. "Landscape, History and the Pueblo Imagination." *At Home on the Earth: Becoming Native to Our Place : a Multicultural Anthology.* Ed. David. L. Barnhill. U of California P, 1999.

Sophocles. *The Three Theban Plays: Antigone, Oedipus the King, Oedipus at Colonus.* Trans. Robert Fagles. Penguin Books, 1987.

Starhawk. *The Spiral Dance : A Rebirth of the Ancient Religion of the Great Goddess.* HarperSanFrancisco, 1979.

Suits, Bernard. *The Grasshopper: Games, Life, and Utopia.* U of Toronto P, 1978.

Sutton-Smith, Brian."Games of Order and Disorder." *Association for the Anthropological Study of Play Newsletter.* Vol. 4:2. Fall, 1977.

Tsing, Anna Lowenhaupt, et al., editors. *Arts of Living on a Damaged Planet. Ghosts of the Anthropocene ; Monsters of the Anthropocene.* University of Minnesota Press, 2017.

Turner, Victor. "Betwixt and Between: The Liminal Period in Rites de Passage," in *The Forest of Symbols.* Cornell University Press, 1967. 338-347

Vernant, Jean P. *Mortals and Immortals: Collected Essays.* Princeton UP, 1993.

Waterman - Duke: Ambassador of Aloha. American Masters. Directed by Isaac Halasima, NITV, 2022.

Watkins, Mary M. *Invisible Guests: The Development of Imaginal Dialogues.* Analytic Press, 1986.

White, Hayden V. *The Content of Form: Narrative Discourse and Historical Representation.* Johns Hopkins UP, 1998.

Wilkinson, Richard H. *Symbol & Magic in Egyptian Art.* Thames and Hudson, 1994.

Winnicott, D W. *Playing and Reality.* Basic Books, 1971.

Yun, Lin. Foreword, *Interior Design with Feng Shui.* Sarah Rossbach. Penguin, 1987.

Image Credits

Permissions are listed by page number. Images not listed below are the work of the author,.

23. Generative AI image of fossil by Everlasting Dreams - stock.adobe.com

42. Photo of milling grain by Maksim Shebeko - stock.adobe.com

52-53 Archetypal sun images, left to right:
Mural painting by Mural painting by Carlos Páez Vilaró, Punta del Este. (Wikimedia Commons, CC BY-SA 4.0)

Photo of Mardi Gras Venezia by Gnuckx. (Wikimedia Commons, CC 0)

Photo of sun above clouds by Jonathan Borba on Unsplash.

Watercolor painting of the Four headed sun god, Sūrya. Early 19th C, Company School. Now housed in the British Museum. Public domain.

A fresco from St. John the Baptist Church in Kratovo, Macedonia. Photo by Raso. (Wikimedia Commons, CC BY-SA 3.0)

Photo of painted gate, Weidenhäuser Straße in Marburg, by Frank Vincentz. (Wikimedia Commons, CC BY-SA 3.0)

"The Sun" by Edvard Munch. Painting in the hall of ceremonies at the University of Oslo. Public domain.

Ganjifa playing card, dated between 1800-1850. Public domain.

New Mexico Zia Earth And Sun. Original Work by Anne Lilje, 2019. (Wikimedia Commons, CC BY-SA 4.0)

Junkanoo 'off the shoulder' dancer costume. Photo by RealJunkanoo, 2007. (Wikimedia Commons, CC BY-SA 3.0)

"Jomfru Maria som gudmor" ("The Lassie and Her Godmother") Illustration by Theodor Kittelsen, 2014. Public domain.

Photo of sun through fingers by Daoudi Aissa on Unsplash.

Fire mark for Compagnie du Soleil Societe Anonyme d'Assurance Contre l'Incendie la Foudre et les Explosions in Paris, France. 1829 or later. Missouri History Museum. Public domain.

Photo of sun by Rajiv Bajaj on Unsplash.

105. Egyptian columns. Collotype by Henri Ernst. 1923. The Miriam and Ira D. Wallach Division of Art, Prints and Photographs: Picture Collection, New York Public Library Digital Collections. Public domain.

118. Wine and Cheese. Based on image by Shomixer - adobestock.

206. Photo of strawberries by Tetiana Bykovets on Unsplash.

220. Lord Ganesha Idol from Belgaum, Karnataka. Photo by Kirti Krishna Badkundri, 2013. (Wikimedia Commons, CC BY-SA 3.0)

221. Hermes Ingenui. Roman copy after Greek original of the 5th century BCE. Museo Pio-Clementino, Vatican Museums, Rome. Public domain.

222. Striding Thoth. Faience statuette. 332–30 B.C Egypt. Metropolitan Museum of Art. Public domain.
Thoth as Baboon. Faience, gold and silver. 332–30 B.C Egypt. Department of Egyptian Antiquities of the Louvre. Photo by Rama, 2007. (Wikimedia Commons, CC BY-SA 3.0)

223. Hermes Trismegistus. Sienna Cathedral Mosaic by Giovanni di Stefano, 1500s . Public domain.

234-235. Cosmologies:
Gulliver tied up by the Lilliputians, from Gulliver's Travels: Coloured Picture Book for the Nursery. Thomas Nelson and Sons, 1883. Public domain.

Cosmic Man Shape of Universe, Jain Cosmology, 17th c Rajaloka or Triloka miniature. British Library. Public domain.

Nun Raises the Sun. Nun, god of the waters of chaos, lifts the barque of the sun god Ra. c 1050 BCE. Public domain.

Yggdrasil: Norse Cosmology. Drawing by Nathanael Weir-Wakely, 2010. https://theincrediblylongjourney.com/yggdrasil-norse-cosmology. Courtesy of the artist.

Map of the Square and Stationary Earth. Orlando Ferguson, 1893. Public domain.

Mount Meru. Bhutanese thanka of Mt. Meru and the Buddhist Universe, 19th century. Trongsa Dzong, Trongsa, Bhutan Public domain.

Sufi Celestial Map. Illustrated Manuscript of "Zubdat al-Tawarikh" from 1583. Museum of Turkish and Islamic Arts, Istanbul. Public domain.

Rabbit Hole. Generative AI by mr_marcomstock.adobe.com

Sky Woman. Ernest Smith, 1936. Produced as part of the "Indian Arts Project" Federal Art Project. Collection of the Rochester Museum and Science Center. Public domain.

Overview of Dante's Divine Comedy. Michelangelo Caetani, 1855. Cornell University Library. Public domain.

A Dog's Idea of the Ideal Country Estate. An imaginative map by John Held, 1925. Public domain.

Hypothesis Tychonica. Illustration from Hevelius' Selenographia, 1647. The Sun, Moon, and sphere of stars orbit the Earth, while the five known planets (Mercury,

Venus, Mars, Jupiter, and Saturn) orbit the Sun. Public domain.

The Big Bang. Imagined by Generative AI, Evon J - stock.adobe.com

Hobbiton. Watercolor by J.R.R. Tolkien, 1937. Public domain.

Temple of Time. Memory Palace by Emma Willard, 1846. Public domain.

Large brass orrery, flat cylindrical mechanism with long winding handle, calendar and signs of zodiac engraved on top, mounted on three legs, brass sun with ivory planets with their moons on right angled arms. Robert Brettell Bate of London, circa 1812. Birmingham Science Museum. (Wikimedia Commons, CC BY-SA 4.0)

Google Cosmology. NYC area © 2024 Google Maps.

249. OH-card from the deck. By Ely Raman, 1976. OH Publishing.

275. Photo of Puppet Parade by Corey Marie Podielski. John C. Campbell Folk School. May 2021. By permission.

Photos of Mary with puppets by Amelia D'Angio. May 2021. By permission.

295. The Bhavacakra or Wheel of Becoming is a symbolic representation of continuous existence process in the form of a circle, used primarily in Tibetan Buddhism. Public domain.

309. The goddess Ma'at, from Queen Nefertari's tomb, c 1250 BCE. Public domain.

316. Dancing figures by hibrida - stock.adobe.com and nosyrevy - stock.adobe.com Fighting figures by AdrianHillman - istockphoto.com

317. Pentheus being torn by maenads. Roman fresco from the northern wall of the triclinium in the House of the Vettii, Pompeii. Public domain.

328. Rider-Waite Tarot cards, The Moon, Nine of Pentacles, The Lovers. From the Waite-Smith tarot deck created by A. E. Waite and illustrated by Pamela Colman Smith, 1909. Public domain.

365. Pattern design by Blaize D'Angio.

Index

A

Abbot, Edwin 293
Abram, David 49
abstraction 100, 115, 239, 290, 332
abuse 84, 292-293, 311, 314
acknowledgment 202, 292, 314
active imagination 59, 67, 71, 138, 142
Adams, Douglas 207
addiction 79, 83
affirmation 140, 161, 162, 359
affirmations 69, 161
agency 62, 286
aggression 308
aggressions 80
aging 107, 118
agreement 207, 212, 233, 339, 346
agreements 339, 346
alchemy 110-118, 223, 329
algorithm 341
alike but different 90, 314, 322, 323
Alsadir, Nuar 81
ambiguity 18, 19, 124, 164, 186, 218, 270, 305, 307, 308, 323, 329
analytical psychology 80
ancestor 107, 216-217
angry mob 316
anima mundi 24, 49, 297, 298
animism 210
antisocial attitudes 310
anxiety 32, 71, 73-85, 166, 211, 311, 333, 335, 357
Apollo 221
archetypal awareness 31

archetypal exploration 168
archetypal images 53, 169
archetypal motifs 328
archetypal numbers 287
Archetypal Themes 168
archetypes 52-55, 169, 250
Arrien, Angeles 202
Assagioli, Roberto 147
astrology 52, 97, 203
Athena 229
atrocities 9, 310, 316
authoring 101, 273
avoidance 77, 79

B

Babylonian exile 209
Bachelard, Gaston 61, 114
Baldi, Ben 14
Balk, Janet 309
Ball, William 190
Barrington, Judith 102, 173
Bateson, Gregory 90
Beck, Guy L. 104
being present 14, 16, 49, 50, 70, 120, 124, 197, 359
Benjamin, Jessica 285, 286, 303
Benjamin, Walter 167
Berger, Peter L. 289
Bergson, Henri 211
between space 124, 296, 325
Beyer, Tamiko, et al 162
Bhavacakra 295
Bible 104, 209, 304

Bly, Robert 119
boundaries 19, 20, 124, 126, 171, 186, 187, 189, 221, 227, 296, 305, 308
Bowie, David 118
Boylan, Patrick 222
bricolage 322
bricoleur 322
Buddha 123
Buddhist ethics 295
Byzantine Empire 209

C

Cage, John 167, 239
Carroll, Lewis 232
Cassirer, Ernst 105, 115
catharsis 314, 315
Cazeaux, Clive 106, 110
celebration 318
chance 152, 161, 166-167, 239, 347, 368
chants 161
chaos 62, 234, 248, 308, 338, 366, 398
ch'i 96
child 15, 52, 74, 87, 90, 139, 172, 178, 212, 251, 262, 284, 286, 287, 297, 306, 362
Chodron, Pema 123
Christianity 207, 210
Christian tradition 15, 207-210
Christo 157
church 205, 209, 210
    Catholic 209
    Eastern Orthodox 209
    Protestant 209
clown 81-82
coherence 102, 285, 322
Cole, Susan Guettel 306
collective 98, 211, 288-291, 302, 307, 316-317, 328, 332, 339, 342, 343, 345
Colman, Arthur D. 309
Coming Back to Life 359

common ground 8, 14, 151, 207, 238, 284, 297, 346, 355
communication 14, 36, 49, 70, 76, 93, 94, 106, 174, 194, 202, 220, 221, 284, 320, 321, 338, 347
community 9, 13, 14, 33, 79, 274, 283, 284, 285, 286, 288, 292, 301, 302, 311, 315, 316, 334, 335, 338, 345, 347
compassion 79, 250, 310, 386
Compassionate First Aid 312
competing wills 286
compost 164, 241
confidence 9, 71-72, 76
conflicts 174, 307
container 66, 68, 74, 88-89, 104, 107, 115, 124, 186-187, 189, 198, 200, 316, 317, 319, 326, 329, 330, 332, 333, 345, 346, 351, 352, 371
containing rituals 316
continuity 8, 18, 19, 22, 24, 28, 72, 94, 103, 110, 230, 296, 299, 329
conversation 32, 49, 50, 56, 61, 63, 70, 72, 90, 93, 96, 115, 124, 126, 142, 144, 145, 146, 150, 155, 168, 212, 217, 226, 251, 286, 300, 312, 313, 321, 335, 346, 356, 370, 374
Corbin, Henri 58, 59
core inner self 313
Cornell, Joseph 176, 396, 398
cosmic cycles 288
cosmology 59, 115, 122, 223, 232, 237, 239, 332, 385, 398
Coyote 224
coyotes 230
Crafting the Mythos-Sphere 332-333, 378-380
Crastnopol, Margaret 80, 81
Creative Collaboration Method 380
creative engagement 4, 5, 7, 13, 14, 30, 32, 33, 40, 67, 79, 114, 345
creative exploration 31, 71, 333
creative group 33, 311
Creative Ritual 352-353
creative sharing 36, 347

creative visualization 72, 107, 138, 138–143, 142, 152, 167, 168, 180, 354, 355
cultural consciousness 311
cultural participation 300, 333
cultural pluralism 321
cultural psyche 22, 300
cultural transformation 327, 329
cultural understanding 320
cultural view 324
Cuna cure 107, 108

D

daimon 93, 206–207, 208, 210–211
Dalai Lama 123, 230
Davis-Floyd, Robbie 181
daydream 117, 123
deep play 88
Deloria, Vine 291
Delphic Oracle 306
dependent arising 295
depth psychology 59, 113, 169, 203, 333
detachment 18, 114, 287
developmental process 284
Dickinson, Emily 172
differentiation 287, 289, 291
disbelief 88
disorder 36, 306, 307, 308, 310
diversity 302, 360
divination 166, 180, 206, 224, 247, 342
divine 34, 206, 207, 209, 220, 224, 231, 309
Djinni 224
Dogon culture 233
dominance 153, 303
Douglas, Mary 305, 307
drama 30, 90, 297
Dr. Bronner 300
dream 170–171
dreams 7, 12, 23, 29, 52, 55, 56, 67, 90, 114, 116, 117, 149, 165, 169, 210, 224, 232, 239, 262, 263, 283, 289, 298, 301, 313, 332

dreamwork 136
Driver, Tom 89, 181
dualism 27
Duke 188
Durham, Jonathan Edward 104
Durkheim, Emile 206
dynamics 19, 303

E

earthly rhythm 285
earth magic 210
eco-participation 31
eco-psyche 28
ecopsychology 297
ecosystem 13, 14, 21, 60, 165, 213, 303
education 39, 40, 75, 220, 385
ego 11, 34, 35, 70, 72, 92, 98, 99, 244, 284, 335, 347
Egyptian culture 104, 105, 107, 115, 233, 309
élan vital 211
Eleusinian mysteries 15
emergence 112, 120, 287
empathy 297, 314
Endless Exquisite Pattern 364
Endless Landscape 364
enframing 60
enlightenment 327, 364
Enoch 223
entrenchment 83, 84
Ermi 226–230
Eshu 224
everyday connection 36, 283
Everyday Creative Practices 351
everyday creativity 30, 36, 49, 68, 72, 84, 130, 153, 283, 345
evil 210
expanding the third 67, 106, 185
experiment 75, 126, 130, 153, 154, 156, 240, 350
experts 341
expressive arts 65, 77, 333

Exquisite Corpse 362–363, 364, 394
extraversion 97, 347
extraverted 75, 97, 98, 99, 113, 341, 343

F
Fable 375–377
facilitator 36, 39, 329–330, 339, 340, 345, 354, 371
fairy tale 80, 91, 173, 197, 264, 375, 377
fears 56, 73, 76
feng shui 96
Ferrucci, Piero 139, 147
Feuerstein, Georg 220
fireflies 285
flaneurie 167
Flatland 293, 385
flow 6, 7, 22, 28, 38, 57, 67, 75, 96, 121, 126, 130, 142, 160, 161, 193, 200, 211, 249, 273, 285, 299, 335, 356, 357, 371
fluidity 84, 97, 99, 100–101, 186, 236, 323
focus 27, 42, 63, 68, 83, 87, 93, 96, 105, 113, 115, 136, 161, 180, 211, 217, 233, 289, 297, 333, 337, 371, 372
fool 52–53, 62, 86, 118, 218, 219, 229
Fortune, Dion 104
Frankl, Viktor E. 82, 195
Franz, Marie-Louise 287
free symbolic expression 65–66, 80, 81, 82, 303
free time 121
Freud 297
Freud, Sigmund 297, 306, 313
Fyleman, Rose 201

G
Ganapati 220
Gandhi, Mahatma 123
Ganesa 220, 229
gathering 283, 335, 337, 339, 347, 370
Gawain, Shakti 69, 143
Gaye, Marvin 123

genies 197, 219
genii loci 206, 207, 208, 219
genius 102, 208, 340
Ghent, Emmanuel 326, 333
Gibran, Kahlil 12
Gilbert, S.F. 26
goddess 107, 205, 309, 339
god(s) 34, 53, 92, 105, 107, 115, 119, 204, 205, 206–211, 215, 220–223, 224, 234, 259, 292, 299, 308, 309, 317, 318, 397, 398
gods and gender 204
Goffman, Erving 175
Goldsworthy, Andy 157
goofing around 86
grandiosity 34, 286, 317
Greco-Roman 115
Greece 15, 206, 208, 221, 306
Greek tradition 61, 110, 194, 206–207, 209, 218, 221, 223, 233, 317, 390, 391, 398
Greene, Maxine 114, 301, 302
grief 316, 318
grok 87
group alchemy 329
group energy 308, 316, 333
group experience 315, 323, 327, 329, 337, 338, 344, 345, 347
group function 338
group mind 316, 339, 345
group process 247, 311, 315, 333, 345, 347, 359
group ritual 319, 352–353
Group Theme 373–374
group unconscious 309
guardian 206, 208
Guggenbühl-Craig, Adolf 310
guidelines 36, 180, 200, 216, 330, 344, 351, 352
  for Being In-Between 200–201
guides 65, 199, 212, 218–230, 273, 365

H
habit 77, 84, 97, 99, 151, 214, 346

Hari, Johan 79
Harrison, Jane E. 206
healing 28, 40, 65, 79, 80, 83, 84, 113, 116, 144, 198, 294, 304, 311, 312, 314, 318, 319, 324, 343, 345
healthy sharing 341-345
Hebrew tradition 207, 209
Heidegger, Martin 60, 214, 215
heka 222
helpful spirits 213-217, 219
Hemphill, Destiny 162
herm 221
Herman, Judith Lewis 27
Hermes 115, 207, 220, 221, 223, 224, 228, 273, 308
Hermetica 115, 223
Hermetic dictum 115
hieroglyphs 105, 162, 222
Hillman, James 54, 62, 169, 170, 209, 210, 211, 221, 297, 299
Hindu tradition 88, 220, 233
Hölderlin 60
Homegrown National Park Initiative 336
Homer 221
hooks, bell 311
Hornung, Erik 222, 309
Horus 107, 222
Huizinga, Johan 88
human nature 3, 6, 8, 38
humiliation 323
humility 11, 13, 34, 57, 62, 318, 344
humus 11, 34, 241
Hyde, Lewis 208, 283
hyperbole 97

I

icon 207, 209, 210
iconoclasm 209
ideals 52, 100
identity 70, 103, 105, 264

idol 209
idolatry 209
Idris 223
imaginal beings 212-217, 226, 274
imaginal content 7, 24, 332
imaginal dialogue 72, 97, 113, 145, 168, 178, 180, 211, 216, 226, 247
imaginal exploration 31, 198
imaginal guidance 144
imaginal impulse 6, 24, 35, 38, 238
imaginal interview 226-230
imaginal others 199
imaginal sharing 344, 345
imagination 7, 52, 58, 59, 60, 61, 62, 65, 67, 70, 71, 85, 86, 90, 93, 95, 100, 101, 138, 142, 146, 179, 210, 211, 222, 230, 232, 293, 296, 305, 314, 317, 322, 335, 343, 347
improvisation 120, 179, 313, 378
impulse 6, 16, 24, 35, 38, 39, 65, 66, 86, 126, 238, 327
independence 284, 296
indigenous tradition 9, 42, 108, 202, 224, 290, 291, 292
individual vii, 14, 18, 19, 34, 59, 87, 88, 94, 98, 99, 107, 114, 206, 284, 286, 288, 289, 291, 292, 294, 296, 297, 298, 300, 303, 304, 306, 309, 310, 311, 314, 315, 317, 319, 323, 327, 328, 332, 333, 339, 340, 342, 343, 347, 359, 378
individual consciousness 284, 288, 289, 294, 296
individualism 33-34
individuation 98, 99, 300, 340, 343
inertia 79, 84
infant 163, 221, 222, 284, 286, 288, 307
infinity 122, 232, 233
inner and outer experience 6, 7, 19, 20, 21, 22, 28, 31, 42, 49, 50, 57, 67, 70, 87, 94, 95, 96, 97, 99, 100, 104, 106, 114, 115, 378
inner critic 74, 178, 199
inner space 69, 114
inspiration 50, 123, 166, 167, 206, 213, 241

integrated awareness 327, 343
integration 7, 101, 114, 222, 311, 327, 333
intention 63, 67, 69, 71, 103, 104, 108, 117, 134, 140, 144, 161, 179, 180, 192, 200, 211, 216, 217, 288, 307, 318
intentional 63, 66, 72, 84, 92, 138, 179, 240, 337, 338, 345
intentions 22, 63, 140, 179, 198, 307
Internal Family Systems 147
internal system 285
introversion 97, 99, 346, 347
introverted 97, 98, 113, 284, 335, 336, 341, 343
intuition 7, 22, 52, 56, 57, 62, 67, 111, 115, 179, 189, 190, 202, 212, 213, 222, 386
intuitive awareness 76, 347
irrational number 233
Isis 107, 108, 222
Islamic cosmology 59, 115, 234
Islamic tradition 59, 209, 223, 224
isolation 27, 33, 36, 50, 304, 311

J
Jackson, Michael 106, 107, 108
Jackson, Shirley 305
Jeanne Claude 157
journal 81, 117, 144, 149, 150, 154, 197, 236, 245, 272, 277, 354
journaling 31, 148-151, 168, 177, 191, 215, 354, 355, 377, 379
Judaic tradition 209, 304-305, 309
judgment 69, 113, 158, 202, 211, 221, 312, 323
Jung 98
Jung, C. G. 56, 67, 80, 82, 98, 112, 113, 115, 211, 287, 291, 296, 316, 317, 327, 328, 342, 345
Jupiter 229

K
Kahanamoku, Duke 188
Kalsched, Donald 27, 311, 313
Kant, Immanuel 110

Karenga 309
Kashmir Saivism 104, 122
Kearney 61, 101
Khanna 88
Kimbles 293
King James Bible 104
kinship 289, 290, 292, 307
Kundalini-Shakti 220

L
Laius 306
Lakoff 106, 320
language 61, 104, 106, 107, 108, 114, 163, 194, 195, 204, 205, 221, 222
laws 233, 301
Levi-Strauss 108
Leviticus 304
Lévy-Bruhl 291
lichen 26
liminality 308
liminal space 87, 201
liminoid 323
limitations 27, 88, 312
limits 66, 68, 85, 86, 88, 89, 123, 124, 187, 188, 189, 200, 221, 232, 233, 237, 241, 296, 312, 330, 345, 346, 375
loneliness 33, 79
lowest common denominator 345
lunar cycles 222

M
maat 222, 309
Machado 119
macrocosm 220, 233
Macy, Joanna 359
magic 15, 88, 89, 91, 96, 104, 105, 106, 108, 110, 124, 162, 210, 222, 229
magic circle 88-89, 124
magician 222, 223
mana 206, 210, 211, 317

Mandela, Nelson 123
manifestation 59, 72, 104, 250, 308
manifesto 338
map 83, 91, 170, 232–239, 255, 376
Mark Making 155
materials 32, 35, 50, 77, 90, 110, 115, 152, 155, 156, 157, 160, 176, 179, 240, 241, 247, 356, 364
maya-lila 88
May, Rollo 85
McNiff 62
meaning 3, 7, 22, 23, 40, 49, 50, 56, 59, 60, 61, 62, 67, 87, 101, 105, 110, 120, 162, 174, 195, 197, 202, 221, 222, 232, 233, 273, 283, 287, 289, 314, 318, 320, 322, 332, 347, 375
measurable experience 233
meditation 107, 203, 339, 354, 360, 366, 373, 377, 379
meditations 15, 16, 35, 48, 57, 65, 78, 84, 93, 95, 108, 117, 124, 192, 195, 199, 219, 237, 298, 325
memoir 173, 177
memory 20, 80, 101, 112, 197, 207, 217, 235, 299
Mending the Web 366
Mercury 224, 273
Merleau-Ponty 110, 112
messages 83, 116, 206, 220, 221
messing around 68, 120
metabolism 315
metabolizing 311, 313, 315, 333
metaphor 22, 28, 52, 56, 90, 91, 96, 106, 108, 112, 114, 115, 171, 194, 195, 218, 220, 222, 314, 318, 319, 320, 322, 366, 376
metaphysical reality 233
microcosm 220, 233
microtrauma 83
mind-body split 27, 112, 114, 329
mindfulness 198, 251, 318
minifesto 338
Mixed Media Memoir 177–178
mixing media 155

model 5, 98, 210, 232, 233
MoMA 363
monoculture 13, 60, 303
moon 98, 222
mother 20, 35, 52, 107, 120, 139, 172, 212, 261, 262, 284, 287, 306, 307, 317, 319
movement 22, 61, 64, 65, 80, 81, 84, 86, 93, 97, 100, 102, 113, 139, 153, 159, 163, 164, 180, 273, 308, 315, 316, 353, 386
Muller-Ortega 104
mundus imaginalis 59
music 66, 80, 135, 137, 140, 160, 171, 180, 217, 221, 315, 335, 363
mycelium 13, 14, 26, 28, 32, 298, 303, 304, 335
Myers-Briggs 97
Myriorama 364
mystery 15, 70, 104, 141
myth 22, 23, 28, 33, 34, 55, 91, 173, 195, 206, 210, 300, 322, 332, 347, 385
mythic imagination 322
mythmaking 194, 196
mythological awareness 8, 22–26
mythology 22, 23, 24, 25, 29, 52, 169, 179, 210, 218, 223, 224, 232, 237, 259, 288, 296, 333
    American 9, 24, 224, 288, 291, 292, 293, 396
mytho-poetic 60
Mythos-Sphere 239, 332–333, 378–380, 385

N
Napper 295
narrative 70, 100–103, 108, 161, 317, 323, 333, 338, 347, 378
nature 3, 4, 6, 8, 19, 38, 52, 58, 61, 62, 70, 73, 75, 76, 78, 80, 85, 87, 89, 90, 96, 99, 100, 106, 107, 114, 138, 160, 186, 205, 208, 218, 223, 284, 288, 289, 290, 292, 295, 297, 298, 302, 307, 316, 320, 322, 323, 327, 332, 375
negative talk 74
Neumann 284, 328
Nhat Hanh 295

Nicaean Council 209
non-rational 56, 110, 114, 171, 210
normalcy 211

O

objectivity 100, 102, 202
Odajnyk, Walter 169
Oedipus 305–307
Ogden 313
Olympian gods 206, 207, 221
oneness 104, 284, 288, 317
Ong 320
openings 96, 124, 221
opening space 1, 3, 5, 198
Open Space 370, 371, 379, 394
Open Studio 152–162, 356
oracle 167, 203, 206, 273, 347, 368
order and chaos 338
"Other" 14, 16, 70, 166, 206, 287
otherness 306
Owen 370

P

paganism 210
Palmer 334
pantheism 203, 210
paradox 90, 93, 211, 212, 218, 308, 323
Parker, Priya 337, 352
parrots 314
Parry, Alan, and Robert E. Doan 102, 173
participation 3, 14, 16, 18, 28, 31, 32, 33, 40, 49, 50, 67, 70, 72, 83, 95, 115, 126, 206, 284, 286, 291, 300, 314, 329, 332, 333, 336, 344
participation mystique 291
Parvati 220
pathology 8, 80, 292
patience 337
pattern 52, 54, 153, 171, 207, 214, 273, 284, 286, 287, 288, 299, 333, 364, 366
perception 59, 110, 122, 191

permeability 28
permission 6, 30, 75
personality 75, 87, 97, 99, 310, 368
personality type 97
physical experience 106, 115, 320
physical space 68, 232, 323
pi 233
Pinch, Geraldine 105, 115, 222
playfulness 75, 88
pluralism 321, 323
poem 48, 55, 61, 108, 162, 168, 176, 360, 363
Poem Circle 361
poetry 30, 104, 108, 161, 180, 360, 362
Poetry Spells 359
poiesis 61, 104
pollution 305–307
power 56, 58, 59, 60, 61, 64, 84, 85, 104, 105, 108, 115, 146, 161, 162, 172, 197, 202, 206, 209, 210, 222, 230, 250, 251, 264, 267, 273, 288, 310, 315, 317, 319, 333, 359

Power Words 359, 360
practices 5, 9, 13, 30, 31, 42, 49, 62, 84, 91, 107, 111, 130, 131, 158, 168, 174, 181, 185, 186, 200, 203, 207, 209, 210, 216, 236, 286, 302, 305, 308, 317, 318, 321, 333, 345, 350, 351

Praise Song 360
prayers and blessings 161
pretend 14, 18, 23, 57, 86, 87, 90, 93, 101, 104, 148, 198, 211
Principles of Design 153
privacy 68, 324
progress 68, 82
progressive relaxation 132–134
projection 56, 115, 211, 291, 308, 314, 344
prophecy 206, 221, 306, 342
protection 77, 95, 107, 114, 123, 124, 200, 216, 217, 222, 224, 250, 319
psyche 12, 14, 16, 22, 24, 28, 48, 49, 56, 67, 70, 80, 110, 112, 113, 115, 210, 211, 214, 218, 221,

291, 296, 297, 298, 300, 317, 327, 328, 332, 335, 339

psychoid 112, 291, 296, 298, 328
psychopomp 218, 221, 224, 228
purification 115, 305–308, 319
purity 42, 305

Q
quantification 233
questions 4, 60, 82, 93, 215, 217, 226, 312, 321, 333, 335, 374, 375, 376

R
Ra 107, 108, 222, 234, 398
rational analysis 32, 67, 211
Re 54, 116, 130, 172, 222, 255, 309
reality 48, 58, 59, 61, 72, 87, 100, 104, 105, 106, 112, 135, 136, 143, 146, 187, 190, 193, 200, 201, 205, 210, 211, 212, 229, 232, 233, 236, 240, 291, 297, 319, 320, 328, 343, 385

reciprocity 297, 310
recognition 90, 303, 309, 314
refinement 42, 111, 115
Re-Framing Narrative 172–173
relational awareness 284
relaxation 87, 95, 132, 133, 135, 136, 138, 140, 142, 354
release 35, 71, 80, 134, 148, 197, 313, 314, 315, 316, 346
religion 23, 57, 123, 206, 222, 317, 333
religious practices 317
repression 27, 73, 292, 297
resistance 4, 47, 68, 77, 78, 79, 80, 82, 83, 84, 85, 87
respect 9, 36, 57, 200, 289, 290, 312, 318, 321, 324, 342
reverie 31, 67, 97, 117, 123, 138, 170, 177, 313
rhythm 40, 50, 52, 65, 69, 97, 124, 153, 159, 160, 240, 284, 285, 287, 288, 339, 347, 358, 359, 369, 378

rhythmic participation 286
righteousness 293, 317
risk 73, 85, 88, 89, 114, 144, 179, 187, 249, 302, 306, 307, 319
ritual 69, 72, 89, 105, 114, 162, 168, 179, 180, 181, 216, 251, 305, 315, 316, 317, 318, 319, 323, 324, 329, 333, 339, 352, 353
    characteristics of 224
    First Ritual 353
    Ritual Objects 180
ritualized trauma 319
Rogers, Carl 65
Rogers, Natalie 65, 152
Rose, Deborah Bird 289
Roszak, Theodore 297
rules 88, 89, 104, 124, 149, 151, 220, 239, 305, 307, 340, 346, 352, 356, 371

S
sacred 15, 69, 70, 105, 115, 152, 170, 180, 206, 209, 210, 211, 217, 222, 267, 319, 352, 359, 385
safe space 65, 68, 88, 94, 114, 188, 340
Salen, Katie, and Eric Zimmerman 86
Sander, L. 285
Saturn 229
scapegoat 304, 305, 307
scapegoating 304–308, 310, 314, 340
Schechner, Richard 88
schema 110, 194, 210
scientific claims 342
scribe 70, 220
sculpture 35, 157, 171
self-abandonment 339, 340
self-awareness 284
self-denigration 73
sense of self 88
sensory information 110
separateness 296
serpent 206, 220
shadowbox 176

Shakti 69, 143, 220, 391
shamanic tradition 108, 250, 319
shamanism 210
shame 81
shared creative practices 345-347
shared extraversion 347
shared introversion 346, 347
shared metaphor 319, 320
shared metaphorical understanding 332
shared narrative 323, 338, 347
shared ownership 347
sharing reality 385
sharing the imaginal 301, 303, 327
Shattuck, Richard 99, 100
Sherman, Cindy 175
Shiva 104, 220
showing up 47, 53, 67, 218, 364
Siebert, Charles 314
Silko, Leslie M. 324
silliness 92
sin 308
SiPSES 240
Śiva-Śakti 122
skill building 66
Smith, Pamela Colman 328
snake 107, 206, 221
social categories 307
social change 303, 308
social cohesion 32, 333
social connection 13, 14, 31, 32, 324
social constraints 344
social contract 33, 310
social discourse 313
social disorder 36
social experience 79, 301, 304, 311, 324, 335
social gatherings 301
social institution 308
social interaction 96, 283, 285, 324
social issues 303, 304
socialization 81

socializing 140, 284
social mycelium 13-14, 26, 32, 303, 304, 335
social opportunities 19, 301
social participation 284
social problems 309
social structure 305, 307
social system 286, 302, 305, 308
social third 94, 286, 311, 323, 325, 328, 336
social unconscious 293
social web 304, 310-311, 366
social wounds 40, 304
society 14, 18, 32, 33, 39, 85, 86, 88, 174, 284, 292, 301, 302, 303, 307, 308, 311, 321, 329, 332, 336, 341, 343
socio-cultural expectations 94
sociopathic behavior 310-311
sociopathy 304, 310, 386
socio-political influences 73, 77, 83, 85, 375
Sophocles 306
sorrow 82
Soup or Compost 241
space of play 87, 88, 90, 211
space of possibility 18, 87, 93, 124, 185, 347, 378
spaciousness 6, 95, 294, 322
spells 104, 161, 162
splitting 290, 292
spontaneous generation 50
stability 301, 303, 366
Starhawk 162, 181, 359
starting a group 335-336
statistics 341
Stone Soup 207, 321, 367
storytelling 375
stranger 249
stress 99, 100, 132, 133, 151, 315, 319
structure 52, 59, 61, 68, 85, 98, 102, 106, 107, 173, 179, 187, 232, 239, 247, 305, 307, 332, 337, 338, 339, 340, 367
subjectivity 59, 99, 100-101, 106, 236
submission 303, 326, 341, 343

subtle body 112
suffering 40, 79, 115, 198, 292, 312, 314
Suits, Bernard 88
Sun Boat 222
surrender 15, 239, 316, 326, 333, 343
Sutton-Smith, Brian 308
symbol 56, 91, 105, 168, 169, 206, 250, 328
symbolic patterns 328
sympathetic magic 105
synchronicity 112, 113, 291
synchronization 285
syncretism 321

T

Tallamy, Doug 336
tarot 52, 167, 169, 203, 213, 215, 250, 328, 368
  Rider Waite 328
Ten Commandments 209
territory 21, 49, 89, 95, 194, 236, 237, 240, 296, 332
Theatrical Frame 176
Themes for Exploration 163
therapeutic approach 147
therapeutic effect 36, 75
therapeutic relationship 114, 313
therapy 36, 312, 313, 333
the third 18, 19, 21, 67, 93, 94, 96, 97, 106, 124, 166, 173, 185, 186, 187, 189, 192, 194, 212, 213, 218, 222, 236, 240, 241, 286, 287, 293, 294, 303, 324, 326, 332, 333, 362, 363
thirdness 8, 18, 22, 186, 197, 285, 286, 288, 303, 325, 329, 339
third space 21, 93, 96, 106, 185, 186, 323, 324, 333, 378
Thoth 220, 222, 223, 229
Toning 357
traditional rites 318, 319
traditions 9, 15, 23, 27, 29, 102, 179, 202, 203, 205, 207, 209, 210, 211, 220, 224, 239, 292, 320, 321, 332, 346

transcendent function 115, 327
transformation 18, 87, 98, 106, 110, 113, 115, 116, 179, 193, 206, 250, 315, 316, 319, 327, 329
transformative group experience 329
transgressions 293, 304, 305, 308
transition 114, 136, 240, 319, 355
transitional space 94, 95
transrational 210
trauma 27, 77, 79, 80, 311, 312, 313, 314, 315, 319, 333, 345
trauma-informed response 313
traumatic experience 319
traumatic memory 80
trickster 52, 218, 221, 224, 227, 244
Trix 226, 227, 228
Tsing, Anna Lowenhaupt, et al. 289
tuning in 49, 120, 131, 283, 354
Turner, Victor 181, 323
typology 97, 98

U

unbearable experience 311
unconscious 16, 21, 23, 34, 47, 56, 67, 71, 78, 82, 98, 99, 104, 105, 112, 114, 116, 142, 187, 211, 215, 218, 239, 291, 293, 296, 308, 309, 314, 317, 332, 345
unconsciousness 98, 289, 333
unfolding 60, 95–97, 99, 229, 286, 289
unity 104, 105, 106, 108, 110, 112, 153, 220, 287
unknown 18, 34, 35, 49, 60, 61, 67, 70, 72, 73, 87, 93, 105, 163, 179, 210, 211, 213, 218, 220, 287, 306, 317, 323, 326, 332, 343
unus mundus 233
Upanisad 220
USDA Forest Service 26
utilitarianism 290, 343

V

Vernant, Jean P. 231
vets 187, 314

visual arts 376, 378
voice 13, 30, 32, 61, 67, 71, 72, 74, 102, 104, 139, 141, 149, 158, 160, 190, 191, 198, 299, 300, 316, 357, 358, 360
voudou 210
vulnerability 73, 79, 114

W

Waterman 188
Watkins, Mary M. 211
weltenschauung 286, 324
western consciousness 99, 100, 290, 291, 297
western culture 19, 20, 22, 26, 27, 34, 42, 59, 72, 100, 110, 112, 120, 205, 210, 233, 289, 296, 315, 318, 320
Wheel of Becoming 295, 399
White, Hayden V. 101
White, Lisbeth 162
wildness 316
Wilkinson, Richard H. 105
Winnicott, D. W. 87, 90, 118, 211, 212
witchcraft 210
wondering 30, 38, 55, 150, 171, 275
word magic 104, 105, 108
word play 91, 195, 221
worldview 19, 232, 286
wounding 304, 309, 314
wounds 27, 40, 81, 118, 304, 309, 311, 312, 324, 330

Y

Yun, Lin 96

Z

Zeus 206, 221
zine space 371
zodiac 52, 399

www.ingramcontent.com/pod-product-compliance
Lightning Source LLC
Chambersburg PA
CBHW042314300426
44110CB00042B/2837